FOLKWAYS
RECORDS

FOLKWAYS RECORDS

Moses Asch and His Encyclopedia of Sound

Tony Olmsted

ROUTLEDGE
NEW YORK AND LONDON

Published in 2003 by
Routledge
29 West 35th Street
New York, NY 10001
www.routledge-ny.com

Published in Great Britain by
Routledge
11 New Fetter Lane
London EC4P 4EE
www.routledge.co.uk

10 9 8 7 6 5 4 3 2 1

Library of Congress Cataloging-in-Publication Data

Olmsted, Tony
    Folkways records : Moses Asch and his encyclopedia of sound / Tony
Olmsted.
        p. cm.
Includes bibliographical references (p.   ) and index.
    ISBN 0-415-93708-6 (alk. paper)—ISBN 0-415-93709-4 (pbk. : alk.
paper)
    1. Folkways Records—History. 2. Sound recording industry—United
States—History. 3. Asch, Moses. 4. Sound recording executives and
producers—United States—Biography. I. Title.
    ML3792.F65 065 2003
    781.62'13'0092—dc21

                                                                    2002155714

To my dearest Julie
For everything . . .

Contents

FOLKWAYS RECORDS was created to document contemporary sounds, be they music, speech or natural phenomena.

Like an encyclopedia, there are over 2,000 record albums that reflect the sounds of the earth and its peoples. Folkways continues to issue recordings that are bought by governments, anthropologists, musicians, educators, etc. Folkways is also like an encyclopedia in that sales criteria are not used. The music of Afghanistan is as important as the music of the Cajun people, even though one may sell more copies than the other. Both are found in the Folkways catalog because they depict the unique music of a culture.

Folkways is also a living archive in that we deem it essential that all recordings be kept "in print." Although *Growing Up with Ella Jenkins* is requested more often than *Sounds & Ultra-Sounds of The Bottle-Nose Dolphin* makes it no more or less valuable. Both give Folkways its reputation and define its unique role.

As Director, I have tried to create an atmosphere where all recordings are treated equally regardless of the sales statistics. My obligation is to see that Folkways remains a depository of the sounds and musics of the world and that these remain available to all. The real owners of Folkways Records are the people that perform and create what we have recorded and not the people that issue and sell the product. The obligation of the company is to maintain the office, the warehouse, the billing and collections of funds, to pay the rent and telephone, etc. Folkways succeeds when it becomes the invisible conduit from the world to the ears of human beings.

Moses Asch,
excerpt of "Folkways Records—
Declaration of Purpose," c. 1980s

Foreword

In his book *Folkways Records*, Tony Olmsted explores and substantially explains one of the great mysteries surrounding my father's company. That mystery is: how did his company stay in business for over forty years? This mystery differs from the one that is inevitably asked about a small business that manages to last for a long time. Folkways was hardly typical of a small business. It is true that the company was small in that it generally employed no more than four or five people, and had a yearly gross typical of a small operation. However, in its scope and reach it was not a small company at all. It developed a catalog that rivaled and, most likely, surpassed that of the largest record companies. In fact, by the time of his death in 1986, Moe Asch had produced roughly 2,200 records or roughly one a week for the 40 years of Folkways' existence. At its heart, Folkways was driven by a mission that required a catalog that encompassed the literary, political, historical, scientific, and musical life of the world's peoples. To succeed in this mission meant that every record must remain in print regardless of sales.

No one ever questioned that the idea of Folkways made sense. It was, at one level, a dictionary or encyclopedia of sounds. And, as my father often said: "You don't take the letter 'J' out of the dictionary because it is used less than the letter 'S.'" It is the economics that does not seem to make sense. According to standard business practice, to survive, a company must delete those items that do not sell and replace them with others that do. Otherwise they fail. But Folkways did not fail. So what was the secret of its success, despite violating a fundamental rule of rational business practice? That is the mystery that this book, *Folkways Records*, addresses and resolves.

To do this, Tony Olmsted could hardly rely on the words of my father. When asked the central question: "How can you afford to keep everything in print?" He would evade, turning the answer itself into a mystery. For example, often he would say: "That is the secret. By keeping everything in print, it is like I have one record that is a best seller." Instead, Tony Olmsted relied on hard data, including business records, company correspondence, and interviews with key individuals. Through a careful analysis of this information, he brings forward for the first time the actual choices my father made in order to keep the business afloat. In so doing, the book explodes a number of myths about how Moe Asch succeeded. There was no secret fund of money derived through family money or through the exploitation of artists or through his ownership of a publishing company. Nor did he rely on the kindness of others to keep the wolves from the door. Instead, we discover that the answer lies in the skill with which my father conducted his business.

In this book, Tony Olmsted teaches us about the real economic problems my father faced and how his abilities as an entrepreneur helped him to overcome them. In so doing, he explains how all manner of business decisions, from the details of his everyday business practices to innovations in marketing, helped to secure the conditions that would best enable a company, whose mission contradicted basic principles of market economics, to endure.

Michael Asch

Acknowledgments

One of the great benefits of working on a project like this is the opportunity to meet and share information with a variety of wonderful people. The generosity of those who contributed to this work in a multitude of different ways is deeply felt and for which I am eternally grateful.

The path from idea to publication of this tale of Folkways Records has been a long and roundabout one. What started out as an idea to study "something involved with music" for a master's degree led to a meeting with Dr. Michael Asch, now professor emeritus of anthropology at the University of Alberta, Canada. As I later found out, he is also the son of Moses Asch, founder of Folkways Records—a connection that I credit for my academic introduction to Folkways. From those early discussions, Michael directed me to Dr. Regula Qureshi, professor of music at the University of Alberta, and close ally with Michael in fostering the interdisciplinary work in ethnomusicology that continues to grow at the University. Through a decade of classes, projects, odd jobs, and two graduate degrees, I am forever in debt (intellectually and otherwise) to Michael and Regula. Both have offered support and encouragement that has been instrumental in guiding me along the many steps that have led to this manuscript. More than just supervisors, they have been mentors and friends that have led by example and shared generously of their talents.

More specifically to Folkways, the research for this project could not have been completed without the generous support of a 1996 predoctoral research fellowship from the Smithsonian Institution, Washington, D.C. The fellowship allowed me to live and work in Washington for the fall of

1996, and provided me with access to the Moses and Frances Asch Collection at the Center for Folklife and Cultural Heritage. More importantly, however, were all of the staff of the Center, who were both welcoming and very helpful, especially Jeff Place (Archivist), Stephanie Smith (Assistant Archivist), Mary Monseur (Production Coordinator, Smithsonian Folkways Records), and, more recently, Harris Wray (music publicist, researcher, and past employee of Smithsonian Folkways Records). Of particular assistance was Curator Emeritus of Smithsonian Folkways Recordings, Dr. Anthony Seeger, whose generosity extended well beyond expectation. His insightful suggestions and comments helped shape my original research into Folkways, and have added elements to this final work that would not have been included otherwise. In addition, a number of other people have added their voices and have played an integral part in helping to tell the Folkways story. For their openness and assistance, thanks to Pete Seeger, Larry Sockell, Marilyn Averett, Sam Charters, Brian Dunsmore, Cathy Ennis, and my editor and a former record producer for Folkways, Richard Carlin.

I have also been blessed with many wonderful friends and colleagues who have provided insight, commentary, support, humor, and camaraderie through often trying times—thanks for all your help. To list names would be to risk omission—you know who you are. I am humbled to be able to call all of you my friends. But to make one exception, I must mention Michael Hamaide and the late Rebecca Rasch-Hamaide. They have stamped this work with meaning and memory that will last a lifetime. I miss you, Becky.

Last, but not least, are my family—immediate and extended—who have meant so much during the course of this work and to my life. To my parents, Dr. Allan D. Olmsted and Noreen Olmsted, my brother Pat, to Bert and Jeanne Golosky and the Golosky family, and to my infinitely beautiful, tolerant, and supportive wife, Julie, I will never be able to express my appreciation for your support.

I would like to thank everyone for their contributions to this work, but as is only fitting, any errors or omissions of fact or interpretation are mine and mine alone.

Introduction

Attempting to tell a story as grand as the life of Folkways Records is a daunting task, to say the least. Nonetheless, these pages contain what I hope is the foundation for such an important tale. It is built largely from what Folkways left behind: sales forms, tally sheets, letters, legal documents, and all those bits and pieces that add up to what famed anthropologist Bronislaw Malinowski referred to as the "imponderabilia of everyday life."[1] It is a story that can launch a hundred other lines of inquiry: the artists and their lives; the recording industry that has surrounded Folkways for the fifty-plus years of its existence; the impact on the cultural groups whose music has been preserved on Folkways, or the loss to those who have not been recorded. All are important avenues to investigate and will undoubtedly find authors to pursue them.

Such stories are important because Folkways Records has come to represent many different things to different people. It is most often the source of a favorite type of music, for example, a treasured Pete Seeger record or a children's record by Ella Jenkins. Or perhaps it has represented a great research resource, providing printed documentation with every record to inform, educate, and broaden the horizons of those who wish to know more about a music, a people, or an instrument. Folkways has been a political force, releasing protest songs and spoken-word recordings from around the world that offer first-person accounts of struggle. Often, however, Folkways has simply been known as that unique company that puts out records of sounds that cannot be found anywhere else.

Founder Moses "Moe" Asch set out early on to create what he called an "encyclopedia of sound"—all the sounds that are important to people's lives—a heady mandate for someone who knew perfectly well that the record business was a fickle one. Moe's early forays into recording with his first company, Asch Records (1939), gave him some success and a solid start on building his inventory. However, the realities of business interfered, and he all but abandoned Asch Records to start a second business, DISC Records of America (1945). Alas, DISC also proved to be a struggle, leaving him in bankruptcy in 1947.

Fortunately, it was Moe's third attempt and the creation of Folkways Records and Service Corporation in 1948 that set him on course to create a catalog of sounds that came closer to being an encyclopedia than anyone thought possible. In Folkways, Moe brought together lessons learned from his earlier businesses, and important early recordings still owned from Asch and DISC. The prosperity of post–World War II America, and the new technology of 33⅓ rpm Long Play (LP) records also contributed to create the Folkways legacy we know today. Eventually sold to the Smithsonian Institution in 1986, Folkways has persisted as Smithsonian Folkways Records, and continues to release fully documented recordings of new material, as well as mining the wealth of historic sound still held in the Archive to ensure its preservation.

This book is a biography of Folkways, the company. The difficulty with this concept, however, is that one person played such an important role in the shape and direction of the company that it is difficult to separate the company from the individual. Moe Asch created Folkways in a broad array of senses. Literally, he put together the business—the recordings, production, distribution—while creating a mythology about the nature of Folkways that continues today. Nonetheless, the company had an existence of its own, and it owed that existence to its predecessors, Asch and DISC, and its partnership with Pioneer Record Sales, the related distribution company that Asch formed in the early 1950s. Folkways was born in 1948 and had its growth spurt in the 1950s and early 1960s. As it matured, it faced a new set of problems in the late 1960s and early 1970s, and then settled into a quieter pace through the mid-1980s. This book will close with its transfer to the Smithsonian in 1987, but it is by no means the end of the Folkways story. Folkways continues to add to an impressive, historically and sonically important catalog.

At the end of the day, this story is about the details of company operations, such as they exist, and the assumptions and logic that span the gaps in documentation. When the Smithsonian Institution took over the operation of Folkways in 1987, shortly after the passing of Moses Asch in 1986, it made available all of the working papers and collected documentation to researchers as part of the Moses and Frances Asch Collection. Moe revealed later in his life that he was well aware that the papers generated during the operation of Asch, DISC, and Folkways were as important in documenting his business culture as his recordings were in documenting sonic culture. Fortunately, the Smithsonian has generously granted access to this Archive, and it is from that data that this book has been created.

This documentation has presented an unprecedented opportunity to look into the details of how a company like Folkways operated. I suppose the more basic question to ask is "why Folkways?" This investigation was undertaken for a few reasons. First, very few independent record companies have survived as long as Folkways has, and therefore, have left behind little in the way of documentation for researchers. Those that have survived for any length of time typically have not been all that interested in keeping documentation longer than is required. Folkways was unique in that its mission was to preserve and document sound, and Moe applied this thinking to his own companies. As circumstances would have it, the Smithsonian generously encourages scholars to use its Archives, to produce stories such as this one. In this regard, for anyone interested in the business of recording, the Folkways Archive offers a rare glimpse into the operations of an independent recording company.

Second, Folkways is more than just a company that produced recordings for the marketplace. It has created a catalog that is academically important to researchers as well as musically important to listeners around the world. Few companies can claim to produce material that has had the kind of global impact on music—that has opened the ears of music listeners and creators around the world—as Folkways recordings.[2] In this regard, it is important to be able to paint a broader picture that will expand the understanding of Folkways for those who only know its catalog. As important as the music is, so too is an understanding of the engine that produced, marketed, distributed, and managed those recordings.

This leads to the third point. In discussing Folkways, many people with even a passing familiarity with the catalog inevitably ask the question, "How did Folkways survive?" More than anything, the motivation behind this book is to answer this question. How does a company that produces recordings that other companies ignore, that consistently has sales figures that would quickly bankrupt other companies, thrive and prosper while insisting that it will always have available every recording in its catalog—even if a recording sells only one copy a year?

It is an intriguing question. To a certain extent, the answers are conjecture; Folkways is still operating, albeit as part of an important government-supported institution. Although many explanations could be convincingly put forth for Folkways' success (in addition to this book), the most interesting facet of the story is how Folkways' survived as basically a one-man operation. What becomes clear is that Moe had a deep understanding of the unusual nature of Folkways' operation. He understood the long sales cycle of some recordings, the value of cheap production, the exploitation of niche markets like educational records or children's records, and he accepted the limitations of his enterprises.

However, in reviewing the documentation to reach these answers, I hope to achieve a second, somewhat unrelated objective. As a researcher, I am frustratingly aware of the lack of published documentation on the economics of independent recording companies. Working with the Folkways Archive, it quickly became apparent that the material would hold great interest and scholarly value to anyone pursuing a similar kind of research. To this end, I have attempted to include as much of the details of Folkways' operation as possible, either in figures within the text or as appendices. Although in some instances information may appear superfluous, its value to other researchers may be apparent and therefore it has been included.

A similar approach has been taken to identify documents in the endnote references. Part of the excitement of this project was being able to go through seemingly endless boxes and file cabinets of material, most of which has not been formally cataloged. As exciting as this may be, however, it can be particularly difficult for other researchers wishing to gain a sense of the kind of documentation held within the Archive. Because there are no accession numbers or cataloguing information available, I have relied on a brief explanation and the date of the documents to give them as unique a description as possible and have used italics to distinguish the citations from other endnote text. I hope that other researchers will build on what I have attempted to do here, and that these descriptions will help guide future investigations.

The work itself is largely chronological. Indeed, the discussion begins some time before Folkways. First covered are some of the important historical antecedents that gave Moe the skills and inclination to found Folkways. I have deliberately avoided much discussion of what might have personally motivated Moe. However, because Moe is such a central figure throughout, some insights are offered into what I see as relevant areas of Moe's background or opinion. I am particularly fortunate to have this volume preceded by an insightful foreword by Moe's son, Michael Asch. I am humbled to be able to have Michael add his thoughts to this endeavor.

The discussion begins in earnest with the histories of Asch Records and DISC Records. Even though considerable space is taken up with these enterprises, it will soon become clear that both Asch Records and DISC records continued to influence Folkways throughout its life, particularly through Moe's introduction to Woody Guthrie, Pete Seeger, and Huddie Ledbetter (Lead Belly). It is at this point that the birth of Folkways is announced.

The Folkways story is then broken into a number of smaller parts, each dealing with a particular facet of its business. These include, in order, pressing recordings, printed material, credit, distribution, marketing and sales, and licensing and contracts which includes the deals that Moe made with Scholastic Magazines and with MGM during the 1960s "folk boom." Following these major licensing agreements in the late 1960s, there was an attempt by Moe to introduce other companies, as well as an attempt to resurrect both DISC Records and Asch Records in different forms.

Perhaps the largest, and ultimately the most important, section is that dealing with the finances of Folkways, Pioneer Record Sales (Folkways' distribution arm), and Moe himself. Inasmuch as the documentation exists, it is discussed here. Finally, the terms of the sale of Folkways to the Smithsonian Institution are discussed. With the terms of the sale, the presentation of the actual data as they exist is mostly complete. The conclusion wraps up this particular story with some broader reflection on the central question of the survival of Folkways.

As is customary with a work of this nature, it is stressed that, above all, this is only one version of the events. I am well aware that there are people and events that are not chronicled here, and that to some, such omissions would disqualify this work. My guide in presenting the events and details of this work has been clear: Is this the story that is represented by the Folkways documentation as I understand it? While the answer in my mind is emphatically "Yes," the truth of the story of Folkways remains elusive. The documentation in the Archive was repeatedly filtered by Moe, his staff, the Smithsonian staff, circumstance (there were a number of moves in Folkways' life and in the Smithsonian Archives' life), and ultimately, myself. One hopes that this filtering leaves behind the important and discards the superfluous, but that is sometimes not the case. In any event, the documents have told a story here. It is one version of the Folkways tale—a version I believe is well worth telling.

1
Early Influences
1870s to 1930s

Much as Moe would have insisted, it is necessary to set the stage with some context before jumping into many of the business details that preceded Folkways. Moe's attitudes to recording and the values that he sought to enshrine did not arise in a vacuum. The vast changes of the Industrial Revolution set the foundation for a myriad of astounding technological innovations. One of these—Edison's invention of the phonograph—can easily be called the seminal event of a now-ubiquitous recording industry. However, as is often the case, the value of such an invention was not immediately apparent. Eventually, its power as a medium for music found footing and began to blossom. It was into this growing technology, and the turmoil of East European expansion, that clearly shaped Moe's vision about the world around him, and what he could contribute to the world in the form of his famous "encyclopedia of sound."

The Phonograph and Sound Recording

The first ten years of the phonograph's existence after its invention in 1877 were quite noneventful, with not a great deal done to take full advantage of its potential. Certainly, the novelty of the phonograph's abilities were recognized, but even its inventor, Thomas Edison, conceived of the phonograph more as a business machine (primarily to be used as a dictaphone) than anything else. However, it was not long before others began to realize the importance of the phonograph, or at least its commercial appeal. In particular, Alexander Graham Bell, with his brother and an associate, were granted a number of patents based on their improvements of the consistency and clarity of recordings.

One of the most important of these patents was granted on 4 May 1886. The patent outlined the substitution of an incising stylus in place of Edison's indenting stylus and the replacement of the tinfoil cylinder with a cardboard cylinder covered with wax.[1] Changing the action of the stylus was critical in allowing the recording of more acoustic detail, based on lateral movement of the stylus at a consistent depth on the substrate. In addition, the substitution of wax for tinfoil on the cylinder further improved both recording and playback by providing a softer, smoother, more consistent surface that could capture the minute movements of the stylus. The downside was that the wax was more prone to damage, but the advantages definitely outweighed the disadvantages. The consequences of these improvements were that, despite the formation of the Edison Speaking Phonograph Company in 1878 to "exploit the tremendous popular interest" surrounding a "machine that could talk," it was Bell and his associates, as the Volta Graphophone Company in the 1880s, who were "directed towards exploiting [the graphophone/phonograph] for the reproduction of music."[2]

It was the reproduction of music that was to quickly solidify the potential popular and academic value of the phonograph. The speed and range of the early efforts by individuals to get out and collect music were astounding, and set the groundwork for the recognition not only of material culture, but more importantly for a growing group of scholars, the expressive culture of a group. Prior to the invention of the phonograph, there was no way for someone to record how a song or recitation *actually* sounded, except through inadequate notation methods developed for Western musical idioms. Needless to say, the value of this new tool in musical collecting was soon discovered in the field, where aural expressions from around the world were directly recorded.

Interestingly, although over a decade old, neither Edison's phonograph nor Bell's "graphophone" were available to the retail market. Recording machines were only available through a commercial lease from the respective companies. Therefore, when ethnographer Walter Jesse Fewkes made recordings on the Passamaquoddy reserve at Calais, Maine, in February and March of 1890, it was through the support of philanthropist Mary Thaw Hemenway, who was also a substantial shareholder of Edison Phonograph Co. stock. It is presumed that she supplied Fewkes with his phonograph as something of a marketing ploy, and a successful one at that. Hemenway was also reported to have funded collecting expeditions to the Zuni (1890) and to the Hopi (1891–1894),[3] presumably using an Edison phonograph.

By the mid-1890s, less than twenty years after its invention, the influence of the gramophone/phonograph had jumped American borders with interest in the new machine becoming international. By 1899, 151,000 phonographs had been made in the United States, with evidence of steadily growing markets in England, Germany, France, and Russia, and even some development in India, Egypt, and Japan.[4] Clearly, the speed with which the commercial recording enterprise was encompassing the globe far outstripped any research projects. With so many machines, and the entertainment potential growing in leaps and bounds, there was a skyrocketing demand for material to play on the machines. The depth of the international penetration of the phonograph is highlighted by a recording engineer, who noted that by 1910:

> In the Caucasus mountains the talker [phonograph] can be heard in every one of the multitudinous villages; the records are played unceasingly and are therefore soon worn out, causing a result which is not particularly pleasing to other than the Cossacks themselves who will never buy another record of the same title until one is actually broken. Even then they retain the pieces and in some cases decorate their huts with them.[5]

There was a growing body of experts in the recording field who found themselves making recordings all over the world for the European and American markets, in addition to the efforts of music scholars.[6] Edison's company, now named the National Phonograph Co., had set up offices in London, Paris, Berlin, Brussels, Vienna, and Milan, and by 1899 many professional recordists had found ready employment in Europe.[7]

In the United States, the Bureau of American Ethnology and the Smithsonian Institution played an important role in supporting early research into Native American communities and in the collection of American folk music from various parts of the United States. In Europe, a similar pattern was developing through several universities and musical organizations. With early collecting expeditions recording Hungarian peasant music in 1895,[8] Tatar and Bashkir songs in the late 1880s and 1890s, and music in the Ukraine in 1900,[9] for example, the early range of recording efforts was quite remarkable.

By the turn of the century, a variety of forces swirled around the phonograph. In the United States a commercial war was brewing over supremacy in the phonograph market. In Europe the home-consumption market for recordings was growing rapidly and needed to be fed with new products. On both sides of the Atlantic, scholars were recognizing the incredible tool that the phonograph represented in terms of ethnographic collecting of music and oral histories. Nonetheless, it appeared that the commercial interests appeared to be dominating the recording market.[10] The cost of the machines and blanks was still prohibitive for many individuals. Support came primarily through either individual philanthropists (like Mary Thaw Hemenway), larger organizations that wished to acquire samples of a wide variety of music, or commercial music companies looking for musical novelties.

After some technical modifications made recording easier, there were areas where the interests of all three groups overlapped:

> Almost immediately, students of languages, tribal customs, and folk lore realized that here was an instrument of great value. Enthusiastically, leading universities and museums sent out recording expeditions to the heart of darkest Africa, to the wilds of the Amazon, and to reservations of vanishing Indian tribes of the South and West.[11]

By the turn of the twentieth century, the academic collection of music began to state its presence in the collection and systematic comparison of the world's music. The first, and most important effort, was through the work of E. M. von Hornboestel and Carl Stumpf at the Berlin Phonogramm-Archiv, founded in 1901. Trained in the natural sciences, von Hornboestel and Stumpf saw analyzing music collected in the field as a way to find common features in music from around the world, and to see whether those features might be based in human psychology and cognition. The Phonogramm-Archiv set the stage for the practice of systematic collection and analysis of recordings from around the world, establishing an important standard that would influence collectors and analysts alike throughout Europe and the world.

Youth and Family Influences

Side by side with the growing phonograph industry was the growing Asch family. Matilda Asch (nee Spiro) and eminent Jewish writer Sholem Asch brought Moses Asch into the world on 2 December 1905. Moses entered the family as the second-oldest of siblings Nathan (b. July 1902), Janek, or John as he was commonly called (b. January 1907), and Ruth (b. February 1910), the only daughter.[12] The early lives of all the Asch children were filled with international elements. The parental and family influences on the Asch children were strong. Both parents were strong social activitists who worked for a variety of humanitarian and nationalist causes. Both individually and as a young couple, Sholem and Matilda were involved in defying Russian control of Poland at the end of the 1800s by teaching Yiddish and Polish—languages forbidden under occupation. Matilda's family were also involved in a wide range of nationalist and prolabor struggles. Although some of their efforts, including the fight for a shorter workweek, seem of less consequence now, strikes and rallies organized throughout Poland could often result in imprisonment or death to both organizers and participants.

In concert with such struggles, Sholem began to find fame throughout the world with a variety of novels and plays dealing with Jewish life and experience in Poland. However, as public appearances and the literary life beckoned, the children were increasingly left behind with Basha Spiro, Matilda's sister, as Sholem and Matilda began their extensive travels in support of Sholem's work—a pattern that continued well into Moe's adulthood. Whether such travels ultimately had a positive or negative effect on the Asch children, and Moe in particular, is open for debate, but there is little doubt that such cultural and political exposure early in Moe's life left a lasting impression.

Moe's first foray into international travel began in 1912, when Sholem's frustration with the labor and nationalist conflicts in Poland finally drove the family away for good. Arriving on an estate in northern France, Sholem began to impose a sort of worldliness on the family by decreeing that they would only communicate in the language of the country they lived in. Political intent aside, it was likely a considerable practical and cultural challenge for seven-year-old Moe and his siblings. Nonetheless, while the location sounds idyllic, there was little contact with Sholem—if he wasn't traveling, he would demand silence from the children while he was writing. Often, most of the parenting was left to Basha.

Life in the French countryside was shortlived. In 1914, World War I erupted, providing impetus and opportunity for Sholem to work in the United States, renewing his ties to the *Jewish Daily Forward* in New York City that he had first established through Abe Cahan after an extended writing tour in 1909. For a year, Basha and the children stayed in Paris, joining Sholem and Matilda in 1915, settling into a home in Greenwich Village in New York City. Exposed to yet another language in less than a decade, Moe, Nathan, and John were left to adapt to life in the United States. The progression of World War I appeared to have little effect on the material life of the Asch family, with the exception that the royalty money that Sholem had collected from Germany, in particular, had ceased. Nonetheless, it didn't stop Sholem from sending Moe and his brothers on vacations with Basha at a union-based summer "resort" run by the International Ladies Garment Workers Union each year until 1918.[13]

Travel, language, and disinterest all seemed to play a part in disrupting Moe's education. Moe struggled through his general education, showing little enthusiasm for the curricula of the day. Eventually, however, he demonstrated great interest and talent in technology, becoming an avid amateur ham radio operator, an interest that would serve him well. Attempts to finish high school first in New York in 1921, then at the Jewish National Farm School in Pennsylvania in 1923, were not successful.[14] Instead, Moe began a trip to Europe that would again expose him to some harsh political realities that would leave a lasting impression, particularly the growing and increasingly overt anti-Semitism that would be directed at him. However, despite the downside of the experience, Sholem was able to again get Moe into school, this time exploiting Moe's interest in electronics. With the growing political and economic difficulties in post–World War I Germany, inflation made American dollars go a long way. Taking advantage of this via Sholem's financial support, Moe enrolled in the highly respect electronics school, the Electronische Hochschule in Bingen-en-Rhine, to pursue his technical education.

During his late teens, Moe would experience some of the seminal moments behind his later Folkways success. Amid the mix of European and international folk idioms that he encountered among the students at the Hochschule, there was criticism from other students that there was no real "culture" from the America that Moe had come from. Knowing this was not true, it was nonetheless difficult for Moe to prove it, until one fateful day in Paris. As Moe recalled:

> Whenever he [Sholem] would travel West, he would pick up books about cowboys and these books would usually start off with a song text or a poem. It wasn't meaningful at first but one day in 1923 I was on vacation from school on the Quay on the Left Bank [Paris] browsing through books, I came across a first edition of John Lomax's *Cowboy Songs* that had an introduction by Teddy Roosevelt which guided me through life because he said that folklore and songs are the cultural expression of a people. So here I had these books and was able to show that we had this kind of uniqueness to our culture which was not just a melting pot, but were part of a whole bunch of other things. All these things stayed in the back of my mind.[15]

Moe was finally beginning to develop the vocabulary to describe the array of cultural encounters that he had experienced throughout his young life. But in addition, he was also being exposed to the process of recording those expressions in a technically and culturally meaningful way. Aside from the political turmoil that was brewing, Germany in the 1920s was also at the forefront of the phonographic collection of music from abroad, with the continuation of the work of von Hornboestel and Stumpf. Moe would also have been exposed to the new forces that were beginning to shape the drive to create and collect music from around the world that would emerge in the 1930s.

Between the World Wars the larger academic community had clearly taken note of these developments. In what Bruno Nettl termed "applied ethnomusicology,"[16] people began to see the possibility of preserving different musical traditions that were perceived to be at risk by dominating cultural forces. An effort was made to collect traditional musics to create programs that would serve to perpetuate the traditional cultural practices of the area: a program that Moe Asch would have found very appealing. For example, in the 1930s von Hornboestel, Curt Sachs, and Robert Lachmann, among others, headed a recording committee in Egypt. Their goal was to set out a plan for the preservation of traditional Egyptian music by identifying and preserving particular musical traditions.

A second motive for collecting arose at this time, based on government policies supporting the collection of "national" musics or traditional forms that could be appropriated and defined in the nationalist agenda. In the United States the Department of Education sponsored a "rescue mission" for ballads and folk songs that inspired academics and amateurs alike to collect music. This effort, too, fit well with the direction Moe would take with Folkways, particularly the value of work by collectors of all stripes, and the importance of getting music into libraries so that everyone could have access to it. In the post–World War I period, this move may well have been a "reaction against the theoretical preoccupations of the earlier generation, and the search for a sense of national tradition in the face of striking regional diversity."[17] Parallel to these efforts were the transcription and analysis of commercial recordings by academics through the 1920s, with regular academic reviews of commercial recordings beginning in the late 1940s[18]—again, part of an important practice that Folkways would later exploit to its advantage.

Moe would have been well aware of the political situation in Europe during the 1930s, partly through his own connections with Germany, but also through his father, who had been writing and lecturing on the deteriorating Jewish situation throughout Western and Eastern Europe, especially in Germany. During the 1930s, strong nationalist policies toward recording were prevalent throughout Europe, driving many groups to collect their sounds with a sense of increasing urgency.[19] Beginning in 1930, projects from the University of Poznan in Poland had collected about 4,000 discs of melodies from western Poland while the Centralne Archiwum Fonograficzne in Warsaw had collected over 20,000 melodies from central Poland. Sadly, all the recordings from Poznan were deliberately destroyed during World War II by occupying forces.[20] The Warsaw collection likely fell to a similar fate.

Moe was very much aware of the history and importance of these collections and was surely moved by their destruction. Indeed, it was a similar history that later prompted Moe to name Folkways Records:

> The name [Folkways] did come to me from the famous book by [William Graham] Sumner [1907]. The idea came to me from George Herzog, who was a colleague of Harold Courlander, my first editor in the Ethnic series. . . . He said Erich von Hornbostel had collected a lot of ethnic music in Germany and . . . [t]hey had lost a lot through our bombings of the libraries in Berlin, where they were housed. . . . So all the early collections of the people's material is lost.[21]

Naming the company "Folkways" served as a reminder that what was available on the label were the sounds of how people lived, celebrated, and worshiped—their folkways.

Training in Radio and Electronics

A crucial element in Moe's life and the development of Folkways Records was his knowledge of and attitude toward electronics. Upon his return to the United States in 1926, after his tenure at the Hochschule, at age 21 Moe put his electronics training to the test. After working a variety of factory jobs in the electronics field, Moe began his own electronics company, Radio Laboratories. Moe was able to struggle along with some degree of success building and installing a wide variety of transmitters and receivers. As part of the business, Moe also became the Eastern repair representative for Stromberg-Carlson radios, which Asch described as the "Rolls-Royce of radios."[22] A side benefit of working for Stromberg-Carlson was Moe's introduction into the world of marketing and radio distribution networks across the country. Radio and electronics retailers of the time were also important distributors of recordings. Thus, in addition to electronic retail markets, Moe would later be able to gain access to the distribution networks of record dealers across the East Coast, retailers that were traditionally dominated by the three major companies: Columbia, Decca, and RCA.[23] He would later use these contacts to distribute his early recordings.[24]

His work through Radio Laboratories also gave Moe expertise in the operation of public address systems. In an interesting twist, it was the burlesque and theater houses in New York that helped Moe develop both the technical expertise and the philosophical approach that made his recorded work so enduring. Moe realized that as theaters attempted to amplify their stages, a fundamental problem arose: "I understood the audience problem and I knew you couldn't put something between the actor and the audience that was false; otherwise the play would suffer. It had to be a natural sequence . . ."[25] Efforts to create this "naturalism" led Moe to make importance advances in microphone technology, including the development of a new type of condenser microphone, as well as an automatic rising microphone for the stage.

Through this time, Moe also involved himself in the radio section of the American Standards Association, working to improve the quality of recorded and broadcast sound. Little of his work in the ASA has been documented, but it is clear that such work allowed Moe to put his energies into developing and defining his philosophy of sound—not only the technological aspects, but also the importance of sound to the people who produce and consume sound. This led to Moe championing acoustically flat, monaural recording as the best way to preserve sound. It was not about sound as entertainment, but sound as meaning and content, the elements so dear to the individuals and groups that identify with the cultural relevance of their aural expression.

Hand in hand with the development of new microphones and new recording techniques came the introduction of frequency equalization to the engineer's arsenal, which Moe vehemently opposed. In an argument that would have resonated with the ethnomusicological recording efforts throughout the world at the time (and since), Moe argued for no alteration of the original recorded frequencies, despite the changing popular tastes that drove companies to boost the low and high frequencies to greater and greater heights.[26] Moe concluded in the 1970s that:

> You are controlled by the economic factor even though you are living in an electronic world. With my records, I think if I am documenting a thing, then I want as good quality as possible, because the person 20 years from that time should be able to reconstruct what I recorded. And in order to do that, the flatter the sound, the better the quality is. . . . You can reconstruct by recording flat the quality that recorded originally, but if you have peaked something you never know how much your peaks have cut it down. When very good equipment will occur in a few years, the flat record will sound like the sound was. If you play some 78s which were made of very good shellac, you will find how wonderful that quality is against an LP. One of the horrors of stereo is that you record with two microphones you unbalance the thing; or if you record eight track, you are creating a sound that wasn't there originally.[27]

Moe was clearly confronted with the popular choice in the music industry to manipulate the original sound during the recording process. In fact, when faced with the pressures that popular music was exerting to manipulate sounds with more elaborate recording techniques, Moe concluded that

"I understand it and take may choice. People come to me and say, critically, this what you have done. I say, 'yes.' I have to stand for something."[28]

Moe put his recording philosophy to practice somewhat by accident in the late 1930s. By 1938, Radio Laboratories had merged with Harry Mearns and another engineer, to more effectively build custom recording and amplification equipment.[29] One job in particular had Radio Laboratories constructing and installing new radio broadcasting equipment in the WEVD Building in Manhattan. Although the installation went well, it left the radio station in the quandary of having equipment but nothing to play. WEVD Radio featured programming directed to the growing immigrant population of New York City, and in particular, the Jewish population. At the about the same time (1938–1939) RCA Records, largely for economic reasons, stopped producing Jewish recordings. Responding to a request by WEVD, Moe took advantage of the opening in the market and began his recording career by producing the Bagelman Sisters'[30] rendition of *Kol Nidre*. After receiving positive feedback from the Jewish community and seeing rising sales of the recording, Moe decided to branch out from Radio Laboratories. On 15 April 1940, Moe filed the business certificate for Asch Recording Studios doing business at 117 West 46th Street, New York City.[31]

There is little doubt, however, that there was more to Moe's transition into recording than simply success with *Kol Nidre* and the Bagelman Sisters. In 1939, several events converged to propel Moe forward into what would become his life's work. World War II was declared in Europe, with European Jews in particular peril. Albert Einstein, an acquaintence of Moe's father, Sholem, was making frequent appeals from Princeton for aid to help Jewish refugees. Moe was enlisted to use his portable recording machine to record Einstein. As Moe recounted:

> One Sunday at my father's home in Connecticut, they [Einstein, Sholem, and others] asked me what I was doing. I told them about my idea of starting Asch records. They all told me the same thing. It's very important for the 20th Century to have someone like me who understood the intellect and who understood the changes of the 20th Century and who understood folk and dissemination. . . . What opened it up was the word "folkways" means that everything occurring on the earth and in the contemporary time is being recorded. I became conscious of history and that folk music always gave you a sense of something that happened before that someone set down for us to remember, for they always felt that there is a moral, a universality, a truth to something that people pick up and sing and talk about and bring back from generation to generation.[32]

2
Beginnings
Asch Records

Moses Asch may have stumbled into the record producing business, but his first two labels gave him quick lessons of the many pitfalls that could come to a small label. Although he didn't know it at the time, Asch Records was formed just as a shortage of shellac—brought on by World War II—would make it difficult for small firms to get the material needed to produce 78 rpm records. For this reason, Asch had to go into partnership with another label, Stinson, and the repercussions of that arrangement taught him to be wary of losing control over his future enterprises, discussed shortly. With his second label, DISC, Asch saw an opportunity to develop a larger business appealing primarily to the jazz audience. However, his gamble on better known artists—and the commitment of larger sums of money to press and promote records—led him quickly to realize that producing hits was a dangerous business. For the rest of his life, he studiously avoided hitmaking and the associated economic risk, preferring to fill the gaps that the larger labels couldn't—or wouldn't—address. Ironically, it would be in the small niches that Folkways would find its success.

The jump from audio equipment manufacturer and installer with Radio Laboratories to full-fledged record company founder was really an enormous step for Moe. His qualifications for making this move were admittedly limited. Although he knew a great deal about how to record, his intuition about what to record certainly came from disparate sources. On one hand, he knew that some Jewish recordings were needed because of WEVD's desire for recordings at the same time RCA was taking their Jewish recordings off the market. Moe recorded Albert Einstein for the Jewish relief effort, and although he was encouraged to keep recording, the business of recording was still left to Moe to discover. Ultimately, Moe was not even a musician, though he admitted that he knew a little about drums through his first exposure to early jazz:

> . . . early in 1919–1920, when I was fifteen in Kingston, New York, picking apples. On Saturday nights, three or four of the pickers had a saxophone, a drum, a bass and a piano, and they played the dances of the day for the fruit and berry pickers. I got along with them because I helped with the drum.[1]

At the same time that opportunities were beginning to take shape for Moe, the dynamics of the recording business were changing. Many small labels that had flourished in the 1920s suffered due to the increased popularity of radio and the coming of the Depression. Larger conglomerates began to dominate the field, led by the "big three" of Columbia (from the mid-'30s part of CBS Radio), Victor (owned by RCA), and the new label Decca. The big labels were less interested in recording specialized acts, such as blues, jazz, "race" or "ethnic," and country singers; folk music barely registered on their radar. An opportunity for new labels came in 1942 with the first American Federation of Musicians (AFM) strike.[2] AFM leader James Petrillo was angered by radios playing recorded music, which supposedly put "live" performers out of work. The AFM "ban" meant that union musicians were not available for recordings; the large labels were unable to settle, and were unwilling to work with nonunion artists. Jazz, country, blues, and folk musicians—all historically not represented by the union—were happy to record for just about anyone, at any time. A new crop of small labels—including Asch's own—were able to take advantage of this demand. A small indication of the range of musicians that Moe recorded can be found in a recording itinerary that was produced for artists that had recorded for Asch in 1944–1945 (Table 1).

That said, if Moe saw opportunity in the recording business, he was soon to discover that the reality of the recording business was harsh. Moe had some initial success with the Jewish recordings, as well as with some service work doing radio transcriptions (producing a set number of copies —usually twenty-five or fifty—plus a master for a flat fee). However, by the early 1940s, with the war continuing, both the production of recordings and the market for them began to suffer from rationing and limited sales and distribution opportunities.

In some respects, Moe's entrance into the recording business was badly timed. Because of the impact of World War II, shellac—the key ingredient in the manufacturing of 78 rpm records—was in short supply. The Asian sources of the material were unavailable due to the political and military

Table 1 Recording Itinerary for Asch Recordings, 1944–1945[a]

Artist	Date	Schedule
Richard Dyer Bennet	Oct. 4, 1945	6 sides
James P. Johnson	Feb. 27, 1945	1:30–3:30
Jerry Jerome	June 6, 1945	8–1 A.M.
Carlos Montoya	Sept. 13, 1945	6 sides
Mary Lou Williams	May 30, 1945	3–6 P.M.
Bob Pope[b]	Jan. 19, 1945	3–6 P.M.
Jerry Jerome	March 7, 1945	7:30–10:30, 10:30–11:30
James P. Johnson	March 26, 1945	2–5
Cecil Anderson	March 31, 1945	6 sides
Mary Lou Williams	April 10, 1945	3–6
Cecil Anderson	April 2, 1945	6–9 P.M.
Tom Glazer	May 11, 1945	7:30–9:30 P.M.
Mary Lou Williams	Dec. 15, 1944	2:30–5:30, 6–9 P.M.
Josh White	Dec. 2, 1944	4–7 P.M.
Stuff Smith	Sept. 8, 1944	2–5 P.M.
Meade Lux Lewis	Aug. 18, 1944	6 hours
Mary Lou Williams	June 12, 1944	3–6 P.M.
Mary Lou Williams	March 4, 1944	3 hours

[a]Presented in the order and format that it appears on the original document. *Recording Itinerary for Asch Recording, 1944–1945.*
[b]This entry is corroborated by a contract signed by Bob Pope and Moe Asch. Pope was paid $60 for the session. *Contract between Bob Pope and Moe Asch, Asch Recording Studios. 19 January 1945.*

conflicts throughout southeast Asia. As a result, shellac was rationed in the United States. The rationing of shellac for recordings was based on a percentage of the number of records each recording company manufactured in the previous year of business. Unfortunately for Moe, he had done little business in the previous years, leaving him in very short supply. Facing a lack of raw material to make his records, Moe entered into one of the more troublesome partnerships that he would ever make with the Stinson Trading Co. (Herbert Harris and Irving Prosky)—one that continues to haunt the original Asch recordings to this day.

The Deal with Stinson

The actual beginnings of the Asch/Stinson arrangement are foggy at best. Stinson had begun its life around 1939–1940 first selling Soviet-made records and then producing records based on master recordings from the

Soviet Union. The quantity of recordings that they manufactured and distributed in the United States was substantial. On one hand, Asch needed an outlet for his recordings; on the other, Stinson had a good distribution network in place and a history of producing records that allowed them access to shellac. The outbreak of World War II would also make the availability of master recordings from Russia and the rest of the world more difficult for Stinson to obtain. The fact that both companies were also "progressive" (as an Asch press release from 1943–1944 stated; see below) didn't hurt, either. So the marriage would seem to have been ideal between the fledgling Asch studios and the more established Stinson label.

Documentation of the early interaction between the companies begins with a draft of what might have been a press release of some kind—written on Asch Recordings letterhead and dated to late 1943/early 1944—which outlines the background of Irving Prosky and Herbert Harris (the owners of Stinson) and their association with Asch. The story begins with the participation of the Soviet Union in the 1939 World's Fair:[3]

> [Mr. Prosky] became the first exclusive American distributor of records made in the Soviet Union. During the next 2 years there were only 2 places in the East where these records were sold to the public. Mr. Herbert Harris who had concessions at the Stanley and Miami Theaters was the pioneer who sold these records directly to the people. It was therefore, inevitable that these 2 men should get together to form a company for the purpose of distributing records made in the U. S. S. R. throughout the country called Stinson Trading Company. This organization is now manufacturing thousands of records made in the Soviet Union to be sold through 12 distributors in the United States and to Canada and Mexico. . . . However, due to the war, the curtailment of records has made it imperative for this progressive company to associate with another progressive firm, the Asch Recording Studios, for a wider variety of social[ly] significant records. . . .

The shortage of shellac during World War II is probably the most commonly invoked reason for the beginning of the recording and distribution arrangement between Moe and partners Harris and Prosky. However, early documents seem to suggest that there might also have been a previous relationship of some kind in place. The initial motivation for the relationship appears possibly to be that Asch was in tough financial straits (not surprising given the shellac shortage and other wartime difficulties) and that Prosky and Harris agreed to bail him out with a loan and a job.

One of the first known contracts executed between Moe Asch and Stinson (signed by Prosky) was essentially a sales commission contract. Dated

25 January 1943, the contract promises Moe a 15 percent commission for all new accounts that he brought to Stinson for the one-year duration of the arrangement[4] (Table 2). This would seem to indicate that Asch was looking for other material to distribute along with his own, both to support his own distribution efforts and to build his financial base. (For example, Asch added Signature Records to his distribution business in 1944; see page 24.) The peculiar feature of this arrangement is that commission payments in the documentation do not begin to appear until well after the one-year agreement had expired in January 1944. Nonetheless, Moe continued receiving the 15 percent commission at least through the end of 1945.

The columns highlight the essential numbers for sales of this period. The first column is the total owed by Stinson in royalty payments to Asch for all the recordings sold in the month prior to the date listed. Whose recordings were actually sold (Moe's or Stinson's) is not entirely clear, but Moe did provide some musical material and production resources, and Prosky and Harris were enlisted to distribute the recordings with Moe acting as saleman. As Moe's material was sold, a royalty was paid back to him, usually ranging between 12¢ and 25¢ per recording. Once the royalty tally was done, a second column—the "profit" percentage—was added from June 1944. There is no documentation of this change being implemented, but, on the surface, it appears to be paid to Moe in part as compensation for his liability for the manufacturer's excise tax. The excise tax was implemented in the United States to tax manufacturers for merchandise produced. As stated in the 1946 printing of the regulations, "In general, the tax attaches when the title to the article sold passes from the manufacturer to a purchaser," and that "Generally, title passes upon delivery of the article to the purchaser or to a carrier for the purchaser." Furthermore, and this was most troublesome for the recording industry, "In the case of sale on credit, it is immaterial whether or not the purchase price is actually collected."[5] As the owner of the master recordings and therefore considered the "manufacturer," Asch was on the hook for the 10 percent tax on all monies billed for the sale of the recordings.

Shortly after the commission arrangement began in 1943, Prosky and Harris gave Asch a $1,000, interest-free loan to be paid back over an eight-month period. A tally list and five of the original eight credit notes signed by Moe and made out to Prosky and Harris still exist and show that the loan was promptly repaid between May and December 1943.[6] The reason for the loan is still a mystery and appears unconnected to the royalty/commission arrangement that was already in place. In all likelihood, however, the loan was connected to Moe's efforts to keep Asch Records alive through the stresses of the World War II period. Shortly after the loan was repaid, Moe began receiving fairly considerable sums from the royalty/commission arrangement with Stinson (see Table 2).

Table 2 Summary of Commissions Paid to Asch by Stinson, March 1943–November 1945[a]

Date	Total Royalties	15% Commission (Profit)	Total Paid to Asch before Federal Taxes	Federal Excise Tax (10%)
March 1943	$892.19	—	$892.91	$81.10[b]
June 1943	124.03	—	124.03	11.07
July 1943	452.86	—	452.86	41.17
March 1944	2,324.09	—	2,324.09	232.41
April 1944	2,580.40	—	2,580.40	258.04
May 1944	1,975.16	—	1,975.16	197.52
July 1944[c]	1,294.60	$258.92	1,553.52	155.35
August 1944	1,163.18	109.85[d]	1,272.93	127.29
September 1944	2,508.26	376.23	2,884.49	288.45
October 1944	2,147.68	322.14	2,469.82	246.98
November 1944	2,115.65	317.35	2,433.00	243.30
December 1944	2,119.63	317.94	2,437.57	243.76
January 1945	1,519.69	227.95	1,747.64	174.76
February 1945	1,875.75	281.37	2,157.12	215.71
March 1945	2,352.11	352.81	2,704.92	270.49
April 1945	2,212.95	331.94	2,544.89	254.49
May 1945	3,186.32	477.95	3,664.27	366.43
June 1945	2,762.21	414.33	3,176.54	317.65
July 1945	1,999.77	299.97	2,299.74	229.97
August 1945	2,757.46	413.61	3,171.07	317.10
September 1945	2,667.88	400.27	3,068.15	306.82
October 1945	3,259.23	488.88	3,748.11	374.81
November 1945	2,766.07	414.91	3,180.98	318.10

[a]Compiled from a selection of sales records and receipts.
[b]The excise tax paid on these amounts for March, June, and July 1943 totals 9.09% of sales, rather than 10%.
[c]No entry exists for July 1944. These values were computed based on a notation in the August 1944 billing indicating "Less 5% of July (Paid 20%)—$64.73." From this value, the total sales, federal excise tax, and the 20% additional payment were calculated. The August 1944 value reflects the deduction of $64.73 for the July overpayment.
[d]This amount reflects the 15% profit of $174.48 minus the 5% overpayment of $64.73 from July 1944.

Table 3 Sample of Asch Records "H"-Series Recordings, 1942–1943

Record Number	Artist	Title	Tally Number (Jan. 1943)
H6001	Cantor Leibele Waldman	A Yidd Darf Gehen In Shul/ Al Tiro	640
H6002	Cantor Leibele Waldman	Eichu/Es Kummen Gute Tzyten	120
H6003	Menasha Oppenheim	Wohin Sol Ick Gehen/ Zulaika	550
H6004	Menasha Oppenheim	Drei Techter/ Reisele	1,050
H6005	Harry Lubin's Orchestra	Lebedig und Freilach/ Erinerungen	140
H6006	Max Klettner	Mein Shtetele Yaass/Yiddish Red Sich Schoen	40
H6007	Max Klettner	Gesselach/ Der Ferliebter	100
H6008	Saul Meisels	Der Badchn/ Reb Dovid'l	460
H6009	Saul Meisels	Hora: Mi Boneh Yerushalayim/ Katonu M'od	475
H6010	Cantor Leibele Waldman	Kol Nidre/Eli Eli	—
H6011	—	—	—
H6012	Saul Meisels	Hatikvah/ Techezakna	60
H6013	—	—	—
H6014	—	—	250
H6015	M. Yardeini	Shirat Haemek/Reitiha	180
H6016	Menasha Oppenheim	Dos Schneider'l/ Nysym	280
H6017	"Pesache" Burstein	Fity Die Ritia/ Proshtchai Odessa	60
H6018	Chaim Tauber	Motl der Operator/ Mein Shtetele Moliff	100
H6019	—	—	

At about the same time that Moe was entering into arrangements with Stinson, he was able to continue to produce his own recordings on a more modest basis. From the beginning of 1943, most of Asch's sales were primarily from material he had recorded in response to the small but persistent demand for ethnic Jewish recordings. Incomplete sales tally sheets[7] for November/December 1942 and possibly January 1943 show that the bulk of the material being sold came out as the Asch Records "H" [presumably standing for "Hebrew"] Series (Table 3).[8] At the same time, Moe was also selling some of his Jewish material through Stinson. Between March and December 1943, for example, a *Kol Nidre* recording released on Stinson sold 7,216 copies, netting Moe $1,841.02 in royalties. Similarly, a recording notated only as "Jewish 10'" sold 17,384 copies, paying Moe $2,411.84 in royalties.

Also in 1944, Moe picked up Robert (Bob) Thiele's Signature Records for distribution. A series of form letters dated 20 July 1944[9] were sent to several dealers by Thiele indicating that distribution of Signature Records had changed and to contact Asch for distribution. Moe was already pushing the distribution of Asch and Stinson records throughout the United States by writing to a variety of local record outlets. In one letter, Moe wrote the Mayflower Novelty Co. of St. Paul, Minnesota, informing them that distribution for Signature and Asch Records was still open in that area. At a distributor cost of 50 percent less 10 percent off the retail price, the offer had the appearance of being a lucrative one for the retailer.[10]

There is no clear suggestion as to why Thiele contracted with Moe for the production and distribution of Signature Records. Part of the reason was possibly because of business hardship, perhaps as a result of diminished resources, including access to shellac. In any event, Asch's association with Stinson gave him the resources to continue to produce Stinson, Asch,[11] and presumably Signature Records. The addition of Signature Records to the lineup might have simply been a way to ensure that Signature would continue to be produced until after World War II, through an association with other labels, where it would likely have failed on its own. In a letter Bob Thiele wrote to Moe in 1944[12]:

> I would appreciate it greatly if you would drop me a short note telling me just how many mothers[13] have been taken from the Scranton Company and shipped to other outfits such as the company at Phillipsburgh. . . .
>
> I am sure you understand why I want this information. I'd like to know, when the war finally does end, just where Signature plates are located throughout the country.
>
> Also, I hope you will commence to send invoices of the amount of records received from other companies than the Scranton Record Co. This information is needed to compile how much money must be paid to the government, music publishers and the American Federation of Musicians.

Controlling where all the "mothers" and "masters" were located was key for any record label because anyone in possession of them could press records. This would become a problem for Asch when his dealings with Stinson soured, as we shall see. In any case, it certainly appears that Thiele wanted to maintain control over Signature Records after the war. Whether he was actually able to do so is not clear.

By any measure, the association between Asch and Stinson was one of necessity rather than choice. Moe likely felt there was an opportunity to be pursued in the relationship, but more than anything, Moe wanted—and continued to pursue—his own direction. In fact, Moe was quick to demonstrate that he was fiercely independent, even in the face of a business relationship like that with Stinson, and was quick to let people know. Perhaps most telling is a letter that Moe wrote to his pressing plant, Scranton Record Co.,[14] on 18 March 1943. In it he clearly wants to avoid the impression of being absorbed into another organization, as well as explicitly identifying the market direction he intended to take. In part Moe wrote[15]:

> For the past 3 years the Asch Recording Studios has worked as an independent organization and we want to maintain that status even though we may from time to time change our distributorship set up. Our records are in demand throughout this country, in Canada and South America. Our present contacts in all parts of the world should materialize into big things after the war since we are the only manufacturers of Jewish records.
>
> We want to maintain a listing in your books in our name—Asch Recordings—which would not conflict with any agreements that we have now. In this way we hope to re-establish the basis for good will between us for years to come.

The tone of the letter would almost appear to indicate that there had been some kind of prior difficulty between Scranton Record Co. and Asch Recordings. The most obvious difficulty would have been payment of accounts. A letter of 21 June 1943[16] suggested that a previous policy of allowing companies to use masters owned by Scranton often led to some companies not paying copyright and royalty payments back to Scranton. This may have been the case for masters that were leased to Moe, and could account for the money difficulties that Moe had encountered and thus explain the loan that Asch received from Prosky and Harris. It may also account for the reference to the change in distributorship, because by this date Asch Records was being distributed through the Stinson Trading Co.

Once again, the context of the letter quoted above may have been related to the shellac shortage. A response to Moe four days later, on 22 March 1943, from John Griffin of the Scranton Record Co. general sales office states[17]:

> I am preparing the order along the lines of your letter of March 18 with the anticipation that it will be accepted at Scranton. As you know, all our customers are on a quota basis and at the present time our complete production is allocated. However, it should be possible for us to work in an additional 1121 records at some time, but our ability to make these records is no guarantee of our ability to make larger quantities at a future date.

Incidentally, have you anything in mind about furnishing us with some scrap for which we will, or course, pay at the regular rate?[18]

A further difficulty that arose in the relationship between Scranton and Asch (as well as all of Scranton's other customers) were changes in the administration and liability of the manufacturer's excise tax. In a letter dated 21 June 1943,[19] John Griffin of Scranton notes that "Under a ruling issued by the Commissioner of Internal Revenue we have been held responsible for the payment of excise taxes on all records made from masters of which we are the owners." However, Scranton also had problems where "in some instances claims have been filed against us for the payment of copyright royalties and artist royalties" after loaning these masters to other companies. This prompted a formal contract between Scranton and all its customers (Asch's is dated 29 September 1943) that clearly explains that[20]:

> Since our company is merely the fabricator of your finished records we should not, of course, be directly concerned with such matters, but nevertheless in some instances claims have been filed against us by third parties in connection with copyright and royalty charges alleged to be due on masters we have accepted for processing. The purpose of the enclosed agreement is merely to indemnify us against the possibility of loss in these matters. . . .

This particular problem may also have prompted the relationship between Scranton Record Co. and the Record Syndicate Trust of Massachusetts to sell off rights to the masters and mothers that it owned. As part of this sell-off, Moe purchased full rights for North and South America (the Trust retained world rights) to the *Wreck of the 97* from Scranton through the Trust[21] for $50, and was waiting for a response concerning licenses for other Scranton mothers or masters.[22]

Asch took advantage of the sell-off, as well as other usage agreements. A further example dated 28 February 1944 (for the period 1 August 1943 to 31 July 1944) entitles Moe to use Scranton matrices for the *Lone County Bachelor* (master US 67) and *Little Old Sod Shanty* (master US 68), for distribution in the United States (plus territories and possessions) and Canada. The ultimate cost to Moe was to be 1.5 percent per side, or 3 percent if the two songs appeared on the same record, of the retail selling price of the recording.[23] It certainly appeared to be a relatively easy way to get material for release in what were arguably pretty tough times. However, these masters may well have been the only masters Moe used under the agreement with Scranton. In a letter to Moe dated 16 August 1944[24]:

> We [Scranton Record Company] do not believe . . . that it will be necessary to send to you a new contract covering the use of US mas-

ters. In dispensing with this agreement we do not feel that it will in any way alter the pleasant relationship we have had and sincerely hope that we may enjoy your continued business in the future.

Early 1945 was marked by the reestablishment of a purchase relationship between Asch Recordings and Scranton Record Co, and the termination of any relationship with the Record Syndicate Trust. In a contract with Scranton Record Co. and Record Syndicate Trust dated 24 January 1945,[25] Moe begins by reminding the parties that:

Reference is made to our agreements dated November 5, 1943 and December 8, 1943 with Record Syndicate Trust and all other agreements or contracts . . . between ourselves and Record Syndicate Trust.

In consideration of the acceptance by the Scranton Record Company of the enclosed order dated January 24, 1945 for four masters and four mothers, and subject to the fulfillment by you of that order, all obligations of the Scranton Record Company, if any, arising out of said agreements and contracts between ourselves and Record Syndicate Trust are hereby canceled and brought to an end.

All obligations of Record Syndicate Trust to furnish to order for us any metal matrices, test pressings or records, if any, are also hereby canceled and brought to an end.

Enclosed with the letter[26] was a purchase order for a handful of masters that Moe wished to purchase from Scranton. Oddly, the list suggests that Moe wanted two sets of the same numbered masters, one for $4 each, the other for $3 dollars each. Why there should be two prices for the same numbered masters is not at all clear. About 8 months later on 16 August 1945, Moe put in another, larger order with Scranton for more masters[27] (see Table 4).

By all appearances, it looked like Moe was attempting to do two things by purchasing these masters. The first would have been to avoid the payment of royalties that would be necessary on the masters licensed from Record Syndicate Trust. Eliminating such payments appears as a lifelong practice for Moe: the less he had to pay out after the release of the recording, the better. This was not a bad strategy at all, considering that a large proportion of cash flow could get eaten up in royalty payments and through the additional staff time necessary to calculate and disburse the payments.

This would be particularly important, given that Moe had very few staff in these early days—perhaps no more than three or four employees. The only well-documented figure was Marian Distler, who joined Moe in 1940, shortly after the establishment of Asch Records. There may have been one

Table 4 Masters Purchased from Scranton Record Co., August 1945

Title	Master Number	Title	Master Number
Mustang Grey	73-1	Sweet Betsy from Pike	79-1
Sam Hall	80-1	Jesse James	69-1
Buffalo Skinners	70-1	Black Outlaw Steer	US 74-1
Bald Faced Steer	US 63-1	Jack O' Diamonds	US 81-1
Joe Bowers	US 72-1	Arkansas Traveler	1823-2A
Bottle in My Hand	USG 13543-D1	Ten Thousand Years Ago	C1146
Old Joe Clark	1840-1-B	Tea for Two	1317-1
Pom Pom	1287-1	Blues	1316-1
Zonky	1319-1	Scratchin' the Gravel	1318-1
Harem Party	USE 859-D1	A Good Man is Hard to Find	US 1113-2
Traveling Blues	USC 16609-D1	I'm Long Gone	USC 16965-D1

or two other employees to help with inventory and shipping, but Marian was by all accounts an integral part of keeping the office running while Moe dealt with the recordings. With such a small staff complement, owning the material outright would eliminate an unnecessary headache from the bookkeeping side of the enterprise.

The second reason for purchasing the masters is a bit more speculative. The demise of the Asch/Stinson relationship was imminent at this point, and certainly Moe had a number of his own recordings tied up in Stinson's distribution and production arrangement. The purchase of Scranton recordings at this time might have been seen by Moe as a bit of an insurance policy, a way of establishing a set of titles that he could easily demonstrate did not have any ties to Stinson whatsoever. As will be shown later, such a strategy would have been a good idea, considering the mess that arose with the breakup in the Asch/Stinson partnership.

As far as Moe was concerned, the relationship with Scranton seemed to be meeting most of his record-production needs, and he certainly seemed to want to keep it that way. Perhaps in anticipation that Scranton might get drawn into the difficulties between Moe, Harris, and Prosky, Moe was working hard to keep a healthy relationship with Scranton, and especially with then–Vice President John Griffin. In a letter to Moe dated 30 January 1946, Griffin opens by writing that "It was most thoughtful and generous of you to give me such a fine cigarette lighter at Christmas time and I appreciate it very much." He then apologizes that Scranton is not currently able to help Moe out, but "please be assured that I am keeping you in mind and that as the situation changes you can be sure that I will be only too glad to do anything I can to make further production available."[28]

The nature of the personal relationship between Moe and John Griffin was likely quite warm as reflected in correspondence spanning several years. The appreciation that Griffin had for Moe's gift is noteworthy, not just because of the personal nature of the business relationship, but also because of its apparent rarity in Moe's business dealings. However, in the larger context of the conflicts that Moe likely knew were coming, it is pretty obvious that Moe was working to shore up some good favor at Scranton. It also stands out in part because Moe didn't typically approach business relationships in this way, but ultimately, it was a move that may well have helped him buy some time to sort out the mess following the collapse of the Stinson relationship.

Overall, the relationship between Asch and Stinson was a mutually beneficial and apparently profitable relationship. However, attempting to follow the flow of money is a little convoluted, to say the least. Referring back to the tally sheets from March 1943 to November 1945 (Table 2) it appears that Moe was paid an amount equivalent to a royalty for every unit of each title that was sold. On top of that amount, Moe added a 15 percent "profit" margin (although on one invoice, it is marked as "overhead," which may in fact be closer to the truth). If Moe had simply licensed these titles to Stinson and then was acting as a salesman/distributor (which he had been certainly been doing in 1943), then the 15 percent might be accountable in terms of general expenses or sales costs. Interestingly, however, all of these invoices have an additional 10 percent federal manufacturer's excise tax added on that, as receipts show, Asch Recording Studios paid on a regular basis. By most accounts, the explanation for this lies in the fact that Moe took responsibility for the production of the recordings on contract to Stinson, who had the access to shellac quotas based on their sales of Russian materials in the years prior to the war and their relationship with Asch Records. Asch Records, on the other hand, did not have the sales to be able to produce its own material, instead "leasing" it out to Stinson in return for a royalty or licensing fee of some kind.

On one level, you might expect that Moe would simply hand over the masters of the material that was being sold through Stinson, collect the percentage fee, and forego the added expense incurred through the production process, particularly the excise tax. In all likelihood, the reason why Moe did not directly license material to Stinson lies in Moe's desire to keep control of production. Had Moe simply offered up his masters, he would have had his material released only under the Stinson label (although they did collaborate on an "Asch/Stinson" label for some titles). Instead, by continuing to produce under the Asch label, he was able to accomplish two important goals. First, although he certainly paid more in taxation, he nonetheless maintained control over his material, even though it was being sold via the Stinson Trading Company. Asch might not have been making as much as he would surely have liked, but as least he was continuing to produce his material. Second, it may have been an important step in a very forward-thinking production strategy. Although there is no direct evidence to support this suggestion, Moe's production strategy may have been to use up Stinson's production quotas producing "Stinson" records. However, in the process he would have been liable for the manufacturer's taxes, ensuring that he would be eligible for the 10 percent shellac quota allotted to a record manufacturer based on the previous years' production. In this respect, had World War II continued, and the shellac shortage deepened, Asch would have been in a much better circumstance than he might have had he not taken on the role of manufacturer for Stinson Trading Company.

Whatever the reasons Moe had for setting things up the way he did, the close of 1945 was marked by a purchase agreement between Asch, Prosky, and Harris.[29] In a contract copy, the three signees, plus two attorneys, acknowledged the sale of 106 items (presumably most or all masters) by Moe Asch to Prosky and Harris (Stinson) for $1, limited to a term of fifteen months. Dated 22 December 1945, the agreement lays out the transferal of license of the items on an attached schedule.[30] Unfortunately, the actual list does not appear to have survived, leaving much speculation about the truth of ownership of many masters pressed during and after this period. More to the point, perhaps, is why the agreement was limited to fifteen months. On the surface, it has the appearance of an arrangement designed to get Asch and Stinson apart quickly and equitably with the eventual return of the licenses to Moe. Unfortunately, it was not to be so simple.

Although there is great confusion to this day about the rightful ownership of many of the masters involved in this and several other transactions, it is apparent that confusion reigned even shortly after the agreement was signed. A letter from T. L. Allen at Scranton Record Co. to Moe, dated 1 February 1946,[31] points out that:

> Recently you sold to Stinson Trading Co. a quantity of masters. From what we have received, it is pretty difficult for me to segregate the Stinson masters which you have sold from your own. . . .
>
> Certainly we cannot segregate the masters based on the incomplete information which we have here and we do not want to be put in the position of finding ourselves in difficulty because of making records for Stinson from something that might be Asch or vice-versa.

Table 5 Asch "H"-Series Masters Pressed by Stinson without Permission

[Date][a]	[Master Number]	[Quantity]	[Total]
Feb. 5, 1946	H 6000	347	
	H 6001	352	
	H 6002	200	
	H 6004	200	
	H 6007	200	
	H 6009	325	
	H 6022	334	1,958
Feb. 6	H 6001	21	
	H 6002	169	
	H 6004	159	
	H 6007	187	
	H 6009	23	
	H 6021	345	904
Feb. 7	H 6003	277	
Feb. 8	H 6003	66	343
Feb. 8	H 6006	326	
	H 6005	200	
	H 6008	307	833
Feb. 11	H 6008	41	
	H 6005	134	275
		Total	4,313

[a]The square brackets indicate that the headings were not included on the original document.

A letter from Asch's attorney J. J. Corn (about whom more will be said later) further reinforced the difficulties that Moe was having with Prosky and Harris. Dated 13 August 1946,[32] the letter indicates that Moe was preparing an "action against Stinson Trading Co., Irving Prosky, Herbert Harris and Stinson Trading Co., Inc." Apparently, Stinson was pressing records from Asch masters that Moe did not sell to them outright. The first item of inquiry in the letter has Corn asking of Moe: "Were any more records unauthorizedly made from your masters than this list,"[33] attaching a list of twenty items from the Asch "H" series (Table 5). Examining the dates in the left-hand column of the list, it certainly appears as though some advantage was taken of the fact that Scranton Record Co. could not clearly distinguish ownership after the 1 February 1946 letter. In the meantime, these records were pressed for Stinson while Scranton was awaiting more information from Moe.

Meanwhile, Moe still had not contacted Scranton Record Co. (now referred to by its new name, Capitol Records, Inc) concerning the identification of the masters. In an exchange with Mary Connerton at Capitol, Moe received a letter dated 18 September 1946[34] that read in part:

> With reference to my letter to you [Moe] of August 23, 1946, I am still awaiting confirmation that all Asch and Stinson matrices—located at our factory—are the property of Stinson exclusively.
>
> Today I received a letter from Mr. Prosky who requests that all metal parts be forward to him. I am holding up this shipment, pending your response . . .
>
> Unless I receive your immediate response, I will assume that you are not interested in the question of ownership . . .

Two days later Moe replied[35]:

> With reference to your letter of September 18, please be advised that we are still investigating this matter and we will have definite information for you next week.
>
> Kindly hold this in abeyance until you hear from us.

Whatever legal action might have been in the works through J. J. Corn and possibly other channels, it is clear that it was not moving forward at the pace that Capitol Records required. On 9 October 1946, nearly three weeks after the promise of the above letter, M. S. Hardy, the plant controller at Capitol, sent Moe the following letter[36]:

> We are extremely anxious to dispense with all metal parts belonging to former customers such as yourself. We find that repeatedly we have requested a list of the matrices belonging to you which are located at the Scranton Plant. We have received from time to time, in answer to our letters, various promises but to date, after a four month period, we still do not have the list. I understand that there is some question as to the ownership of certain parts which our records indicate belong to Stinson Recording. Stinson has acknowledged the ownership of some 700 odd metal parts; the question of ownership of a portion of this 700 parts has been brought up by your office. In order to alleviate our storage problem and to comply with Stinson's request for the return of the metal parts to them, it is imperative that we have a similar list from your office immediately . . .
>
> . . . we are now insisting that your office give us the information we desire; otherwise, the responsibility of possession of the metal parts will no longer be ours as it is our intention to wash our hands of the whole affair. As a matter of fact, we have a signed release for

all parts belonging to Stinson Company; therefore, any miscellaneous disputes and assignments as to the ownership should be handled directly with Mr. Prosky of Stinson.

It appears Moe must have failed to let Capitol know about any progress that was being made concerning the question of ownership as legal proceedings were already underway at this time. By 7 January 1947, a statement of agreement was signed by the lawyers of Moe Asch (plaintiff) and Irving Prosky and Herbert Harris (defendants).[37] To briefly summarize the terms relating specifically to recordings in this historically important agreement, Asch was given, free of charge, a number of 78 rpm albums, presumably drawn from his back catalog of recordings that Stinson had pressed under the original agreement, plus the right to purchase additional sets at a reduced price. Presumably, this was as punishment to Stinson for illegally pressing titles from Asch's earlier "H" series. The agreement also specifies that all "H" masters (with one exception) are owned by Asch, not Stinson, and that "on or after 3 March 1947 [Stinson] will not directly or indirectly use the name 'Asch' or trade names 'Asch Records' or 'Asch Records-Stinson.'" Furthermore, Stinson was required to sticker over these names on any remaining stock that they continued to sell. The timing of this agreement appears to coincide with the expiration of the fifteen-month license from the previous agreement, though it does not explicitly refer to the earlier transfer.

Despite the appearance of a clear-cut termination of the Asch/Stinson arrangement, there continues to this day to be confusion over ownership and control of many of the recordings. These difficulties with Asch Records may have been part of the impetus for Moe to take another shot at record production, and form DISC Corporation of America in late 1945. This would have allowed Moe both a change of emphasis in material, from being known for predominantly Jewish records to focusing on producing jazz recordings through DISC. More importantly, however, it also would have removed Moe from any obligations—legal or otherwise—arising from the relationship between Asch and Stinson. It is not surprising to think that Moe would not want to put any new masters at risk of being lost to Stinson. The legal wrangling marked an unfortunate end to Moe's first foray into the recording business. By the time this last lawsuit was filed, Asch Records was essentially dormant, although by no means forgotten.

The problems with Stinson would continue to gall Asch for decades to come. Stinson continued to market its Asch recordings on LP for decades, including Woody Guthrie and Lead Belly sessions, at discount prices. They also occasionally licensed material to others that Asch considered his own. For example, in the early 1960s, Moe was involved in some legal problems revolving around the unlicensed release of Folkways material by Dansk Grammofonpladeforlag, Copenhagen, that they had received from Stinson Records. In the first notification on 15 June 1962,[38] Moe's lawyer Harold Orenstein informed K.E. Knudson that Moe had found out about a record released in Europe by Dansk (*Storyville Blues Anthology,* Vol. 7, SLP 124). The recording contained Lead Belly material recorded by Moe and noted on the jacket liner that it was "A Stinson Master."

As Orenstein stated later in this letter:

> If, in fact, you purported to acquire the rights contained in the aforesaid album from Stinson Records, we call to your attention the fact that Stinson had no authority from Folkways Records, nor does it itself possess legal title or property in the master records referred to above. The unlicensed master records are as follows:
> TALKING AND PREACHING [TALKING, PREACHING][39]
> BRING ME A LIL WATER LILY [BRING ME A LITTLE WATER, SILVY]
> JULIE AND JOHNSON [not listed]
> LINE 'EM
> WHOA, BACK, BUCK [WHOE BACK, BUCK]
> COW COW YICKY YACKY YEA [COW COW YICKY YICKY YEA]
> OUT IN THE WESTERN PLAINS
> GREEN CORN
> JOHN HARDY
> BIG FAT WOMAN
> MEETING AT THE BUILDING
> BOTTLE UP AND GO [BORROW LOVE AND GO]
> WE SHALL WALK THROUGH THE VALLEY [not listed]
> NOTED RIDER [NO GOOD RIDER]

In a letter shortly after, dated 29 September 1962[40] Moe admonishes Dansk (Knudsen) directly for not having made payments to Folkways for the lost royalties on the records that had already been released, as well as their failure to address the legal issues through Moe's lawyers. Moe was quite upset at the weak attempt to get around determining ownership:

> On volume 7, SLP, which you have on Storyville, you will find the marking, "Recording date unknown." You know that in spite of this legend the recording was made after my contract with Stinson expired. In your program notes you state that the recordings were made in 1942 and in 1946. In 1945 I have a signed court order by a Supreme Court Justice in the State of New York forbidding Stinson records to use my name or my assets.

The final letter in this series is from Moe's lawyers to Jack Kall of Stinson Records on 23 January 1963.[41] Of course, the letter follows the same pattern as the previous two directed at Dansk. The letter reads in part:

> Dansk has advised us that your company purported to license certain rights to it to release these recordings. These performances were first recorded by Lead Belly for our client after March of 1946, at which time your company no longer had any rights whatsoever to release Folkways masters.
>
> Notwithstanding this fact, you have purported to grant rights in master recordings in which you have no rights. . . .
>
> Unless we hear from you within ten (10) days after your receipt of this letter, we shall have no alternative but to take all steps which the law allows to protect our client's property rights.

Although this is a somewhat *pro forma* kind of letter, it does clearly highlight the difficulties involved in rights protection. It must be said, however, with respect to many cases of unlicensed releases like this one, the punishment is often worth the infraction. In the Dansk case, it may have been something of a fluke that Moe found out at all. Had Moe not found out, the release may have continued to make money for both Dansk and Stinson, leaving Folkways uninformed and uncompensated. According to these and other cease-and-desist orders, the standard procedure is for the offending companies to pay back royalties on the released material and to stop production. By these standards, unauthorized releases would still be a profitable proposition for the offenders.

First Recordings by Lead Belly, Pete Seeger, and Woody Guthrie

Asch's early output mostly focused on Jewish material, the so-called "H" series of records. Then, through Charles Edward Smith (and later Frederic Ramsey), he began recording jazz. However, it was his introduction to the musicians of the first folk-music revival during the early 1940s—specifically Lead Belly, Pete Seeger, and Woody Guthrie—that would be defining events for Asch and ultimately for the development of Folkways Records. Within only a few years of each other, these three individuals changed the course of recorded American music and did so largely through Moe Asch. They also provided Moe with a core of material that would, particularly with respect to American folk music, provide for many years of releases and re-releases. As the folk revival began in the 1950s, Moe was not only able to capitalize on the growing interest in Seeger and Guthrie, but Moe's early recordings of American music provided much of the musical fuel that drove the revival in the first place.

Despite claims to Dansk (above) and others, it is pretty much accepted that Asch made his first recordings of the blues singer Lead Belly in May 1941.[42] (Although there is often some disagreement about this date, especially from Moe, himself; see below. Whether it is an honest mistake on Moe's part or an effort to place the date after the Stinson agreement so Moe could maintain control of the material is open for debate.) Nonetheless, significantly for the future of Folkways Records, Moe had Lead Belly focus on children's material. The children's market would become a major one for Asch throughout his career, and this initial success must have helped point him in that direction. Despite Seeger and Guthrie being perhaps better known, it was Lead Belly that Moe credited for putting Folkways on the map for folk music. As Moe put it:

> John Lomax heard about him and went down to Louisiana and got him out of prison, where he was serving a sentence after having been convicted of murder. Lomax dressed him up in a convict suit for his performances. Lead Belly was a very acute, very intelligent person, and he realized he was being used, but he didn't mind as long as he was getting something out of it. Then Lomax more or less dropped Lead Belly, and he was introduced to me. This was around 1946. I recorded him singing children's songs that he knew, since I had had some success with recordings for children. Walter Winchell got a hold of that and wrote: Here is this convict, this murderer, and he's associated with a record company that puts out children's records! Everybody got interested in us after that.[43]

Aside from the publicity, Lead Belly also added an important voice to the music from the South. Moe felt very protective of Lead Belly. Anecdotes abound of Moe going out of his way to ensure that the individuals that he believed in had a roof over their heads and something to eat, offering up the occasional "advance" during hard times.

Moe first recorded Pete Seeger in June 1943, when Seeger was on leave from the army. Like many other artists who recorded for Moe, Pete Seeger (and other members of the Seeger family) became almost a partner in Folkways. Coming from an important musical family,[44] Pete had set out to discover his own musical path, performing a wide variety of early American music and writing important topical songs, as well as a range of songs that for many have become part of the soundtrack of the twentieth century, including the seminal arrangement of the Civil Rights anthem, *We Shall Overcome*. Moe's first meeting with Pete certainly set the tone for a long and important musical and personal relationship.

> The way we met was like this: there was a session at Decca about Lincoln, *The Lonesome Train*. I got a phone call from Alan Lomax,

who said, "Stay in your studio because Pete Seeger is in town, and we're coming to record." He said Pete had to go back to army camp in New Jersey, and then he may go overseas. So I stayed in the studio. They got through at Decca about four in the morning, and Pete had to be back in camp about nine that same morning. So from the studio where they did the record for Decca, he came to me. And we were introduced, and he did the first album we did together, 2003 [10" *Darling Cory*]. That's how I met Pete. . . . He always wanted to do what he wanted, immediately, right at the moment. And I had to pay attention to what he wanted to do. And as a result he created my whole folk music concept. Because he created ideas and songs and every time he had an idea I went along with it—and there are those fifty albums that we did. Every one is Pete's idea. I tried to work with all my artists that way—I wanted to know what they had to say and how they wanted to say it. That's what it meant to me to be a documentor.[45]

Seeger would record prolifically for Asch through the 1950s until 1960, when he signed with Columbia Records. Albums like *The Goofing Off Suite*, an all-instrumental outing that featured selections from Beethoven and Irving Berlin as well as traditional numbers, were planned entirely by Seeger. It is interesting to note that Asch's notion of "documenting" extended to the idea that the artist should control his own albums, from packaging and liner notes to the selection of theme and material; this would become a hallmark of small labels in the future, but was virtually unheard of at the time. Eventually, Asch released dozens of albums credited to Seeger alone, along with many collaboration and compilation albums.

The third event was Moe's introduction to Woody Guthrie, a prolific writer of topical political songs in the 1930s and 1940s, which came in March 1944, after Woody recorded material for Alan Lomax, music curator at the Library of Congress. Shortly after Woody recorded for Lomax, then briefly for RCA, he introduced himself to Moe. As Moe recalled[46]:

In his own way Woody was the most antisocial person I ever met. He didn't like people, especially middle-class, bourgeois people. When he came to New York, he didn't meet people of his own kind, his own background. But he had a driving force and a knowledge of what he stood for. He felt that he represented a group of poor people that needed to be spoken for, and he wanted to give them exposure. . . . He was a terrific writer. As long as I didn't bother him and contradict him but listened to him and used his idea, he felt comfortable with me. Woody could create a song right there in the studio. When Woody got in front of a microphone, he knew exactly what the guitar was going to sound like and what he was going to sound like. He was using me like a pen, to make a book. I was working the machinery, but he was using it for himself. I never looked at his hair, his way of dressing. That was Woody, you accepted Woody the way he was. He had just walked into the studio one day, sat down on the floor, and said, "I'm Woody Guthrie." I said, "So what?" Later on we became good friends. I helped him in the sense that as soon as he wrote down the song, he would rush to the studio to record. We were always ready for him. He would try the song immediately with the tune that he had in his head. He always used a folk tune for the words he wrote. He'd made two or three versions of the thing until the tune sounded right to him. He could say, "I like this song, I don't like this song, and put this album out.". . . And he appreciated that what I had to say had validity, and I treated him like a human being who had something important to say. But generally you would think he was the strangest person in the world.

Guthrie recorded both alone and with larger groups for Asch, often in informal sessions. As Moe mentioned, Woody liked to record several versions of tunes and try out a number of different arrangements to find one he liked or to experiment with different lyrics. Of all these recordings, Asch issued only a handful at the time, primarily focussing on Guthrie's better-known songs and his children's material. Eventually, the Smithsonian would reissue the best of this material in a four-CD series of *The Asch Recordings* (40100–40103): *This Land Is Your Land* (Vol. 1), *Muleskinner Blues* (Vol. 2), *Hard Travelin'* (Vol. 3), and *Buffalo Skinners (Vol. 4)*, along with *Long Ways to Travel: The Unreleased Folkways Masters, 1944–1949* (40046). In addition to Guthrie's own recordings, he contributed collaborations or single songs to compilations for nearly twenty other Folkways releases.

Of course, one of the common threads between Woody, Pete, Lead Belly, and others was an enduring vision of the importance of individual expression. Moe developed relationships of trust and respect with people that others in the record business had cast aside or ignored. Moe was only interested in the legitimacy of what they had to say, and that reputation became a very important beacon in musical circles. Woody, Pete, and Lead Belly— along with countless others—believed in Moe's vision of documentation, just as Moe believed in what they were trying to accomplish. The fact that Moe had established this reputation so early in his recording career, while he was still recording as Asch Records, became a pivotal factor in Moe implementing his business model later on with Folkways.

On a more pragmatic level, it also became an important part of Moe's ability to procure material for release. Very often, it was those who simply wanted to have a voice that came to Moe, knowing it was not about money, but about expression. Moe, for his part, was also interested primarily in legitimate expression, although he would often turn down material if he though it had already been well-accounted for on record—either his own or from another company. But the ability to gain access to material without explicit concerns over production costs or sales returns would later prove to be an enormous advantage for Moe. Moe's studio was also very accessible to anyone who wanted to record, or, alternately, would provide Moe with an opportunity to make a quick dollar. As Moe himself once described the early days[47]:

> My studio at that time at 117 West 46th Street was very open. Marian Distler, my assistant, did the books, and I had the equipment. . . . There was a window, and my equipment was against it; Marian was close with a desk and files. And on the other end was a studio that I insulated and built, about fifteen by ten feet. The door was on the other side and you walked into the studio. That was the famous studio where so much work was done. So we were always in the place, either Marian or me, and people used to come in and say "I want to record," so all I had to do was get off the desk and put the equipment on and record. Nobody ever had to call beforehand to make appointments, because they all knew I was there twelve to fourteen hours a day.

This openness played a critical part in Moe's ability to capture many early performances. Not only did such recording arrangements favor his own preferences for recording, he was able to avail himself of performers who might never have been recorded if faced with the delays found at other studios.

3
Broadening the Mandate
DISC Records of America

The motivation behind Moe forming a second record company apart from Asch Records likely came from several events. Escaping the legal and practical difficulties that had come to be associated with Asch Records and the Stinson Trading Co. agreements would be understandable. At the same time, however, Moe was demonstrating a change in musical direction as well. Later on in his career, Moe would again create other company names when directions for new material would arise. Whatever his motivation, however, Moe still believed in the possibilities of recording, and after weathering the demise of Asch Records, he formed his second label: DISC Records of America.

In addition to the Stinson affair, Moe was occupied through the first months of 1946 with the promotion of his new company. Moe clearly worked very hard at trying to promote DISC.[1] Among the surviving documents, it seems that DISC was the only one of Moe's many companies that had a regular and extensive series of promotional bulletins, with well over forty bulletins released in only a few years. What was likely the first of these bulletins was released on 20 August 1946.[2] Marked for immediate release, the bulletin was done on DISC letterhead and contained " 'DISC quotes,' NEWS CAPSULES for editors, TREND TIPS for record dealers, 'Disc 'n' dat' for everybody in music."

In this bulletin there are some interesting bits of information that set the tone for much of what was to come later with Folkways. The bulletin trumpets:

DISC Company of America since its inception by Moe Asch in January, 1946, has shaped a record catalog comprising all phases of folkways, rare classics, documentary scope, children's music, and basic jazz. Across the DISC record workbench the folkways of the world, from backwoods to conservatory, are made into recordings of permanent value and immediate importance.

However, there is a discrepancy in the founding date of DISC records. Although the bulletin suggests it was January 1946, on 19 June 1945 one of the first references to DISC Company of America was made in a contract between DISC and Charlie Ventura—on DISC letterhead.[3] The January 1946 date is further contradicted by a statement, shown later in this section, that DISC began in December 1945. The evidence would suggest that DISC was in the works for some time before mid-to-late 1945, given the additional time needed to print stationary and other office paperwork.[4]

The actual start date of DISC Records notwithstanding, what is more instructive is Moe's promotional "mission statement" for DISC. Existing only in draft form, the statement clearly sets out what Moe envisioned for DISC and for his larger directions in the music industry. In separate paragraphs, Moe wrote:

> With the end of the war and opening up of new sources of musical and documentary material it was felt that a new label was necessary to cover an enlarged recording program. The DISC label presents an expanded listing of music of all countries while continuing releases of American music with special attention to folkways.
>
> DISC represents a catalog that makes sense. Provocative and listenable records for a satisfying record library with ample variety for all tastes. Pre-school children, long-hairs, followers of musical Americana and the quest of musical means to spread world peace and understanding.
>
> With the advent of DISC folk music became a recognized factor. After its first "Songs to Grow On" children's albums appeared on the market everybody began thinking in terms of activity records for children. Its jazz records broke ground for old and new fans and in the classics DISC produced one of the first complete opera albums as well as the first recording of the now famous Masquerade Suite by Khachaturian.

Moe seemed to be working as a one-man public relations machine. From a series of draft copies of "DISC DIGEST #1 (The baby is growing up),"[5] it is clear that Moe was working hard to promote DISC within the larger music-selling industry and to introduce DISC Records to the music-buying public.[6] Among other items, Moe notes that:

> With tireless effort and unshaken belief from a modest beginning—successful results. A new venture was established throughout the country with overseas contacts. DISC supplies the know-how. Expansion has not come cheaply but with most of the industry singing the blues about the spring and summer slumps DISC is carrying on in its selected sphere. . . . DISC has been able to ride it. Building up a steady clientele that is continually growing. In the Swim; the call for unusual and hard to get items that first attracted customers to DISC is a steady and fast growing one. A force in American life today.
>   Families can keep up with modern cultural trends with DISC just as they read their everyday newspaper. A sure guide to the better people everywhere. The people who count are the ones who read and are interested in culture. They prefer DISC. Leaders in Amer[ican] life. The company is not worried about the future in spite of new inventions or the Petrillo ban. Asch is proud of his part . . .

Another factor in the growing success of DISC was Moe's efforts to put cover art on his records. This was not only celebrated by Moe himself in a number of interviews, but also in contemporary news items like Bill Gottlieb's 1947 *Down Beat* article, "Cover Art Sells Albums."[7] There is little doubt, both from insiders and the media, that cover art did indeed make a tremendous impact in the identification of the albums by the consumer, and thus helping to create an identity for the albums within the marketplace.

However, along with the importance of promotion and cover art, it was the growing use of accompanying booklets that really helped to distinguish Moe's recordings from others on the market.[8] A clearly thought-out piece stressed why the relationship between the booklet and the music was so important:[9]

> The packaging of discs in albums, now an accepted part of the record industry, may have begun with concert music. This would have been a logical beginning, to keep intact the records of a set. And the booklet, or inside cover description, may have grown from this, at first to include merely a few facts, later to deal as well with analysis and background. For as time went on album introductions became as erudite as intermission commentaries, but more useful since they formed a part of one's permanent record library. . . .
>   Today, more than ever, music is music in context. . . .

In the preparation of written material a dual function is performed. First of all, the writing footnotes the contents of the album, giving the background of performers and music. But in describing the latter one can hardly escape the inter-relatedness of one song, dance or type of music to another. Presented clearly and popularly, the writing points up the historical and environmental framework.

Booklets on performers, performance and background accompanying DISC jazz albums, for example, acquaint the listener with jazz as it is today and the pattern of its growth from the early beginnings in New Orleans. . . .

An interesting aside to the text above is the brief mention of a newsletter-type release called PERISCOPE (see Appendix 1 for an outline of material to be included in PERISCOPE).[10] PERISCOPE had every appearance of being a dead-end, as there appears to be only a single direct reference concerning the goals of such a release,[11] along with a few other items serving as potential material for inclusion in the newsletter. The potential material for the newsletter has the provocative heading "FOR PERISCOPE: CONTINUATION OF 'HUMBLE-PROUD' COPY" and notes that:

In recording our own music and that of the world, DISC believes, as do many companies large and small, that they are helping Americans to feel at home with themselves and with their global neighbors. For its own part, DISC has set as its goal a selective, informative and entertaining catalog of albums and records. Along with this have been issued background booklets and releases, and such practical copy as illustrated instructions for dances and for children's games. In *Periscope* we bring you what others as well as ourselves feel about records and recording, give you an inside look at what goes on inside our plant, trends in the industry and any "briefs" that will be helpful or interesting. We look forward to your reactions and ideas for we do not intend to narrow the range of vision to DISC doings or the DISC catalog. The columns of *Periscope* are open to readers in all branches of the industry. We feel healthy enough so that we probably do not need a shot in the arm but we'll always need, and welcome, food for thought. [Signed DISC].

The final comment is both interesting and fairly perplexing at the same time. It would be pure speculation as to what purpose or audience Moe might have wanted to direct this release, especially given the prevalence of the DISC release notes. The "broader-issues" theme might have been strong enough to push Moe, but overall it seems unlikely.[12] A more cynical view might support the suggestion that PERISCOPE might be part of a plan to give the appearance of the financial health and stability of DISC when, in fact, things were starting to look bleak, as it most certainly would have prior to DISC's bankruptcy.

It should be apparent by now that Moe was very focused on DISC's success and to have been intent on developing the specific issues of promotion and strategic business plans for DISC. Two examples in particular are of interest. The first is a draft of a strategic plan. Many observers of Moe and Folkways over the years have implied that Moe was less that organized when it came to business. In a formal sense, this might have been true, but Moe was very aware from an early date of the value of strategic planning as a means of maintaining some control over the direction of whichever company he was directing at the time. In this instance, he clearly has asked for some suggestions on the direction to take with DISC. Given the suggestions that are being made within the text of the letter, the DISC plan appears to have come from DISC sales manager Nelson Lewis.[13] If this is the case, the letter was likely directed to Moe:[14]

> In the summer time one has to stabilize the catalog and set the policy of the firm for the fall. I believe that Disc will be a factor in the children line there fore I believe that as soon as possible a children set should be issued in plastic. Also a single record in an envelope has to be issued in the children's series.
>
> We are established in the unusual Classic field therefore I believe that the 876 should be at all times available for this item shows the most interest from dealers stand point also I believe that the Charles Ives should be prepared for fall issue with all the preparitory [sic] work done now.
>
> I believe that the Summer Day suite should have a release sheet and be plugged on the air, sent to major reviewers and albums displayed wherever possible for this is an unusual set and can have a good summer movement. I think that the Lennie Tristano Album should be issued as soon as possible because the followers of that type of jazz will buy at all times as I do not believe that there is a special season for him.
>
> Calypso should always be in our mind because the buyers of this kind of music are legion and expect and will buy new releases. However, main stores want these records in albums. We have broken the prejudice of 12" jazz records with the 2500 and I believe that the Red Norvo "The Man I Love" will be another hit of the same nature.
>
> Disc is a major factor in the industry in its folk series I don't think that a new item should be issued in this series till June or July and then the item should be Van Wey in Louisiana folk songs for she is light on the ears and very melodic as an alternative I would suggest her Smokey Mountain ballads.

> We have a blues record made by Brownie McGhee which could
> be issued for the Harlem trade. A test record should be made and
> sent out to the various Distributors who would go for such item.

The author obviously knew DISC well, both in terms of markets and
also the inventory, which is a task in itself. From this point of view, it is
tempting to think that Marian Distler could have written the letter to Moe,
offering her point of view on the future of DISC. If this were the case, it
would certainly elevate opinions of her as simply the office manager and
all around "Girl Friday" for Moe. Some have suggested that she was, in fact,
the motivating force behind Asch, DISC, and ultimately, Folkways, and
that Moe was only the hired hand. Though more will be said on this concerning the origins of Folkways, it simply is incorrect to suggest that much
of the broader vision of the recording mandate that Moe followed was anything but his alone. Marian's contributions were unquestionably important to the success of Moe's early ventures, but there seems to be little
doubt that she was following Moe's direction, not the reverse.

All that aside, the content of this letter is quite incredible. The letter is
one of the earliest documents to set out a marketing plan that, in essence, is
devoid of larger social values. The content is directed solely at exploiting a
set of markets as efficiently as possible with existing musical resources—
much of which appears to have been left over from Asch Records. The
writer is also very supportive of the incredibly wide range of markets, from
children's to classical to jazz to folk. On the face of it, any sensible entrepreneur would try to find a few areas of strength that could be clearly identified and exploited. DISC aimed at the opposite goal: to issue some
recordings in all musical areas. Perhaps it is only at this level of abstraction
that Moe's original idea of creating a sound encyclopaedia is evident
through efforts to produce something different in every genre.

New Products and Directions

DISC marked something of a new beginning for Moe, and offered further
indications of the type of product he would eventually issue on Folkways.
He made two important partnerships during the DISC era: the first with
jazz producer Norman Granz, in mid-1945, that would result in DISC issuing the first live recordings of jazz; and the second with ethnomusicologist
Harold Courlander in July 1946, who began assembling the first "Ethnic"
recordings that Asch released.

The deal with Granz initially appeared to offer DISC a great opportunity: to release top-quality jazz performers, in concert, based on Granz's
successful Jazz at the Philharmonic (JATP) series. Although live concert recordings are commonplace today, they were unheard of when Granz ap-

proached Asch; many critics were dismayed by the poor quality of the recordings, and the inclusion of audience noise and reaction. To Asch, this documentation of a real event would fit perfectly into his recording philosophy: to present a "real" performance, not one manufactured in the studio. Plus, he was shrewd enough to recognize the commercial possibilities in obtaining top-flight jazz performances. The Granz deal continued through early 1947, and eventually the expansion into more popular music would cost DISC dearly, but at first it seemed like both a golden business opportunity and a nice fit with Asch's overall philosophy.

Courlander brought to Asch a different opportunity: "authentic" recordings of music from around the world. Undoubtedly, the scholarly/documentary quality of these recordings would appeal strongly to Asch. The educational mission was underscored by Courlander's careful documentation, included with the initial 78 albums released in the new "Ethnic series." In the DISC catalog, the series was trumpeted as "the Folkways of the World on Record"—an early appearance of the use of the term "Folkways"[15] (see also Appendix 2). Also, the low-cost of producing the material—scholars who made recordings in the field were rarely looking for much in the way of payment, and the performers themselves were largely unpaid—would have fit in with Asch's overall need to minimize expenses. Again, at the time, the idea of issuing nonprofessional "field" recordings was a radical one, and Asch was taking a risk in releasing material for which a market was not known.

Bankruptcy

Despite the innovations in content and packaging that Asch made with DISC, he still faced some difficult economic realities. His expansion into jazz left him particularly vulnerable. During 1946, Granz approached Asch with some early sessions recorded by Nat "King" Cole; perhaps foolishly, Asch paid a $10,000 advance on the recording, according to one account. This was a very large amount of money for DISC, and Moe was left holding his breath that he would be able to recover his costs. However, with the holiday season approaching, a violent winter storm and a New York trucking strike prevented him from getting the record into stores. By the time the records arrived, the holidays had passed, and sales were not sufficient for Moe to carry the debt.

Facing increasing financial pressure, Asch apparently prepared four pages of notes that addressed the need to refocus DISC on marketing as well as to clarify his own thinking. With no date or author, or any type of identification on the pages, it is very difficult to determine their position within the document trail. In fact, of the four pages, it does not seem likely that more than two of them actually belong together, other than appearing as though they are answers to a questionnaire of some type. However, the importance of these documents is that they again point to the concerted efforts that were directed at planning a strategy for the DISC releases. The items on the pages amount to little more than collections of statements: however, they provide an interesting glimpse into the types of questions that needed to be addressed in planning recording releases and future projects[16]:

Artists associated on Disc in the Race field that are also on other, acceptable labels

Lonnie Johnson	Calypso
Brownie McGhee	Spiritual
Lead Belly	
Sonny Terry	
The Two Keys	
Ernestine Washington	

Artists associated on Disc in the Hillbilly (Folk Field)

| Cisco Houston | Ralph Page the singing caller and group |
| Chet Tyler | Paul Hunt and group |

Potential artists that are on Disc Label that should be in this group with old releases
Woody Guthrie
Pete Seeger
Tom Glazer

We billed over 500,000.00 and returns with bad pressings bad handling unbusiness [sic] management is less than 2%.
Therefore Disc is associated with salable merchandise new approach, customer acceptance, trade acceptance.
For the purpose of fast turnover merchandise (records)

It is my belief that we keep the present label because:
Present label in existence 2 years we gave 100% ret (good will)
It is now acceptable with about 30 distributors.
and is acceptable to new ones. (Jazz and Race)
Who at the present time consist of 13 who are the sole distributors namely:

Virginia	Buffalo
Atlanta	Utah
Florida (when we get one)	Denver
Texas	Oregon
Tenn.	Washington
South Carolina (Rixon)	California
Louisiana	Oklahoma

St. Louis   Cleveland
Detroit

While in Chicago there is a choice of 2 others
In New York of 4 others
Connecticut 1 other
New England 2 other
Pennsylvania 2 other

It is the type of merchandise that has to be exploited
Types:
Popular field (general)
Novelty
Tune
Lyric

Specialty field
Hillbilly (fastest sales turnover)
Race most concentrated group
Jazz Acceptable to both white and Negro
Latin American the most potential
Polka very regional
Foreign smallest group but concentrated.

Artists associated on DISC label in the most acceptable group.
(Jazz)

Jazz at the Philharmonic	Mary Lou Williams
Illinois Jacket [sic]	Howard McGhee
King Cole	Slim Gailard
Charles Ventura	Les Paul
Charlie Parker	Dizzy Gillespie
Lester Young	Mel Powell
Errol Garner	Meade Lux Lewis
Mugsy Spanier	J. J. Johnson
Bob Haggart	Red Norvo
Vic Dickenson	Willie Smith
Sidney Bechet	Lennie Tristano
Gene Krupa	

C. issue records in the types most suited for present distributors
and in demand by them.
race
be-bop
hillbilly

1. by purchasing masters
   licensing of masters from other recorders, individuals, companies
2. recording new masters
3. issue from catalog records with most potential sales by recoupling of the most salable two sides.

E. in each category we are interested in a new release is necessary not later than every three weeks.

F. we get constantly hints and suggestions from our present sources of sales as to what, when, and how items that these sources are interested in merchandising are to be issued.

The importance of outlining this rather disjointed set of statements is twofold. First, it gives a second, very interesting glimpse into the process that Moe might have used to review the position of DISC in the marketplace. There is no question that there are very clear directives with respect to what should be released, when to release it, and the kinds of stylistic or topical areas that are to be highlighted. Second, it reinforces that, from a production point of view, Moe was not at all hesitant to use whatever sources of music might be available to him: recording new material, buying or licensing material, or repackaging existing material. Moe again appears, even at this early date, to be fully committed to the material and less focused on the manner in which he is able to acquire it for release.

There is also the reference in the document to "keeping the present label." There might be, in my view, two possible reasons for making this kind of comment. First is the possibility that there was some question about the success of DISC in the marketplace and that perhaps a name more reflective of the material should be chosen. Much of the material being released had moved from jazz, which, by some accounts, was largely the reason DISC was formed in the first place. Thus, there might have been discussion about beginning a different label to better reflect the broader range of material.

The second and more ominous reason might have been the rising threat of bankruptcy. The reference to the state of affairs at "two years" puts the date of the reference at something close to 1948—the year that DISC ended.[17] If this is the case, then the text may point to some discussion concerning the future of the label and perhaps whether a name change or some alteration might not improve matters. Clearly, the decision was made to remain as DISC, possibly because of the relationships that had already been established and the reputation and goodwill that DISC had earned.

Whatever the intent of the marketing plans and the efforts to remain viable, they were not successful. Unfortunately, 1948 brought heartache for Moe with the demise of DISC. High production costs and the increased risk associated with Norman Granz and the Jazz at the Philharmonic (JATP) series was the likely cause of Moe's bankruptcy and the end of production under the DISC label (see Appendix 3 for a production summary of DISC material at this time).

Maybe it was the Nat King Cole recording, or a marketing plan that pushed too far, too fast, or simply that DISC was extended to far to be able to handle the problems that came with JATP. In any event, in early 1948, Moe was forced to send out an agreement form to all his creditors to work out a settlement of accounts. Moe offered two options to his creditors: (1) 25 percent of all said claims; or 2) 10 percent of said claims "at the time hereinafter specified and five percent monthly thereafter until the entire claim of the undersigned is fully paid."[18] According to Moe, DISC was some $300,000 dollars in debt when it folded. Although there is a series of lists that accompanied the copy of the creditor letter that indicated names and amounts, it is unclear exactly how the two are connected. It certainly appears as though the list indicates payable amounts, but they do not come anywhere close to $300,000—in fact, they might total a few thousand dollars at most. That said, there is no real reason to doubt the $300,000 figure, given its frequent invocation and the fact that DISC's $500,000 annual sales could place the debt figure into this range. However, based on material contained in the DISC history document discussed below, it would appear that a figure between $100,000 and $200,000 might be more in line with the actual debt incurred. Nonetheless, $300,000, although high, is plausible.

A critical document was prepared in anticipation of the bankruptcy proceedings for DISC and titled "Operations of the DISC Company of America from its Inception to Date of Proceedings."[19] Unfortunately, the bulk of the document is in draft form with only one page appearing to be part of the final copy. Nonetheless, this document sets out in detail the economic steps that Moe took to try to maintain control of DISC. It also provides an absolutely classic example of the difficulties that success can bring upon a small record company.[20] Due to the importance of the document, it is presented below in its entirety[21]:

| Started in business | December 1945 |
| Assets: | $6,000.00 capital, recording studio [Received?] guarantee of $10,000.00 worth of credit for record pressings from Clark Phono. Record Co. arranged through Joseph Corn, Atty. |

	[Had a] guarantee of $500.00 a day income from Interstate distributors.
Standing in industry:	The first releases got rave notices from nation's press. Time Magazine wrote profile on the ~~young~~ Disc Company and Moe Asch.
First business adjustment:	In the late spring, early summer of 1946, about 8 months after inception of the company, because of continually growing sales and expanded distribution it became necessary to make arrangements for additional credit.
With record producers:	Through Joseph Corn, I made the following arrangement from pressings: $30,000.00 worth of credit payable in 90 days instead of the original 30 day terms [through] (Joseph Corn) ~~formed~~ Pioneer Records Inc. [they were] to hold masters through assignment as security. Pioneer Records to pay federal tax ~~and Clark Phono. Rec. Co.~~ and Moe Asch to pay Pioneer [who would pay] (Joseph Corn) ~~of~~ (Pioneer Records) was not to dispose of these masters in case of non payment of bills, without the written consent of both Moe Asch and Clark.
With Printers:	Gave dated checks to Perfect Printing and started with Globe Printing who gave me extended credits.
With album manu.:	Worked long term payments with Howard Matthews, Globe Albums, [Progressive Album].
Second business adjustment:	In the early fall of 1946, as the demand for my merchandise kept increasing so also the complaints about poor quality pressings and albums given to me by my manufacturers made it imperative for me {to} seek new sources of supply to prepare for the winter season. Consequently I needed additional credits. Through Mr. Minton of Putnam's and my father I was able to arrange with the Nat'l Bank of Far Rockaway a loan for $10,000.00

[and a $25,000.00 credit on] trade acceptances from my distributors [and personal notes].

With record producers:
At this time I made a deal with Eastern Rec. Mfg. Co. (Mr. Erlinger) for $5,000.00 revolving credit in which I gave him $2,500.00 advance notes, leaving $2,500.00 open and paying the balance on the 10th of the following month.[22]

With printers:
With Globe Printing I arranged to split bills due into 3 or 4 equal payments giving him dated checks payable 30-60-90-120-180 days which he [said he] was able to discount.

Third business adjustment:
The winter of 1946 through 1947 was a good one. However, because of the truck strike around this time, my sales manager[23] whom I had hired several months previous and myself, felt that it would be advisable to move the warehouse to New Jersey and accordingly I made arrangements to do this. As I had reached my limit with the Far Rockaway bank, I had some accounts receivable discounted at the Pennsylvania Exchange bank in New York.[24]

In the spring-summer of 1947 I went to California to open up new distribution. At this time also because my distributors were demanding classical merchandise I made a deal with Jacques Rachmilovich and the Santa Monica Symphony Orchestra to issue their classical recordings giving him dated notes. I made a deal with Allied Records in California for what they told me would be good quality pressing absorbing the extra freight charges since I could not get quality 12" material from either Clark or Eastern. As my account with Corn (Clark) was running 6 months behind I made arrangements to pay him for current bills plus something on account of old bills.

On credit:
At this time, because the Bank of Far Rockaway gave me assurances that I could have

$50,000.00 worth of credit, $25,000.00 guaranteed by my father, and $25,000.00 worth of trade acceptances from my distributors, my father put up $25,000.00 and 2 additional notes of $7,000.00 each payable in 1947 and in 1948. After he signed they limited me to $25,000.00 covered by my father's guarantee.

With distributors: I also borrowed money from my New York distributors, Malverne (who was just beginning to handle the Mercury line) on the basis of large orders they guaranteed me in the fall and winter of 1947 [especially on classical sets].[25]

The Fall of 1947: Business in general instead of picking up started to slack off. I started getting back defective merchandise from my distributors in lieu of payment and cancellations particularly on my classical items. {Beginning of later version} However, my distributors assured me that this was simply a readjustment period as they felt that my line as a whole would always be in demand. I accepted trade acceptances from Don Sherwood in California in anticipation of Christmas orders. In order to clear some of the pressing creditors so that I might get merchandise for anticipated good winter season, I made an arrangement with Mr. Erlinger whereby he gave me $10,000.00 as an advance against the masters that he was pressing and guarantee of another $10,000.00 for possession of the masters, on demand. This was to enable me to carry on and see if I could bale {sic} myself out. I also arranged with him to help me run the distribution by participating as a consultant.

The Winter of 1947: My New York distributor (Malverne) on whom I had counted for a large income now dropped more than 50% in orders for my merchandise as they had made a deal with

Mercury to push their stock and as I would not consent to have Mercury press and distribute my records on the west coast. There were many innuendoes. In desperation I decided with Mr. Erlinger to create my own distribution and accordingly (together with Mr. Erlinger and myself) Mr. William Avar created the Phoenix Disc Distr.

With the severe winter of 1947, bad business and bad merchandise returns from my distributors it became increasingly difficult for me to meet my obligations.

In December of '47 Joseph Corn put a padlock on my warehouse in New Jersey and refused to open it until I gave him a release on my merchandise on hand pressed from my masters at Clark and albums pertaining thereto, and he put my sales manager as custodian of this merchandise.

At this time Mr. Erlinger took over complete distribution. I was put on a salary of $125.00 a week to create new sales outlets so that Disc could carry on but I was in no way permitted to have any contractual or business relations with the distribution of Disc records.

In February 1948, Mr. Erlinger agreed to loan me money to pay my creditors on condition that the masters from which he pressed records belonged to him (this did not include Allied or Clark) and he gave me $10,000.00. A plan was offered to my creditors for 25% as total payment or 10% down and 5% a month until amounts due were entirely cleared. It was understood that I would get half of Disc Distributing when all my creditors were paid up. {This is the end of the extant document}

This sequence of events gives a telling picture of the problem faced by small labels. Asch began with rather meager assets: his recording studio (presumably remaining from Asch Records) and a small amount of cash on hand. He relied on his record presser, Clark Phonograph, to advance him credit. Within eight months, this was insufficient to continue the business, so Asch's lawyer, Joseph Corn, advanced him further funds, while forming a separate company, Pioneer Records, to "hold" DISC's masters as collateral for the loan. By the fall of 1946, reacting supposedly to complaints of the poor quality of Clark's pressings (and perhaps unable to get them to perform further work due to delinquent payments), Asch made a new arrangement with a Mr. Erlinger of Eastern Record Co. for pressing and further credit. Bank loans and loans from Asch's father followed, along with further expansion (including a deal to market classical recordings by the Santa Monica symphony). Asch switched to a larger distributor in early 1947, Malverne Records, who promised him a good deal of business. However, Malverne then became involved with a new major label, Mercury, who apparently insisted that DISC recordings be pressed by them. Asch refused, and the business from Malverne failed to materialize. Asch turned to Erlinger for help, and the two (with another party) formed the aptly named Phoenix Disc Distribution company to try to salvage the situation, but it was too late. Original lien holder Corn seized the inventory and Erlinger took over its distribution, putting Asch on salary.

A complicated set of events to be sure. The amount of effort that Moe put into maintaining DISC was impressive. However, a couple of important connections come out of the DISC storyline. The first is the fact that, now in his early forties, Moe was able to approach his father to help with financing. It is hard to say how difficult this might have been, given the apparent desire of the Asch children to demonstrate their independence. That Moe would approach Sholem in such a fashion might indicate even more dire circumstances than appear on the surface.

The second relationship that raises some questions is that between Moe and attorney Joseph (J. J.) Corn. A considerable amount of documentation in the Archive around this time period suggest that Corn was simply Moe's attorney, dealing with the everyday matters that confront a small business owner. However, with his involvement in the 1946 Stinson agreement with Asch Records, and his financial involvement in the attempts to keep DISC alive, Corn certainly seems to have a stronger connection to Asch than would be initially assumed. The fact that Corn was behind Moe's financing at Clark and was responsible for locking him out of his warehouse in New Jersey speaks more to a type of partnership, not unlike modern venture capitalists of today. More would need to be done to explore the range of Corn's financial involvements, but it is clear that Corn played an important role both in keeping Moe going—at least for a while—as DISC, then ultimately forcing Moe's hand to protect his own investment, which may have been the final push that led to Moe's creating Folkways Records.

Lessons Learned and New Strategies

The eventual death of DISC Records and the strangulation of Asch Records represent what might be called the "learning curve" for Moe. From the Asch/Stinson debacle, Moe learned to be careful with whom he partnered and how he formed these partnerships; from DISC he learned the danger of high production costs and chasing the elusive hit record. The late 1940s were undoubtedly very tough times financially for Asch. However, there were a number of other events occuring at the time that helped to set the stage for the formation of Folkways and an associated distribution business, Pioneer Record Sales, Inc.

One factor in the DISC bankruptcy was the problem of collecting from outside distributors. In Chapter 5, we will examine how the record label–distributor–record store relationship works, and how payment can be slowed by this chain of business relationships—a deadly problem for smaller labels. To alleviate this problem, Asch must have decided to become his own distributor. Not only could he sell his own product in this way, he could pick up other small labels with similar product; the distribution business could therefore support the recording business, and ease the cashflow crunch. As noted in the chronology prepared in light of the failure of DISC, Asch had tried to form a distribution business, somewhat tellingly called Phoenix Disc Distribution, but it was already too late; returns and unpaid bills sank the DISC label.

Even as DISC was crumbling, on 2 December 1946, Moe filed a business certificate with the New York County Clerk's Office as the sole proprietor of another distribution company, the United Record Service (URS).[26] This was among his first efforts to formalize a distribution company for his own material and outside product. There are several items that indicate business was being done by Moe under this letterhead by 1948. One letter to the Peabody College for Teachers on 28 June 1948 states that, "United Record Service offers for distribution the enclosed catalog of records and other items in the Folkways and specialized category. We would be glad to perform any service in this field for you."[27] A further letter indicates to a prospective customer that "Recently you made [an] inquiry regarding available Disc records. We [United Record Service] are pleased to enclose herewith lists of these records which we believe you would be interested in. We would be glad to take your order on any of these items."[28] This clearly indicates that United Record Service was up and running and operating at the same address as DISC and Asch had previously been located: 117 W. 46th Street, New York City.

URS was one way for Asch to keep a hand in the DISC business, even as he was supposedly divorcing himself from it. Once distribution became an issue, and Moe was not allowed to participate in the promotion of DISC materials as stated in the summary of events, URS may have been his only outlet to retain some control over the management of DISC in the midst of its collapse.

Another question arising out of this period concerns the small, but controversial Union Records label. Some authors have suggested that Moe set up the label to release contentious material. However, there is strong evidence that it was not Moe's label, although Union Records and DISC were neighbors. Biographer Peter Goldsmith[29] contends that Moe created Union Records as a means to release politically sensitive material (predominantly union-related material like that contained on *Roll the Union On*). Moe then listed this Union Records release in the DISC catalog as an "Asch" release. However, when the business certificate was filed with the New York County Clerks Office on 19 January 1946 creating the Union Record Co.,[30] the proprietor was not Moe Asch, but a man named James Dietz. Dietz listed his business address as 119 W. 46th Street, which made the label neighbors with Moe and DISC Records.

Although the handwriting on the certificate filed with New York County bears a striking resemblance to Moe's, it would be careless to suggest that Moe had anything to do with filing the certificate. Obviously, Moe would be placing himself at considerable risk if he did deliberately forge or otherwise falsify the certificate. It is even more improbable that he would do so, when he could have simply created a new label to stick on these releases and create the illusion of separation without the aggravation of filing a separate business certificate.[31]

However, a different scenario to explain the connection might be more plausible. Assuming that the certificate is authentic and that James Dietz did run Union Records next door to Moe, it would not be unreasonable to suggest that Dietz could have had access to the recording facilities at WEVD. While it was Moe who recorded the material that is on Union Records, Moe would easily license his own material if it was appropriate to do so. Additional suggestions by Goldsmith and others that Union Records was also connected to the printed music of People's Songs (a group of "left-wing" folksingers and songwriters who formed a collective to book concerts and publish a small newsletter) would also seem entirely appropriate. Perhaps Moe was acquainted with Dietz and assisted him in setting up the company for mutually beneficial ends, including Moe's distribution of the recordings. In any event, it is too easy to write off Union Records as simply "one of Moe's labels." Unless the deliberate falsification and notarization of the business certificate can be proven, Moe's role in the company is most likely once removed from its origins and its operations.

Reflecting on the demise of Asch Records and DISC Records, one is left with a sense that Moe faced a run of bad luck. Asch Records seemed to be enjoying a relative amount of success recording primarily ethnic records with no reason to think this strategy would not continue to be successful. However, the exigencies of a wartime economy forced Asch into a partnership with Stinson Trading Co. that, on the face of it, worked well. It often seems out of anyone's control when such relationships deteriorate as the Asch/Stinson arrangement did. Moe was left to salvage what he could of his masters and inventory and attempt to regain the control that he once had.

DISC appeared to rectify many of the problems that Moe had encountered with Asch Records. There seemed to be no need to enter into any unusual distribution partnerships to make it work. Moe was able to expand into other musical areas to broaden the range of his catalog. However, in being well aware of the pitfalls of the Asch/Stinson arrangement, Moe still seemed willing to overlook the potential risk offered in a creative partnership to produce records. Norman Granz offered a unique set of recording opportunities to release live jazz recordings of a type that greatly interested Moe. Again, the risk turned against Moe, highlighting the dangers of investing too much in the production costs of recordings. When bad luck struck again and Moe was unable to get the Nat King Cole recordings to the stores for the Christmas rush of 1946, he was unable to recoup his costs and was pushed into bankruptcy.

There is no question that these events stood prominently in the decisions that Moe made with respect to other enterprises that he supported. Moe learned his lessons. The history of Folkways Records illustrates both his caution in creating different distribution and production relationships, as well as his tireless efforts to keep production costs down. Folkways stands as the testament to Moe's development as a business man and as a creative entrepreneur. This will be shown clearly as, from this point on, this work will be focused on the details and relationships that comprise Folkways Records. There will be the occasional reference to other concerns of Moe's, but we have now arrived at our main concern: the life and times of Folkways Records and Service Corp.

4
The Birth
of Folkways Records

Moe needed to start over after all of the difficulties with Asch Records and
DISC Records. Unfortunately, one of the conditions of the bankruptcy
agreement with DISC was that he was forbidden to be an officer of a record
company for a considerable period of time. The creation–story of Folkways Records begins at this point. Although there are a several variants to
the tale that Marian Distler purchased the assets of DISC Records and
started Folkways, perhaps the only "official" story can be found in an undated affidavit signed by Marian Distler.[1] From this source, the story goes:

> When Mr. Erlinger took over the operations of Disc Company
> through Disc Distributing Corp. he needed my services to advise
> him about certain details with which I was familiar having been
> with the Disc Company since its inception.
>
> In the spring of 1948 when I felt that I was no longer needed, I
> resigned and went into business for myself at 117 West 46 Street as a
> matter of convenience. Mr. Erlinger having need of my services
> from this address had agreed to pay the rent until May when he had
> believed he would no longer need me. I formed the Folkways
> Records and Service Co. and assumed full payment of the rent noti-
> fying WEVD (owners) that I was the rent payer and possessor of the
> premises. I did not use any of the assets of the Disc Company and
> Mr. Asch paid me for my services whenever he needed me for
> stenographic purposes in connection with mail or business of the
> Disc Company and for use of my premises whenever he had a re-
> cording job.

Mr. Asch had been paying off a judgement against assets of the Disc Company at 117 West 46 Street including equipment, furniture and fixtures, books and records. When he was unable to continue these payments the Marshall gave notice of a public sale and came to 117 West 46 Street to auction off these assets. As I was already operating from this address and felt it would be to my benefit to continue doing so, I borrowed money from a friend, Mr. George Mendelssohn of Vox Productions, and offered the Marshall a sum for the complete assets at actual resale value. At the time of the sale there were no bankruptcy proceedings. The Marshall verified with the attorney for the creditor that it was satisfactory and legal and upon payment of this sum sold and turned over the assets to me. In order to guarantee Mr. Mendelssohn his money I formed a corporation (naming him as one of the officers) and the corporation took a mortgage and paid back Mr. Mendelssohn.

As I sincerely believe that Mr. Asch is one of the best men in the record business (that the circumstances which have forced him into bankruptcy were actually beyond his control) I have made arrangements with him to advise me in the creating of a new record label. I have allowed him in return to use my premises giving him a desk for his use and a place to keep his own books and records pertaining to the Disc Company, to receive his mail and take messages for him in connection with any matters which pertain to his own operations, concerning either the defunct Disc Company or any other business which he is able to conduct.

Thus, with Marian as the owner of the DISC assets, Moe was hired as a "consultant" to the new company so as not to violate the terms of the bankruptcy agreement. Nonetheless, the creation of Folkways Record and Service Corporation was certainly driven by Moe Asch—the circumstances in the above affidavit seem a little too manufactured. Nonetheless, the ownership constraints were such that Marian Distler was listed as the sole officer of the company on the business certificate filed at the New York County Clerk's Office on 30 July 1948.[2]

Marian's sudden interest in buying the DISC assets in light of Moe's bankruptcy order caused some to doubt the legitimacy of the new company. It is easy to see why few believed that Moe was merely an "employee." Yet, Marian worked hard to establish the perception of propriety in the creation of Folkways. In a letter of 6 October 1948,[3] Frank Borut (also the person who notarized the identity of Marian Distler for the business certificate application) wrote the following "To Whom It May Concern" letter:

I am the attorney for Folkways Records & Service Co., having its office at 117 West 46th Street, New York 19, N.Y.

Folkways Records & Service Co. is a trade name owned and operated by Marion Distler [*sic*] at the above address. The above company has no connection with either Moe Asch, Disc Company of America, or Disc Distributing Co., Inc. That the said Marion Distler is the sole owner of certain masters and properties with which she is now doing business and which are in her possession. That the said Marion Distler has taken over the premises at 117 West 46th Street, at which place she is doing business.

That the certificate of doing business of Marion Distler under the firm name and style of Folkways Records & Service Co. is filed in the office of the County Clerk of the County of New York.

In spite of the economic turmoil and the trying circumstances of the day, Folkways Records was born.

The broader world of technology was also on Moe's side during the early years of Folkways. There is no question that Moe's considerable expertise in electronics from both the technical and retail operations of Radio Laboratories helped immensely in the day-to-day running of a small studio. Moe was able to build, maintain, and manage his equipment in a very efficient and economical fashion. However, there were external changes that came to work in Folkways' favor. The shift to the 33⅓ long-playing (LP) record format—introduced by Columbia only months after the formation of Folkways in 1948[4]—proved to be a huge advantage for Folkways.

Both the Asch and DISC labels had only 78 rpm records available on which to release records, allowing only perhaps 3 minutes of recording time per side (for the standard 10-inch disc) to 4½ minutes on 12-inch discs. This forced the inclusion of several records into an album in order to present complete works or collections. With the introduction of the 33⅓ rpm format, Folkways was able to include as much as 20 minutes of sound per side. This meant that a single LP could often hold the same amount of sound as four or five 78 rpm records. This new format permitted Moe much more freedom to explore a wider range of sonic expression because it did not need to be cut up into 3- or 4-minute parts. Also, the cost of producing these albums was lower than it would have been in the 78 format.

The switch to LPs changed the way people listened to records as well. The pop market was increasingly focused on the single record—now in the new 45 rpm format developed by RCA—whereas more "sophisticated" listeners—of classical, jazz, and folk—were drawn to the album as an integrated musical expression. Folkways' philosophy of including extensive notes and putting together an album of related material—rather than making albums of out a hodgepodge of "singles" as was done in the pop market—perfectly fit the new format.

Perhaps best of all, it was a technological change whose associated costs had to be borne by the pressing plants and other producers as the first adopters of the new technology. Moe certainly had to make some concessions with respect to the formatting of material that he sent for pressing, deciding how releases would be ordered on the LP, and organizing the presentation of the now-ubiquitous liner notes. However, once the risk of using the new format became acceptable and the choice was made to release on LP, all of the other technological costs were carried by others. This gave Moe further advantage not only in exploiting the new technology, but in developing the relationships necessary that would permit him to produce the kinds of recordings that he wanted without becoming tied to the capital costs involved in implementating the new technology.

Another new technology that came after World War II was a new means of recording on flexible plastic tape, as opposed to the cumbersome acetate discs used to record 78s. Tape allowed for longer recording times, which complemented the longer playing time of the LP record. And, although initially tape machines were heavy and expensive, they soon became at least somewhat portable and more available to the average person. Amateurs could begin making their own recordings at a reasonably low cost; by the 1960s, these would become important sources for Folkways. By the 1970s, Asch would cease to maintain his own recording studio at all because he had no need to provide these facilities.

The Business Model

Most record companies survive by issuing hit recordings that, in essence, underwrite the many failures and flops that are part of any business. It is said that the success of Elvis Presley for RCA in the mid-1950s supported the balance of the label's output, while also providing a healthy profit. However, the pitfalls of hit making for a small label were many. High demand for records would strain the small outside suppliers of records and covers; plus the cashflow crunch of producing records (many of which might eventually be returned and therefore be valueless) was onerous. Asch learned this the hard way with his attempt to release a Nat King Cole album for the Christmas 1946 season on DISC; he knew he had to come up with a different model for Folkways.

With Folkways, Asch turned the conventional record-industry model on its head. The major labels attempted to sell millions of records quickly; Asch decided instead to sell hundreds of records slowly, but to have such a large catalog that the overall size of the business would be sufficient to meet its costs and provide him with a reasonable living. Rather than printing thousands of copies (and potentially saving on the unit cost of each

LP), Asch made what were for the industry minuscule pressings, sometimes as low as a few hundred copies. Album booklets were printed separately in small quantity; and the what-would-become familiar Folkways package of a plain black sleeve with a simple cover glued onto it (not even covering the entire back of the sleeve) was also a unique economy measure—and one that would be copied by other small labels, including the Origin of Jazz Library (OJL) in the late 1950s, and by Arhoolie in the early 1960s.

This business model also supported Asch's philosophy of making all types of music accessible. In order to sell small numbers of an album over a long period, he had to keep it in print. The advantage to having a diverse catalog—including everything from nature sounds to spoken word and blues and jazz—was that different parts of the catalog would sell at different times. The early 1960s blues revival led to an increased sale of the back catalog in that area; the old-time music revival of the 1970s led to renewed interest in albums that were by then over a decade old, and so on.

Keeping every album "in print" did not always mean that there were literally copies of each album kept in a warehouse—although Asch's inventory was impressively large for a small label. Rather, because he had the flexibility to do small runs, Asch could repress records quickly on an as-needed basis. Because these were not "hit" albums—where demand was immediate and likely to also immediately drop—he could make his customers wait until he could supply what they wanted. And the customers were willing to wait because the material was simply unavailable elsewhere.

Another way to protect Folkways was to form several related businesses. Although it is unclear exactly when it was formed, Pioneer Record Sales, a record distribution company owned by Asch, had a symbiotic relationship with Folkways. Distributing Folkways product, it could shield Folkways against its creditors, and advance money against future sales. Plus, Pioneer could pay some of the office expenses—and part of Asch's salary—further supporting the operation. Later, Asch would also form subsidiary labels to protect Folkways from problems with reissuing some of his original 78 material or to take advantage of discount markets—something he never did with Folkways.

The model of combining a record producer with its own distribution company was copied by other successful small labels. The Rounder Co-op in the early 1970s included a mail order distribution business (which incidentally sold Folkways and other small labels), a direct distributor to record stores, and a record label. By controlling all of these aspects, Rounder could keep their album prices low and not be too squeezed for cash at any one time. The various Rounder businesses eventually separated when the label was economically secure enough—and large enough—to support its own operation.

Overview of Asch's Businesses

Because of the long history of Folkways—and the often confusing relationship among Asch's various enterprises—a brief description of the relationships of Folkways to other Asch-owned and independent businesses will be helpful.

Depending on how you define its beginnings, Folkways began as an independent operation in late 1947–early 1948, supposedly owned and operated by Asch's assistant Marian Distler but, in fact, owned by Asch himself. Nonetheless, Distler remained with the company until her death in early 1964, and was in many ways Asch's partner in developing the label. Pioneer Record Sales, the distribution arm for Folkways product, was formed sometime in the early 1950s, although an exact date has not been established. It is entirely possible that it grew out of United Record Service that Moe had started in the late 1940s. On the other hand, the similarity in name with attorney J. J. Corn's Pioneer Records, makes one wonder if perhaps there wasn't some influence by Corn behind the scenes. Nevertheless, Asch used Pioneer as a means of better controlling cashflow to Folkways and to take some of the burden of office and salary expenses off of the label. Pioneer seems to have folded around 1970, and was subsequently replaced by new entities (see below).

Asch later formed two major subsidiary labels for Folkways: RBF and Broadside. RBF was formed in the latter part of 1958,[5] with the initials being short for Records, Books, and Films Sales. Blues collector Sam Charters provided many of the first albums, and they were related to books that he had authored or planned to write. The original idea seems to have been that each record would be accompanied either by a book or film or both, although not many (if any) films seem to have been developed. Another reason for the separate label has been suggested by some: because many of the first RBF releases were reissues of earlier 78s, Asch used the subsidiary label to protect himself from charges of illegal piracy that he had faced when releasing earlier reissues on Folkways. As Moe recounted in an interview around 1983[6]:

> I don't censor anything. If something comes to me, and I think its worthwhile to issue, I issue it, if I feel its part of the mosaic that makes up Folkways. Now with Scholastic, they had a problem with Pete Seeger, because at that time, there was the controversy, Red Channels and everything else, but I wrote them a nasty letter saying "you're not going to tell us what to issue or not issue, we stand on what we issue." But, they did not issue certain material, and therefore they allowed me to issue under RBF label.

A variety of country and blues titles were also released on RBF. The number of titles released on RBF was never very high, but it did provide Moe with an administrative way to manage certain types of recordings that were outside of the Folkways purview.

Broadside enabled Asch to release social-protest and other politically sensitive material. Asch had long envisioned releasing records that would be "living newspapers," first suggesting such a project to Woody Guthrie in the 1940s, and later producing several *Gazette* albums in the late 1950s with Pete Seeger and Ewan MacColl to address current events.[7] When Gordon Friesen and Agnes Cunningham launched Broadside magazine in 1962 as an outlet for political songs, Asch partnered with them to release the homemade recordings that they used to make the transcriptions for the magazine. Again, the quality of the actual recordings was of little concern to Asch. By putting this music on a separate label, Asch again protected Folkways from any political or economic repercussions that might have occurred.

The 1960s saw further developments in Folkways reflecting the folk revival and the new interest in Asch's earlier recordings. In mid-1964, Asch decided to relaunch DISC as a means of reissuing some of his more popular albums in a more conventional format and at a lower price than the Folkways versions; the first DISC releases appeared in early 1965. However, soon after, Asch entered into a licensing deal with MGM to reissue select Folkways titles on a new label, Verve/Folkways, and also with Scholastic, the educational magazine and book publisher, for distribution of Folkways releases to schools and the education market. In both instances, Asch maintained the right to release material on Folkways, although as part of the Scholastic deal he licensed off much of his inventory to them. The MGM deal failed first, in early 1967, and the Scholastic deal ended soon after, around 1970. Before he could retrieve the Folkways name and inventory, Moe briefly revived the Asch label, using appropriate Folkways catalog numbers for his new releases (so the records could easily be incorporated back into the complete catalog once it was retrieved). He also continued to release material on RBF and Broadside, both of which were unaffected by the distribution deals.

From about 1971, Folkways was restored to Moe and he continued to operate the firm until his death in 1986. RBF and Broadside were eventually incorporated into the Folkways catalog and bore the Folkways label as well. Two other firms that arose in the 1970s seemed to replace Pioneer as distribution arms for Folkways. First came Blue Giraffe, a somewhat mysterious partnership which involved another party (who perhaps helped finance it), which apparently functioned from about 1971–1974, and then Aschco

Records, which existed from about 1977 through Asch's death and both collected money from Folkways and paid some of its bills and expenses.

Asch was also involved with other businesses that complemented Folkways. In 1958, he formed a partnership with Irwin Silber to take over the publication of *Sing Out!* magazine. This led to the formation of Oak Publications, originally to publish songbooks drawn from material that had appeared in the magazine. The business continued through 1967, when Oak was sold to Music Sales and *Sing Out!* sold to its editorial board. There is also some evidence that Moe was quite closely connected with The Richmond Organization (TRO) and Telra Film Sales, Inc. Both organizations were primarily involved with licensing music to other sources: TRO to other discount labels including those under its own ownership umbrella, and Telra Film Sales to movies and television productions. For example, Moe often bragged that four Russian Red Army songs that he had released were licensed for use in the Warren Beatty film *Reds*. These were, by all indications, additional outlets through which Moe could license the use of Folkways material of which he had control.

Building the Catalog

Procurement of material is probably the most important process that a recording company faces. During the Asch Records years, Moe was able to attract a wide variety of artists who wanted to record, either because of his reputation, whether he just happened to be in his studio when someone might want to record, or whether, in the case of the American Federation of Musicians strike in 1942, he provided a nonunion outlet for striking jazz musicians to record. During the early 1940s, Moe recorded some of the most influential names in jazz in New York, including Mary Lou Williams, James P. Johnson, Art Tatum, and Coleman Hawkins. Similarly, recording Pete, Woody, and Lead Belly could be viewed as equal parts luck and genius. In any event, they, along with a wide variety of other artists at the time, were able to propel Moe through the disasters of DISC Records, and give him a musical foundation from which to build Folkways.

Another, somewhat controversial, source for material were recordings made by the "major" labels in the 1920s and 1930s that would be reissued by Asch on LP. The notion of reissuing 78s was a brand-new one, and some in the industry felt that it violated copyright laws. Asch, on the other hand, viewed it as a question of the right of the people, based on the United States constitution, to hear music that the major labels would not issue on their own. One of his first reissues was Woody Guthrie's *Dust Bowl Ballads*, which RCA had originally recorded and issued on 78. Guthrie did this recording for RCA before coming to Folkways, but RCA refused to reissue it or to allow Folkways to do so. Nonetheless, Woody and Moe both agreed it should be released, so it came out on Folkways as a copy of the RCA record. Some years later, RCA discovered this "piracy," but apparently when Moe explained his reasoning, RCA agreed that it should have been released and let Folkways continue with the release without penalty.

Another controversial reissue was the 10-LP set History of Jazz that was edited by Frederic Ramsey. Moe began issuing this series in 1950, drawing on earlier recordings by the major labels. Ramsey was a scholar and fan of traditional jazz, and wanted to make available the best early recordings for a new generation of listener. At the time, the notion of reissuing earlier jazz recordings was simply unknown; Asch's initial forays into this market inspired other record collectors to from reissue labels, notably Bill Grauer, an editor of the jazz-enthusiast publication *The Record Changer*, who formed his own Riverside label in 1952 expressly to reissue 78 recordings.

The charge of "piracy" that was leveled against Asch rankled him. As already noted, he did not view it as an act of piracy to reissue recordings that were currently unavailable; rather, he saw it as an issue of freedom of expression for the artist whose work could not be heard because it was unjustly held by the original recording company.

Moe was certainly not above releasing material on Folkways without license or permission if he felt that the material was not being made available by the rightful owner and that the merit of the material warranted its release. In 1983, Moe discussed the few recordings that were different from the rest of the Folkways catalog:

> For instance, I issue material that comes from other labels, major labels, the History of Jazz and things like that, where there is no license or anything else because there is no such thing. The only people that permit license are Columbia. RCA won't answer you. Decca is out of business and so forth. I have about 20 items which are not licensable, and those are out on the RBF. Folkways has a history of jazz which has many labels on it, but Columbia, the majority they gave me permission on and I pay them a royalty on. There are in the catalog, I should judge, about 30 items . . .

Asch's reasoning is somewhat peculiar here: The fact that RCA refused to respond to him did not end his obligation to pay a fee, and Decca most certainly was still in business as part of the MCA Group. Moreover, he states that he paid a license fee to Columbia for using the material in the History of Jazz series (first released from 1950 to 1953) as well as the RBF albums. However, the evidence shows that this did not occur until apparently Columbia caught up with him and made a retroactive license. An agreement, in force as of 30 December 1974, set forth pretty stringent terms for Moe's continued release of the History of Jazz series (2801 to 2811), as well as tracks on some other recordings. Columbia agreed to a $2,500 lump-sum payment from Folkways in lieu of a 2-cent-per-track per item sold royalty rate that was in force as long as the Folkways albums were in print. However, a clause in the agreement stated that once the base price rises above $6.98 per record, a formula would kick in to add a pro rata additional licensing fee to each selection. Paying a lump sum for essentially a 30-year retroactive license would have likely seemed fair to Moe. However, four years later when the base price of his recordings went up, Moe was clearly not happy.

In response to a letter on 27 September 1978 that indicates "Since you have increased your base price from $6.98 to $7.98 (or $8.98), the new licensing fees are as follows" (see Appendix 4 for a list of fees), Moe responds to John Franks, General Manager for Columbia Special Products[8]:

> Your letter re raising the fee came as a terrible surprise to me.
>
> First we raised the price of $6.98 to $7.98 when Columbia raised their prices and the printers and pressers raised their prices and every thing went up so my income did not go up.
>
> Our distributor prices for $6.98 is $2.81 while for $7.98 is $3.19 so how can I pay you such an increase as for RF 1 from 14 to 26¢ From RF 10 28 to 77¢????? From 32 to 96¢ Is this a new way of you telling me that I should get out of issuing old recordings that have been the forefront of the whole new interest in the history of music of America. You do remember the time no one cared till I came along and I suppose that the time will come again. Then if I eliminate who will carry on?
>
> By the way on the 4000 series they always were 8.95 I raised them 3¢ to 8.98 in order to make it easier for the billing people but on 4510 I am charged 10¢ instead of formerly 6¢ and all I get back is .005¢ from my distributors. WHY??
>
> In any event I cannot meet the increase on 10 items please let me know if we can adjust this or is this your last word.

Even with some of the spelling errors corrected, the air of haste and irritation is evident in Moe's writing. It is not known what the outcome of this letter was, but as the 1983 comments indicate, Moe seemed to have come to terms with Columbia. That said, one of the last things that Moe wanted was another monthly expense. True to his pattern, I believe Moe hoped that Columbia would take the $2,500 and leave him alone. I suspect that a big part of his surprise was the fact that Columbia even took notice of his change in price. Nonetheless, Moe might have railed a bit about the apparent unfairness of it all, but in the end, Moe paid his bills and continued producing records.

There is one additional part to the early years of Folkways that secured Moe's reputation for creating a product that simply could not be found anywhere else. In his role as a documentor, Moe was very much interested in combining music with text that could explain why the sounds on the record were important. Not just the who, what, when, and where of the recording, but also the ever-important why. Why were the sounds on the record being made in the first place? Explaining the why of the recordings became the catalyst: Why are these people performing? Why are they using those instruments? Why are they performing this song at that time of the year? Adding written context to the music completed the documentation in a way that no other recording company could match.

One of the earliest and most important examples of how the combination of text, music, and theme could come together was the 1952 release of the three-volume, six-LP *Anthology of American Folk Music* (rereleased in 1997, Smithsonian Folkways 40090). This set was also drawn from earlier recordings made in the 1920s and 1930s, but it was the unique way that it was put together that made it a seminal new product for Folkways—and the nascent folk revival. As Griel Marcus stated so concisely, "The whole bizarre package made the familiar strange, the never known into the forgotten, and the forgotten into a collective memory that teased any single listener's conscious mind" that was ultimately "an elaborate, dubiously legal bootleg, a compendium of recordings . . . generally long forgotten . . . it was the founding document of the American folk revival."[9]

The key to the whole anthology was *Anthology*'s editor, Harry Smith. It was his vision, his collections of original recordings, and his knowledge and desire that drove the project. As Moe later recalled, " [Harry] came to me and said: 'Look, this is what I want to do. I want to lay out the book of notes. I want to do the whole thing. All I want to be sure of is that they are issued.' Of course, I was tremendously interested. Harry did the notes, typed up the notes, pasted up the notes and did the whole thing."[10] A good part of Moe's genius was recognizing the value of what Smith was offering. Not only was Smith willing to do the work, which would save Moe a large amount of capital, Moe knew that Smith was the guy to do the project. He acknowledged and respected the fact that expertise was to be found in a variety of places, and in deference to the documentation, Moe was quick to rely on the desires of others to document important sounds. Sadly, it was exactly this lack of documentation that stalled volumes 4 and 5 of the original project. Smith needed money and had sold off half of his collection, unable to get the information he needed. As Moe put it, "I have the tapes of Volumes 4 and 5, but I can't get the documentation. There is no sense in just issuing it without the documentation."[11]

Long after *Anthology*, Moe continued to rely on a number of editors and their expertise to ensure the quality of the documentation that went with the recordings. Key collaborators in the early 1950s included anthropologist/ethnomusicologist Harold Courlander, who oversaw the Ethnic Series, which ultimately numbered several hundred recordings.[12] For jazz music, Moe often relied on commentary by Frederic Ramsey and for contemporary twentieth-century music, Henry Cowell. Many others also contributed, either creating documentation for their own recordings, or by lending some expertise in a particular area that Moe was interested in recording. For example, ethnomusicologists like Richard Waterman and Jaap Kunst often corresponded with Moe on African or Javanese music. Indeed, it has been said that once Moe developed a relationship with a contributor and trusted in the work that they would submit, that he would release their material with virtually no intervention of his own.

Ramsey supplied Asch with another valuable product: the so-called "last sessions" made by blues guitarist Lead Belly. Ramsey had procured a tape recorder in the early days of their availability, and during a period in 1948 recorded lengthy sessions with Lead Belly reminiscing and performing dozens of songs. He wanted this material to be issued as a coherent package, not just cut up into individual performances, and he wanted the package to be accessible to ordinary listeners. The success of the Weavers's recording of "Irene, Goodnight" in 1950 made the major labels take an interest in Lead Belly, but they were unwilling to meet Ramsey's conditions. Asch was happy to oblige; not only did he issue the tapes in their complete form, he eliminated many of the "tracks" on the standard LP to squeeze in 30 minutes per record side, making the entire package a four-LP set (a more conventional approach would have required six LPs—and thus cost more to the consumer). Rereleased by Smithsonian Folkways (40068), the 1953 set was a landmark in blues scholarship, and did much to solidify the reputation of Lead Belly during the folk–blues revival of the 1960s and beyond.

Another important event in 1953 was the first album made for Folkways by audio documentarian Tony Schwartz. Schwartz was another innovator: he took a tape machine into the streets and neighborhoods of New York, producing sound documentaries that remain classics to this day. These unusual products would not have appealed to conventional record labels, but Asch immediately recognized their value as part of his attempt to document "the whole world of sound." Schwartz would continue to produce landmark albums for Folkways through the 1950s and early 1960s, and they would continue to sell for decades to come.

To say that Moe produced recordings that were educationally important is something of a defining statement. But there is a more detailed point to make. Many of the Folkways releases in the Language Instruction, General Instruction, and Historical categories, for example, emphasized learning more about the world. Indeed, virtually all of the Folkways's catalog categories could fall under the general heading of "educational." Although Moe produced many recordings that would make others scratch their heads and wonder what was the point, even these releases have come to have substantial importance. Sound effects and the sounds of science (FX), in particular, seem to hold their share of oddities. Even as early as 1955, Folkways had released the *Sounds of Frequency* (FPX100) and *Sound Patterns* (FPX130) recordings, as well as the ever-growing "Sounds of . . ." series.

Educational priorities were also the foundation behind the children's records that Moe produced. As previously mentioned, Moe had begun recording albums for children very early on and continued throughout his lifetime. As Marilyn Averett (Folkways office manager through the 1970s and 1980s) recalled[13]:

> He had a great pride in having childrens records. Because he had this thing, when he told me years ago that it had to do a lot with childrens poverty, also, that people always said children of poverty never learn or minorities couldn't learn, stuff like that, and he just had to prove a point that if they could learn from the music they could learn from anything. And that was his role to play.

By 1957[14] there were nearly 50 children's titles listed in categories that included "Children's Americana," "Folk Tales for Children," "Children's International Series," "Children's Special and Historical," and simply, "Children's Series." Such a categorical breakdown is clear evidence that Moe had a very specific idea about the kinds of children's recordings he wanted to release and the role that he wanted those recordings to play. By the time Folkways was acquired by the Smithsonian Institution, 210 recordings were listed under "Children's Recordings" and "Children's Recordings Collections" (with esteemed children's entertainer Ella Jenkins contributing 23 titles to this list).

Many people have also pointed to the importance of the political positions that Moe was willing to support. Beginning with his recording of Franklin D. Roosevelt in the 1930s, Moe was never shy about releasing politically or socially important material, provided that he felt there was some justification for its release. Moe took a very strong stance against releasing any material that promoted hatred or subordination of a group, while actively promoting material that supported a variety of causes. Moe's very earliest releases on Asch Records of the Liberation Poets, his many Americana releases by Pete Seeger, including the famous *Talking Union* (5285), as well as *Songs of Struggle and Protest, 1930–50* (5233), *Where Have All the Flowers Gone* (31026), and *Wimoweh and Other Songs of Freedom and Protest* (31018), all speak to Moe's commitment to social issues.

Of course, there were an enormous number of other contributors to this body of work. The release of material like *Anthology of Negro Poets* (9791, 9792) and *American Negro History* by Langston Hughes (7752) in the early 1950s was an important step in the foundation of an African-American identity beyond that of "race" music or stereotyped entertainment. Indeed, Moe produced one of the first recordings that helped to set the groundwork for the civil rights movement in 1960: *The Nashville Sit-In Story* (5590) which included the anthem *We Shall Overcome*.[16] Moe was well aware of the seriousness of race relations in the United States and was quick to issue material that supported it.

From a business perspective, what is most important to note is that Moe was both able and willing to rely on more knowledgeable individuals to help him create the very best documents that he could. This helped Moe to quickly establish Folkways as the preeminent creator of musical documentation, and in doing so, he was able to attract others like Harry Smith, who only wanted the material to be available. The end result was that Moe was able to attract what would normally be very expensive help in creating his documentation. But because the goal for those contributing was not wealth, but longevity for the material—a goal held in common with Moe—they were willing to provide their work at very low or no cost to Moe.

In this fashion, Moe was able to establish a reputation that attracted all the necessary elements to create a unique product, but it did not cost much at all in up-front expenses. For example, when an ethnomusicologist approached Moe with his or her field tapes, Moe would often release the record, paying the individual perhaps $100 outright for their recording rights. In exchange, Moe required a master tape, which he would often request to be in the order the songs were to be on each side, and with all the notes for the songs in virtually type-ready format. This was perhaps the classic strategy that Moe would use to keep Folkways afloat by keeping production costs down, while releasing such a large number of recordings every year.

Also, once Asch made contact with one specialist, it was likely that others would be recommended. Jazz enthusiast Charles Edward Smith introduced Asch to Fred Ramsey; Ramsey, in turn, "discovered" a young blues enthusiast named Sam Charters while he was in the South in the mid-1950s on a Guggenheim grant. Charters would supply Asch with dozens of recordings. Pete Seeger's half-brother, Mike, became a key collector and performer for Asch, and brough along others including John Cohen and Ralph Rinzler, a collector who would later work for the Smithsonian Insitution and was instrumental in negotiating the purchase of Folkways by the institution in the 1980s.

Folkways Records themselves became advertisements for the type of recording that interested Asch, so that the consumers of Folkways product often became producers on their own. By the time Folkways was well established in the later 1950s, Asch could release seventy-five to one hundred new albums a year without looking far beyond his normal collaborators—and without employing an artists and repertoire director! By the mid-1970s, he was faced with more material that he could possibly issue. However, given his declining health and the economics of his operation, much of this material has not—and sadly, perhaps never will be—commercially released.

5
The Business
of Making Records

To fulfil his mission to release all the world's music, Moe had to deal with the essential features of the creation of the recorded product: the manufacture of the record and then its distribution and sales. These mundane facts of life are rarely documented for most labels, big or small, but—as Moe learned the hard way through Asch and DISC—they would be very important to Folkways and its survival. Besides finding reliable vendors who were flexible enough to meet the unusual demands of Folkways's business structure, it was also necessary to negotiate ample credit so that the company's cashflow was not unduly burdened. This often meant dealing with multiple suppliers and juggling them as bills became due.

Another obstacle in the successful management of his cash flow, however, was the system of taxation implemented in the United States during Moe's tenure as a record producer. Certain forms of tax that were applicable to Folkways do not seem to have been particularly troublesome: income tax for himself and employees, New York City municipal taxes, and various use taxes for shipping and production items. However, as alluded to earlier, there is solid evidence that the implementation of the manufacturer's excise tax was punitive on the operation of Folkways, and was likely punitive to other small record companies as well.

The implications of this regulation on the cash flow within Folkways was tremendous. As recordings were produced and sent to various distributors and dealers within the distribution network, payment for these shipments was due on credit (typically 30, 60, or 90 days). According to the tax regulations, this constituted a sale and the tax must be calculated and re-mitted to the government. As the tax was to be paid at intervals not exceed-ing 30 days, the tax payment was due on material that had been shipped, but had not yet been paid for (and may not be for another 30 or 60 days, depending on the payment schedule). As a result, a serious cash-flow prob-lem was created that was particularly difficult for a cash-strapped organi-zation such as Folkways.

Second, there is the question of returns and exchanges, a notoriously frustrating condition given that Folkways allowed a 100 percent return/ exchange policy to its customers. This in itself created difficulties with cash flow as it typically would tie up merchandise in the shipping/exchange/ shipping process, or would simply put Folkways in a condition of owing money to be refunded on the returned merchandise. However, the tax must nonetheless be paid, despite provisions for the refunding of taxes al-ready paid.[1] The amount of paperwork involved, combined with the delays in processing, would likely have made applying for tax refunds an unusual event (only one document suggests that it was ever done[2]). One would sus-pect, especially in the case of Folkways, that most overpayments would simply be left on account to credit against other amounts owing.

An important example of the difficulties with this type of taxation was explained by Larry Sockell, who was then selling Folkways to national ac-counts (more will be said about Larry's role in Folkways later).[3] On one occasion, Moe needed $21,000 to pay his excise tax. Larry called Moe from California and said that he had found someone who would pay $25,000 for 25,000 items as soon as the merchandise was delivered. Larry had spent the afternoon with the man writing up orders, and, sure enough, once the merchandise arrived, Moe received the check for $25,000 and was able to pay his taxes. This is also remarkable in light of Moe's antipathy towards "cheapening" Folkways product by selling it more cheaply—at least at re-tail. Were it not for the contacts and resourcefulness of Larry Sockell, an incident like this one could have quickly pushed Moe over the edge.

One means of circumventing at least some of the tax burden was through an exemption of tax on sales for export. Section 316.25 of the reg-ulations state that "To exempt from tax a sale for export it is necessary that two conditions be met, namely, (1) that the article be identified as having been sold *by the manufacturer* for export and (2) that it be exported in due course." Further in the same section, "The exemption provided herein is limited to sales by the manufacturer for export and is not applicable in cases where sale of taxable articles are made from a dealer's stock for ex-port even though actually exported."[4]

Even though a substantial number of Folkways records were exported to overseas dealers and retailers, Folkways was nonetheless not eligible for the exemption because the recordings were not made specifically for export and labeled to reflect this. All stock was made for domestic sale, and if a foreign order came in, it was filled and shipped, thus falling under the latter qualification to the legislation. As a final insult, even in cases where Folkways might have been able to actually apply for the exportation exemption for certain orders or recordings, several letters illustrate the problems with importers in other countries being saddled with their own domestic import duties that would make the importation of Folkways records impracticable. The solution to this problem was to negotiate a licensing arrangement and to ship master tapes to the partner country and have them produce Folkways recordings domestically. This effectively exempted Folkways from the excise tax, but it also reduced the profit potential from sales of finished product to a payment for use and a percentage for royalties from the licensee.

Manufacturing

In one respect, the previous history that Moe had in the record industry with Asch and DISC Records already put him in contact with many of the small pressing companies in the New York area that he could utilize to produce Folkways recordings. It must be remembered, of course, that it is not simply the pressing of the record that is required: labels, sleeves, covers, booklets, and slicks (the album cover without the jacket) also need to be printed to produce the final product.

The documentation for Folkways Records in these areas is slim at best. There are a few pressing orders, some printing orders, and the occasional price list from various manufacturers. What is intriguing, however, is that far more invoices and the like exist for DISC Records during the early and mid-1940s, just prior to bankruptcy, than for Folkways itself. The reasons for this are not clear, although the legal proceedings of bankruptcy may have prompted Moe to hang on to his DISC documentation in case there were additional problems later on—not unlike the common habit of keeping old tax receipts or moving unopened boxes year after year, while discarding newer items.

It is important to note that Moe had established a pattern during the DISC days of using several different pressing and printing plants at any given time. Through the 1940s, pressing was done predominately at Scranton Record Company/Capitol Records (Scranton, Pennsylvania) and Eastern Record Co. (Laurel Hill, Long Island, New York), with other work going to Clark Phonograph Co. (Harrison, New Jersey), Bart Laboratories (Belleville, New Jersey), Muzak Co. (New York City), and possibly Progressive Album Co. (Brooklyn, New York), to name a few.[5] Printing at this time was also spread out among several companies including Keystone Printed Specialties Co. (Scranton, Pennsylvania),[6] Globe Printing (New York City),[7] and Kaltman Press (Woodside, Long Island, New York).[8]

From a financial point of view, it is easy to understand why the economics of record production are so precarious. One of the curious features of pressing plants at this time was the allowance for up to 10 percent above or below the requested order number to be pressed and billed to the customer. This practice is mentioned in several places ranging from the detailed price list of the Record Manufacturing Corporation of America[9] to an invoice from Custom Record Sales—RCA Victor that lists 769 records shipped on an order of 750 (which resulted in difficulties settling the account).[10] However, what is particularly notable about this practice is the pressure that it put on the small record company, forcing it to absorb unanticipated costs in record production. In a letter to George Clark of Clark Phono. Co., Moe wrote that:

> On August 25th, I placed an order for 200 #4010 records. Please be advised that on your bill #40003 you sent me 450 records and on #39994 an additional 50. This extra 300 records amounts to about $93.00 above and beyond the amount of records that I need and puts undue and added burden on me which is hard enough to carry now.[11]

Perhaps the only feasible explanation is that the presser is adding extra pressings to cover some number of faulty recordings that would be returned by customers and replaced—and Folkways certainly had complaints about faulty pressings. On the other hand, if the pressing plants were compensating for some percentage of recordings that were faulty, it hardly seems reasonable that the customer who places the order has to bear the cost of the pressing plants' production difficulties. It does appear to be a peculiar practice in any event.

By the 1950s when Folkways Records had become a relatively stable company, the use of various pressing plants had somewhat changed. The documentation concerning the pressing of Folkways recordings emphasizes Custom Record Sales (a division of RCA Victor) and Plastylite Corporation of North Plainfield, New Jersey. Although there is not a lot of material remaining about the relations between Folkways and either company, the date span certainly suggests long and active partnerships. Correspondence dating from early 1955,[12] as well as a 1954 price guide,[13] suggests that Folkways' use of Custom Record Sales was well under way.[14] A second item—a letter by Custom Record Sales to Folkways in 1968 regarding the complete physical inventory held by Custom[15]—illustrates the enduring nature of that relationship.

Plastylite appears to be one of the original pressers used by Folkways Records. The archive contains a wide variety of invoices and shipping documents related to the movement of recordings and tapes between Folkways and Plastylite. A 1952 list of the 12" stampers, their condition (amount molded), and the number of labels on hand at Plastylite illustrates the considerable extent to which Plastylite was being utilized by this time.[16] A letter from 1959[17] not only confirms the continued relationship between Folkways and Plastylite, but also provides a sense of the volume of recordings that Folkways was selling by that time. The letter from Plastylite confirms to Folkways that, "We see no reason why we cannot take care of your required 1,000-10" and 2500-12" records per week and, starting in January, supplying you with an increased amount to 1500-10" and 3,000-12" records a week."[18]

This is a substantial volume required of Plastylite, in addition to the other pressings that were being done at other companies. One interesting letter to Moe from H. Weinraub of Plastylite in 1963 sheds some light on the type of relationship that Folkways and Plastylite were able to maintain.[19] In the letter, Weinraub reveals that:

> Some of our record companies make unreasonable demands and we have no other choice then [sic] to follow their instructions. Without them we are out of business.
>
> We are quite aware of your situation and are trying to fit you in, in spite of these things. You may think we are ignoring you but we are not. Believe me, we are doing everything possible to get you out of the hole. Please bear with us.

This statement highlights a couple of important issues. The first is the scale of the production managed by Folkways. Even though the numbers in the previous letter sound substantial, Folkways appeared to be in the minority with respect to the attention that they can command from the pressers. Second, although it sounded like Plastylite had already accepted the order and then were having problems filling it, they are nonetheless sensitive to the needs of the smaller producer. Obviously this is a sensible business position for Plastylite to take with respect to Folkways. But it still points to the importance to Folkways of having a relationship with its suppliers above and beyond economic ones to ensure that Folkways could meet production targets. What is not clear is the extent to which Folkways was "in the hole" and the exact nature of the demands being made on Plastylite.

A compounding factor in the production process, in addition to finding reliable outside vendors, was the negotiation of credit. As discussed earlier, the money chain in the recording industry of the time seems to have been built on the principle that nobody gets paid until the customer pays for the recording. At that point, the money begins to flow back toward the producer—the one furthest from the source. Typical credit arrangements were based on 30-day units: 30-, 60-, and 90-day periods were fairly common, whereas 120-day credits were nearing the exceptional. In that time period, the hope was that enough capital would flow back from the retailer/dealer to distributor to producer/manufacturer that the pressing plants, printing plants, and assorted overhead costs could be paid.

Situations could become very difficult if each step in the chain had a different credit period. One example in the early 1960s found Moe in a letter exchange regarding a credit account with Allied Record Manufacturing. Moe claimed that he had understood there would be a 90-day payment deadline, not a 60-day deadline, "as we have such arrangements with RCA Victor, Sonic Rec. Pro., Plastylite Corp., and others."[20] It is likely that such disputes were fairly common in the negotiation stages of a relationship, notwithstanding that differing lengths of credit could also be part of the utility of having contracts with a variety of pressing plants. If payment with one plant became overdue, pressings from another on a second line of credit could generate the sales to pay the first presser. It certainly seemed as if Moe was more than familiar with this type of strategy. In fact, Moe's reference to Sonic Record Production "and others" indicates numerous pressing arrangements in addition to those Moe used regularly in the early days of Folkways.

Domestic Distribution

Of course, generating product is only part of the business equation; the second issue is how the product gets to the market where it is sold. Distribution becomes the second crucial component of record sales. The business of distribution creates a number of difficulties for producers of all sizes, but especially small producers. Typically, distribution for the independent company follows one of two courses.[21] The first is to use the distribution networks of the major corporations. Often, major companies are more or less vertically integrated, allowing them to control all aspects of the creation/dissemination/sale of recorded product. As a result of their size, major companies often provide production and distribution services to other companies. Thus, independent companies often make agreements with major companies to get access to national or international distribution arrangements. Unfortunately, this type of arrangement puts the major company—as owner of the distribution chain—very much in control and does not allow the independent company much flexibility to pursue different avenues of sale.

The second possibility is the independent distributor. Independent distributors operate at various sales levels, from local to national, and are generally not affiliated with any major record companies; their income comes from a straight commission on the product they sell. However, because of their independent status, distributors often run into conflict with the majors, because the majors can often undercut the independent distributor's cost on product. Independent distributors are also in conflict with "subdistributors"—so-called rackjobbers and one-stops—who deal with retailers at the local level and can take up retail space that might otherwise go to the larger distributors. Independent distributors also cost the record company more, because they do not normally deal in the kind of volume that makes the majors competitive, nor can they offer up-front payment to the producer, because they have to wait until a retailer pays an account before they pay the producer.

In either arrangement, however, the producer is somewhat limited in the number of typical connections that the distribution network offers. As most distribution is geared to the material released by the majors, pop records do well in this type of distribution network. The product can get to the retailer quickly and in high volumes to best capitalize on the hype that might surround a "hit" record—clearly not the sort of system that would work well for Folkways. On the other hand, utilizing the traditional independent contractors was not always the best way for Moe to get Folkways into stores. With a catalog as eclectic as Folkways', a standardized distribution arrangement was simply not sufficient. The net result was that Moe utilized virtually every avenue of distribution available to him: some larger distributors, some local-level distributors, direct-to-retailer with occasional price incentives, mail-order, as well as self-promotion and a number of foreign licensing arrangements.

An overview of some of the relationships that Folkways entered into in order to get recordings to where they were sold shows that it was largely a piecemeal affair. Accounts were opened and closed with considerable frequency. The arrangements that ultimately made up the full range of dealer/distributors agreements for Folkways were complicated and mostly undocumented. The long periods of activity or inactivity of dealer/distributors and the wide geographic distribution of sales territories makes a complete accounting of the relationships virtually impossible. The sheer volume of retail outlets across the United States for Folkways was considerable, with the vast majority of these outlets only carrying a few titles, or some only making orders at a customer's request.

The combination of a very large and very eclectic inventory put Folkways at a considerable disadvantage when working within the existing distribution networks because of the reliance of the distributors and dealers on relatively fast-moving product. Folkways clearly did not produce such popular product. This forced Moe around many of the typical distribution networks and directly into retails stores, where a few select Folkways titles would draw customers to inquire about the Folkways catalog. Although Folkways always faced the difficulties of a slow-moving inventory, in its early days it would have been possible for a distributor or dealer to carry virtually the entire Folkways catalog. However, by the time Folkways was more than a decade old, the size of the catalog (nearing 600+ titles) was beginning to become a serious distribution liability.

However, Moe had one key ally in getting Folkways into a wide range of retailers across the country. At the beginning of the 1960s, Moe began an important association that would prove to be extremely helpful in the overall sales of Folkways Records. Larry Sockell, an independent record sales representative who worked for a number of record companies, contacted Moe and inquired about adding Folkways to his list of clients. Fortunately, Moe saw the wisdom of this arrangement and hired Larry on commission as a national sales representative for Folkways. By all accounts, a very fruitful and mutually beneficial relationship was born.

An important part of what Larry offered was sales exposure for Folkways (along with a number of other accounts) across the United States. According to Larry, he typically traveled around the United States at least twice a year, four times a year in certain locations like Chicago, Boston, Minneapolis, or Washington, D.C., ultimately hitting most of the major cities in the United States at least once a year.[22] Larry ended up working with Moe and Folkways until the early 1980s. It is clear that Larry's intervention made a significant impact on the overall sales and image of Folkways.

Moe's relationship with Larry was exactly what Moe and Folkways needed. Moe could rely on a personal relationship with Larry, as well as trusting him to manage his sales affairs effectively. Moe did pay Larry a significant amount of money in commissions over the years, but these commissions were based on actual sales. More importantly, Moe was also paying for the relationships that Larry was able to establish and manage with the customers. Thus, in many respects, the kind of interpersonal relationship that Moe had with Larry was another essential step in maintaining the degree of flexibility that a larger, more hierarchical or bureaucratic distribution arrangement would not have allowed.

In one instance, Larry recalled that he caught Moe making a cash deal with one of his customers. After pointing out to Moe that he was to get his commission from the deal even though Moe did it behind Larry's back, Moe quickly paid Larry the commission and brushed the event under the table.[23] Moe knew full well that he should not have been undercutting Larry, but, as an astute businessman, he would cut a deal whenever he could, particularly if Larry was working on his accounts for other manufacturers. In fact, Larry's tolerance for such events certainly helped Moe immensely. Cash deals were critical for Moe, especially when money was tighter than usual. Larry's tolerance of these deals not only worked out for Larry, but it gave Moe the room to maneuver financially when it was necessary.

In my estimation, Larry was instrumental in getting Folkways out of many of the standard record distribution channels and directly into the retailers. This was a key move on Larry's part, because centralized distribution was simply not economically feasible with Folkways. There were too many titles to carry and the rate of turnover was, comparatively speaking, very low. By his account, record distributors at that time would need to turn over their stock four times a year to be profitable. In the case of Folkways, only a small number of distributors could turn over the Folkways inventory more than one and half times a year.[24]

This is very likely the reason for such patchy and inconsistent documentation of distributors. On the other hand, very little was recorded about the retailers that did quite well with Folkways inventory, either. Sam Goody's in New York was an important, early Folkways retailer. Goody was one of the few retailers to carry all Folkways titles in regular inventory, and did so from the early 1960s. At one point, Moe was also renting warehouse space from Sam Goody, further cementing their relationship. In the 1970s and 1980s other retailers, Tower Records in Los Angeles, for example, also carried the majority of Folkways' inventory, though not many retailers could handle such a large catalog. Aside from these, there were a few domestic distributors that stand out for their longevity in distributing a very difficult product (see Appendix 5, for example).

An illustration of some of the difficulties that Folkways faced with distribution can be seen in one of the more established distributors for Folkways, K. O. Asher of Chicago. Asher[25] is one of the few early outlets known to have been used by Folkways in the Great Lakes area. After some apparent problems in 1959, Marian Distler assured K. O. Asher that, "Since the inception of Folkways Records in 1948 you have been our distributor and there has never been any question as to our accepting our records from you for credit on your returns."[26] The issue of returns continued to be the topic of correspondence for many more years. As the catalog continued to grow, it became increasingly a financial liability for Folkways to give dealers full credit for records they ordered but could not sell. In 1960 the issue came up again with Asher inquiring whether an account that they were servicing (Lyon and Healy, Inc. of Chicago) would be entitled to full-cost returns through Asher, even in the event that the Asher/Folkways deal were to terminate.[27] An interesting issue arising out of this inquiry was with Asher seeking assurances that such arrangements would also apply to Pioneer Record Sales, Inc., the sales branch set up to handle the distribution of Folkways and other labels that Moe was distributing himself.

The Asher/Folkways arrangement began to experience some troubles in 1964. The renegotiation of their contract "had at least a dozen amendments." In this contract, there are a couple of references made by Asher that are of interest with respect to the operation of Folkways. First was an unsubstantiated reference to the fact that the contract "eliminates Marian Distler's guarantee." It is not known what aspect of the contract the guarantee might have referred to, but it could well be related to the earlier issue of full-cost returns. Following this, a second comment by Asher to Moe that "I assume that you are now president of Folkways and Pioneer" likely arose from Marian's death. The comments from Asher also highlight the issue of control within Folkways. Marian had been listed as Folkways sole officer and president from its inception, whereas Moe was almost always the "production director." Whether these roles were effectively maintained within the Folkways office between Moe and Marian is unclear. Despite clearly leading Folkways, Moe did not regularly sign correspondence as president of Folkways until well after 1960, preferring his listing as production director. Asher's impressions of Folkways' management might have had a grain of truth as far as the outside world was concerned, despite the fact that Moe was clearly at the helm of Folkways from the beginning.

The Folkways/Asher contract is notable for a couple of other reasons. First, it is the only signed contract that I have seen that includes Folkways Records, Pioneer Record Sales, and Moe personally as signatories to the agreement. Virtually all other contracts would be between another party and Folkways or another party and Pioneer. It is highly unusual to see both Folkways and Pioneer as signatories to the same contract. Why Moe would commit himself in this fashion is a bit of a mystery; perhaps Asher wanted a bit more assurance that Moe was going to adhere to the terms of the contract. The second interesting feature is that the contract is quite short and hastily typed with several errors. Physically, it does not have the appearance of a carefully negotiated contract. However, its brevity allows its terms to be summarized here, giving more of a sense of the nature of Folkways' domestic distribution contracts[28]:

1. K. O. Asher, Inc. shall have the exclusive right during the time of this agreement to distribute the recordings issued under the name of Folkways, Broadside, RBF in: Illinois, Indiana, Iowa and Missouri.
2. As long as K. O. Asher Inc. has not been advised to the contrary, they shall be entitled to sell your recordings anywhere.
3. Supplier [Folkways/Pioneer/Moses Asch] shall not be permitted to wholesale these recordings in the territory listed under 1).
4. K. O. Asher Inc. will pay for all purchases not more than list price (less excise tax) less 55% plus excise tax f. o. b. New York, properly packed. Terms: 5% 10 e. o. m. [10 days from end of month].

5. Catalogs, replacement jackets and replacement notes will be furnished by Supplier free of charge.
6. Supplier grants a 100% exchange privilege. However, in case of termination of this contract, Supplier agrees to take back all merchandise from K. O. Asher Inc. at the original cost price and pay for it in cash. The merchandise has to be returned to Supplier prepaid.
7. This agreement goes into effect immediately and constitutes as contract between Supplier and K. O. Asher Inc. All previous agreements are superseded by this agreement and shall be void.
8. This contract can be terminated by either party by giving 6 months notice by registered letter, notice to be given to the end of the calendar month.
9. In case there should be a credit balance in favor of K. O. Asher Inc. on our accounts, Supplier shall not be entitled to give notice to K. O. Asher Inc. until the end of the third full calendar month after the credit balance has been paid in cash to K. O. Asher Inc.
10. All parties listed as Supplier guarantee the proper consummation of this contract.

Not two weeks after this contract was signed, troubles began. In a rare admission of difficulties by Moe, he sent a short letter to Asher to inform him that "due to the terrible situation in the sales of phonograph records this Spring, please do not deduct $500.00 from the $1,000.00 I still owe you on our loan. We would appreciate payment of your invoices as soon as possible." On a separate line, Moe concludes by asking "whether we can open up the matter of a new $10,000.00 loan as soon as convenient to you."

This is quite a suggestive piece of correspondence. There is no other information about the loan, but the timing of the agreement and the reference to the loan from Asher to Moe makes one wonder about a possible connection between signing the agreement and receiving the loan. Asher and Folkways would be nearing twenty years of dealings by this point. If sales were so bad, perhaps Moe felt that he could approach some of his old distribution contacts for loans to help him through the rough patch, using future releases and credit as collateral. That would account for both the hasty nature of the contract, as well as the fact that Moe entered into the contract as an individual, in addition to signing on behalf of Folkways and Pioneer Record Sales. With the closing comment about discussing a $10,000.00 loan, times must have been very rough and cash flow very tight. This further supports other directions that Moe headed at this time, including the Scholastic and MGM agreements he signed less than a year later in 1965.

However, things were not resolved with Asher. On 23 September 1964 Asher wrote to Pioneer Record Sales, Inc. that they had just received a letter from Roberts Record Distributing Co. of St. Louis addressed to "dealers" stating that they were now the exclusive distributors of Folkways Records in St. Louis—part of Asher's territory. Understandably upset, Asher followed by stating, "Referring to our contract of April 27, 1964 we advise you that this is a violation of our contract. We will keep you and the co-signers of the contract responsible for the damage inflicted on us."[29]

The letter from Folkways to Asher dated two days later (25 September 1964) seems to address the St. Louis situation, but not in the manner that Asher would have liked, as its full text indicates:

> Dear Mr. Asher:
> We find that we are now in a position to service the St. Louis area as an important outlet for Folkways Records.
> Therefore we would solicit your indulgence in permitting Folkways to make direct sales to this territory.
> It is our feeling, and we hope that you will agree, that the sales potential of the St. Louis area may be more fully realized in this manner.
> May we expect an affirmative reply?

There is no documentation suggesting how or if the situation was resolved, nor is there mention of the two loans previously referred to by Moe. The obvious conflict and handling of the agreement with Asher raises more questions than the documentation can answer. Perhaps it was a case of Moe feeling it was better to ask for forgiveness than to ask for permission from Asher. If he was offered distribution on better terms than Asher could or would offer, it might well have been too much to ignore. Such scenarios leave tantalizing trails to follow. Unfortunately, at this point, the resolution of this conflict remains unknown, as does the nature of the Folkways/Asher relationship beyond 1964.

A further illustration of some of the general distribution difficulties can be shown by examining only a couple of years in the life of the Folkways' distribution network in the Midwest. It begins with a letter of appointment[30] to Cosnat Distributing Corp.[31] in December 1959 to become Folkways' exclusive distributor in the Cincinnati area. The letter outlines the terms of product cost and payment,[32] along with the terms of the relationship: "We reserve the right to cancel this arrangement on the grounds of delinquent payments or less than normal sales in any period of time."

The next—and only other—piece of correspondence in the archive is a February 1961 termination letter.[33] Addressed to Ed Rosenblatt, Moe states:

> Please be advised that from this day on you do not represent Folkways Records. Our business relationship has been impossible and

our sales have been most disappointing. You will be hearing from I. K. Distributors who is going to be our new Cincinnati distributor. I understand that he will take over your stock. Please let me know what this will be so I can give you proper credit.

Our personal relations have been the best, but our business relationship has been terrible.

Following the termination of Cosnat Distributing, Moe welcomed I. K. Distributors of Cincinnati, Ohio, aboard in 1962. Moe closes the brief letter to I. K. Distributors by outlining the transition from Cosnat and reminding them that "I am expecting an order from you shortly." Here, too, there is no evidence of what sort of relationship may have developed.

Attempts to cover other areas of Ohio, through a relationship with Keynote Distribution Co. of Cleveland, Ohio, also proved short lived. Beginning in May of 1960 following an offer from Folkways through Larry Sockell, Keynote began to cover the territory of Northern Ohio with the occasional product order from Pennsylvania and Indiana.[34] However, only nine months later, a memo to Moe from Larry suggested that:

If you're determined to change Cleveland I believe Duncan Sales will be our best bet. Note list of lines and they have 4 salesmen (Keynote is one (1) man). Advise Keynote of termination with a copy of letter to Shelly Haims and myself that we may know of the change.[35]

Two days later, on 24 February 1961, Moe sent Keynote a letter terminating their distribution agreement. Overall, the reason for Keynote's termination appears to be simply poor performance on their part.

In January 1961, Music Merchants, Inc.,[36] an earlier distributor of Folkways, returned to pick up the territory just to the northwest, in Detroit, Michigan. It is not known why the original agreement was terminated, although it was likely due to an inability to generate enough sales—the constant problem with the Folkways catalog. In a letter confirming the change in distribution from Aurora Distributors back to Music Merchants, Marvin Jacobs adds that "It's nice to be associated with you [Folkways] again and this time we can look forward to a long and mutually profitable relationship."[37] Whether the relationship turned out to be either long or profitable is unclear, as no other references to this arrangement are known.

Of course, the arrangements that Folkways was making with these distributors may also have been an impediment to success. One of the best descriptions of Folkways' expectations of its distributors can be found in a 1958 letter to Kay's Record Distributors[38] of Baltimore, Maryland from Marian Distler[39]:

We would be pleased to have you represent us in the Baltimore-Washington territory and the following is an outline of our working arrangements. Enclosed please find our catalog and brochure. All items are available and should any be out of stock at any time they are back ordered for delivery in ten to fourteen days. We ship directly to the dealers from New York upon receipt of your instructions. We do not require any minimum, but for orders of 5 or more albums we pay the delivery charge. We reserve the right to solicit and do business with educational institutions such as schools, libraries, universities, museums. We do not prohibit you from taking such orders; our billing to such organizations is 20% from list. Our regular billing is 2% 10 days with credit reference or c.o.d. We expect that you will take care in sending us accredited accounts. We will pay you 10% of the monies we collect from your orders once to twice a month depending on the volume. You will receive a duplicate of every invoice for your own checking purposes. We will send you samples free of charge and will be glad to send you sales aids, and any brochure that you may require and catalogs.

We prefer to have the stores order what they need and not overstock. We allow exchanges and in some cases return privilege. Some stores may wish to send us orders directly in which case you will be credited for same. We expect you will have some c.o.d. accounts and possibly be able to enlist some standing order accounts.

I will be glad to answer any further questions and please acknowledge receipt of this letter and acceptability. Thanking you, we are, Truly yours, Folkways Records, Marian Distler.

The completeness of the instructions to Kay's would have been very helpful for any Folkways distributor, and on its surface appears to be a very reasonable set of requirements. The expectations of Folkways were quite clear with respect to timelines, order processing, and the development of new sales outlets. There is little doubt that although Moe was well aware of the process, Marian seemed much more in control of the detail management that was so important to keeping such an intricate distribution network functioning. Perhaps some of the hiccups over territory overlap, timeliness of orders, or even perceived sales efforts might have been allayed if more care had been given to the details. It might even be the case that many of the problems after 1964 were a result of Marian's passing and the changes in the Folkways offices that resulted from it. Nonetheless, with Folkways being such a small organization, it is still quite remarkable that a national—and in a limited way, international—network was functioning at all.

There is a considerable amount of information concerning domestic distribution with virtually all of it echoing the examples given here. Arrangements were terminated very quickly, largely on the grounds of a failure to bring in enough orders, which is precisely the difficulty recognized by Larry. Without such a strong emphasis on the educational component, and the support that Larry could offer to get the rest of the catalog into individual retail outlets, particularly in the 1960s, Folkways would have likely suffered a fatal blow. Larry continued to represent Folkways nationally in the 1970s, even recruiting salesmen as needed for specific regions.[40] Even as late as 1979, Moe continued to negotiate regional representation deals for Folkways, excluding existing Sockell and Folkways accounts. A signed agreement with Herb Goldfarb Associates committed HGA to (1) the taking of orders, (2) following up their delinquent accounts, and (3) "showing new releases and generally act for the benefit of encouraging and promoting Folkways Records' for a 10% commission on all basic $7.98–12" LP record sales.[41] Slightly before, and for a short time after the sale of Folkways to the Smithsonian in 1987, domestic distribution was taken up nationally by the Birchtree Group (a music publisher known for its publications on Suzuki training), then by Rounder Records. From the early 1990s, Smithsonian Folkways recordings have been distributed in the United States, Canada and the United Kingdom by Koch International, along with a number of other distributors worldwide (Appendix 6).

The Educational Market

Despite all the difficulties with distributors across America, the one area of Folkways' catalog where strong distribution was quite effective was for the educational markets (see Appendix 7, for example). As late as the 1980s, Moe claimed that educational sales, including children's albums, accounted for 50 to 60 percent of his total sales. Although the specific sales percentages are not available for the 1950s and 1960s, it is clear that, in Moe's mind, the educational market was a persistent and important market to both tap into and to produce for. Such a goal was also very much in line with Moe's overarching mandate of preserving sound for the world.

One of the earliest documented educational relationships was with Sid Fox and the Children's Music Center in Los Angeles. In an important letter of August 1959,[42] Fox outlines the terms of an agreement that was being negotiated between Children's Music and Folkways. The main areas of concern in the letter are of pricing, educational certification, and distribution. Fox's competitive wholesale pricing was $1.75 for 10" LPs and $2.50 for 12" LPs, pricing that, as Fox pointed out, "was done [in part] on the basis of an expanded promotional campaign . . ."[43] In fact, Fox goes on to note that Children's Music was already giving promotional copies of recordings to KPFK, a "new, non-commercial FM radio station."

Perhaps coincidental, but definitely advantageous to Moe's efforts to expand Folkway's education market, was the exemption to excise tax that was granted to producers of educational material. The educational certification of the vendor was an important part of the educational distribution plan of Folkways, in large part because of the importance of taking advantage of the excise tax exemption. As Fox notes later in the same letter:

> Enclosed you will find a copy of our Certificate of Registry which makes it unnecessary for you to charge us excise tax. However, we will still continue to supply you with the necessary Affidavits of Ultimate Vendor listing records purchased by schools.

Aside from the market and various advantages that Moe wished to exploit, most important were the conditions of distribution. In point 4 of the letter, Fox points out that "On our paragraph 5, this should have read, 'The Children's Music Center will be the distributor of Folkways Records to educational dealers in the Southern California area only.'[44] I am sorry that this was not included in the original because that is exactly what I meant." Furthermore, there was the advantage of Fox's other arrangements[45]:

> We will have as national distributors of Folkways tapes for foreign language study all of the Caliphone dealers who sell the Caliphone Language Laboratory. This means about 75 dealers covering the entire United States. We can also supply these to dealers who sell other language laboratories of which there are now a few hundred.

In spite of the evidence of only a single document, it is clear that the Children's Music Center was poised to play an important part in distributing Folkways Records.

Allied Music Co. was also an important educational distributor for Folkways Records in the Los Angeles area, with its location just down West Pico Boulevard from the Children's Music Center. This first became clear in a letter from Moe in 1960 that first instructed Irving Shorten of Allied that Sid Fox of Children's Music would be placing orders through Allied directly.[46] More than that, in his typically testy tone, Moe described the difficulties of the educational market that they are dealing with:

> . . . Enclosed please find a card from Spencer Press, exclusive Columbia records school distributors who cater to educational institutions throughout the country. As over 50% of our business is educational and since we only give a 10 to 25% discount on orders over $500.00, I feel we must find a method of counteracting this competition. As you see such organizations as American Seating Company, Brunswick, Pocketput [sic] and others are entering into this field, they carry records.
>
> Please bear in mind that there is such a thing as excise in this industry which we have to pay to the government which is 11% [sic]

of the monies we get in that this is more than our net profit. With certification of school sales we are excused from this percentage by the government. Therefore, in order for us to maintain our discounts, may we please ask that you request of the customers you service, who sell to schools, for certification of such sales that you can send to us and which we in turn can get some slight compensation for from the Internal Revenue. I assure you that the more you are able to do for us on this, the more co-operation we will be able to give you.

With both the material and the financial landscape favoring the exploitation of educational markets, it is no wonder that recordings for children and the post-secondary markets did so well.

Foreign Distribution

Selling records abroad involves developing similar relationships in many respects to the domestic market, given that both systems of relationships are based on a similar directive: the dissemination of recordings. There is, however, a distinctive shift in the construction of distribution networks for foreign markets compared to domestic markets based on the balance between the exploitation of specialist markets in foreign countries—the "import" market—and the degree of impediment that was encountered in the importation of foreign goods across those borders.

There is proportionately little documentation on the rest of the non-North American market.[47] Much of that documentation falls into one of three categories. The first and most straightforward are the letters that discuss matters pertaining to deals already in place. However, outside of the archival material there is very little supplementary information available to flesh out much of the context of these agreements. The second category is the solicitation letters sent to Folkways from various distributors. These documents are of considerable interest because they often outline where Folkways was being distributed at a given time. It is important to note that they implicitly support the contention that Folkways' reputation was starting to grow and to gain the attention of those interested in wider markets.

Making up the third category are the legal documents. This is a particularly interesting group primarily because it focuses on the importance of controlling the product even though it may be in a market that is perceived to be very distant and unconnected. Oddly enough, such legal constraints often worked both for and against Folkways depending on the circumstance. There is no doubt that the legal wrangling is an important part of the control over both recorded product and the raw materials—artists, tapes, and masters—that circulate within the recording industry.

The following discussion on foreign markets is divided into two sections. The first section covers in some detail the arrangements between Folkways and Transatlantic Records and Topic Records, respectively. This combination of relatively well-documented relationships with the fact that both companies were based in England helps to paint a good picture of many of the issues faced both in England and in continental Europe. The second section outlines some of the other, less-documented distribution relationships that Moe had in other parts of Europe.

Reaching the UK Market: Transatlantic and Topic

The origins of the contracted dealings between Folkways and Transatlantic Records are found at the beginning of the 1960s. In 1960, Folkways was dealing with at least two other distributors/retailers in England: Agate & Co. and Colletts. In two letters to Moe from Ken Lindsay of Agate & Co., Lindsay expressed frustration with the efforts of Colletts to become the exclusive distributor of Folkways in England and force Agate & Co. to cease direct orders from Folkways and instead to order through Colletts.[48] There seems to be no evidence that dealings with Colletts continued and the agreement was likely terminated by the time the arrangement with Transatlantic was made.

Negotiations with Transatlantic appear to have begun with a request from Transatlantic Records asking Moe to consider distributing European product in the US. In a letter of 5 September 1961,[49] Moe expresses interest in an arrangement of some kind, but "due to the fact that there is a 15% duty and a 10% excise tax, it is impossible to merchandise European made records and sell them to distributors and then to dealers in the United States."[50] Moe then outlined an arrangement that he had developed with another European record company, Jupiter Records, whereby Moe imported their tapes, pressed the records in the United States and paid a fee for the tapes and a per-unit price for the license.[51]

The U.S. distribution deal seemed to go by the wayside, but by spring 1963 Folkways and Transatlantic Records were negotiating an agreement in which Transatlantic Records would act as a licensee of Folkways.[52] The first contract set out that "Folkways agree[s] to grant the agents the sole rights to distribute and sell Folkways Records in Great Britain . . ." for a period of two years with automatic renewal pending mutual satisfaction with the arrangement.[53] On 16 April 1964, however, Transatlantic Records broadened their arrangement with Folkways to gain "the exclusive right to manufacture, release, sell, distribute and promote records containing the material on the attached schedule," which was, in fact, a very short list: "Cisco Houston Sings Folksongs, Pete Seeger / Big Bill Broonzy Concert (2 Records), Art Tatum, Memphis Slim, Jazz At Town Hall (2 Records),

Brownie McGhee and Sonny Terry, Sing with Seeger, New Lost City Ramblers (Capitol)."[54]

One of the clear concerns in both the contractual agreement and in implementation was the effort Transatlantic put into the promotion of Folkways. Although Moe made some efforts to help out Transatlantic (he included sixteen records free in one order because he thought they might be marketable[55]), it was clearly up to Transatlantic to pick up the promotional ball. In a letter of 14 October 1963,[56] Nathan Joseph, director of Transatlantic Records, outlined the how they were pursuing promotion on a set of 17 selections, in addition to the full Folkways line. These efforts included:

- 15,000 catalogs with emphasis on the seventeen-title set, sent to "every dealer in this country," as well as every branch of the trade and made available to the general public.
- Advertising in the major trade magazines *Gramophone Record Retailer* and *Musical Industry News*; folk magazines *Sing* and *Spin*, and concert programs at folk shows at Royal Festival Hall, London.
- Setting up a booth at the British Gramophone Record Retailers Association Annual Conference and Trade Fair and the Midland Dealers Trade Fair.
- Setting up window displays at the shops of several leading record dealers.

Such an effort was certainly in Moe's favor. By the 1960s, Folkways' reputation was starting to gain some momentum overseas, together with interest in American culture generally. British interest in Pete Seeger, along with his sister Peggy Seeger and her husband Ewan MacColl who were actively performing in England, also helped the promotion of American folk records. In this respect, Folkways would seem to be a relatively lucrative distributorship to have in England. Transatlantic Records agreed. Nathan Joseph noted in the 14 October 1963 letter, "All this, together with the mailing out of thousands of your own cataloges, has I can assure you cost us a good deal more than the allowance which we are to receive under our contractual agreement."[57]

While promotion appeared as an on-again, off-again problem, the second difficulty that came to light with the Folkways/Transatlantic agreement was the sorting out of copyrights and payments. This was certainly not a unique problem, by any means,[58] but some of the details are of interest. In response to Nathan Joseph's request[59] for some advice from Moe on how to address the problem of payment of "outrageous" copyright fees on importation by the Mechanical Copyright Protection Society (MCPS), Moe responded:

This has not yet been resolved internationally. The record industry in the U.S. has been working with the federal government to come to some international agreement. All record companies have this difficulty.

The MCPS is naturally trying to collect for themselves while we have to pay over here. The contracts with the publishers in the U.S. have a clause that states Royalty shall be paid on records manufactured. This has been upheld by our courts in the cases of non-payment of royalty. The compulsory payment . . . this is Supreme Court ruling . . . which states that the manufacturer is to pay and the seller is liable for at least 2¢ per record made, per selection plus 3 times the rate as a fine.

All this means that in case of non-payment the Society will have a hard time collecting the fee as manufactured in the US and as imported to Great Britain. Naturally they want this fee—what I call double taxation. The more you resist this pressure by showing them that the US law is as stated above the better chance you have of this being the accepted practice. . . .

I would however show my letter to your attorneys. And have them get in touch with people who are specialists in this field of international intrigue.

In a letter of 4 June 1964,[60] however, Joseph asks for a price reduction of 40 cents on import costs "to compensate for the copyrights which we are now going to have to pay." This increase in cost for Moe was an unfortunate example of the impact that the changing business universe could have on international production and distribution. On the plus side, Transatlantic Records was doing its part to offer a little in return. Later in the same letter, Joseph closes by telling Moe, "We are at present pressing claims with the B.B.C. and four of the I.T.V. companies for mechanical copyright fees on Folkways records . . . we hope to have some results for you within the next three weeks or so."

The final reference to copyright in the context of the Transatlantic Records documentation is an interesting one. A letter of 18 August 1969[61] from Joseph makes note of "the Bob Dylan recordings"—almost certainly a reference to the recordings that appeared on Broadside Records[62] that Dylan did under the pseudonym Blind Boy Grunt.[63] On first appearances, there should have been no difficulty in releasing the Dylan/Grunt songs in Britain. However, Joseph's letter continues:

Having reconsidered the whole matter, we feel it's too risky. Firstly, if these tracks were recorded during Dylan's contractual obligation for CBS, I don't want to cross CBS and secondly you say that the composers rate on the compositions is to be paid through you to Broadside Magazine New York. Unfortunately these compositions are copyright to Warners Music in Britain and I certainly wouldn't like to cross them in a copyright battle. The establishment giants win again!

In the continuing effort to find new angles to sell records, a new facet of the relationship between Transatlantic Records and Folkways was revealed in the launch of the discount label Xtra by Transatlantic in the early part of 1964.[64] As has often been reported, Moe would not discount Folkways recordings at retail. As a result, if Transatlantic wanted to release Folkways material as part of a discount line, it would have to be through license.[65] At about the same time, Joseph also warned that the shift in England to a Labour Party government could lead to restrictions on "unnecessary" imports[66]—an unfortunate term to associate with the arts. So, pressing Folkways product in the UK would make sense.

At the end of 1964, Joseph had almost finalized further licensing deals of Xtra (Folkways) material to major companies in Australia, New Zealand, and South Africa.[67] However, Moe's activity at home started to complicate things for Transatlantic Records. Moe announced that he had made major licensing deals with both MGM and Scholastic Magazine. Both had existing distribution around the world that potentially would overlap with markets that Transatlantic already reached. Nonetheless, Moe approached Transatlantic about distributing Folkways into Benelux,[68] Spain,[69] and South Africa.[70] Needless to say, there was much confusion about licensing material through Xtra, given the scope of the licensing arrangements being made at home through Scholastic and MGM.

After Joseph asked Moe about the deal, Moe replied that "it would be detrimental to Scholastic if I made a deal with you on the above.[71] Scholastic has an arrangement with SONY-PLAY (sic) in Spain. They are issuing Folkways Records."[72] Joseph then replied on 31 October 1969[73]:

> This is to inform you that we obviously have the same agent in Spain. Our agent is Discos Sonoplay . . . and are fairly obviously the same as the one you mention in your letter as Sony-Play. This being the case, it is easy to see why they would like to add some of the excellent early material which you licensed to us, to the material they are already getting from Folkways/Scholastic.
>
> . . . since the circumstances are now somewhat clearer, they might reconsider their decision . . .

It is not clear how much beyond the early 1970s Folkways/Transatlantic relationship continued. The last items of documentation, however, are quite interesting. A 1971 Transatlantic catalog lists both Folkways records at a recommended retail of £2.75 (about $6.60, U.S.), and Transatlantic's discount label XTRA, for which they licensed Pete Seeger and a number of blues artists from Folkways, at £1.47 1/2 (about $3.50, U.S.). At 12 cents per copy sold, the XTRA licenses did not amount to much income for Moe, but certainly every little bit helped. As the 1973 sales figures for XTRA indicate, there was a small, but persistent market in England and abroad for Folkways' American material, especially blues and other Americana that might have been available by license or import (Appendix 9). XTRA ceased activity in 1976. Transatlantic Records itself was taken over by Logos Records in 1980.[74]

The second major relationship that Folkways had with British record distribution was through Topic Records. The relationship with Topic Records predates that with Transatlantic, but it does not appear to have been quite as involved; certainly there is a lack of correspondence to indicate much involvement. The Topic relationship began in the late 1950s, although the company itself began two decades before in 1939.[75] With a history and a mandate similar to Folkways, it is not surprising that Topic and Folkways began a relationship. Like Transatlantic with its XTRA label, Topic licensed select albums from Folkways for release in the UK on their own label. Not surprisingly, as in most licensing arrangements, there seemed to be a lot of little problems that plagued the relationship. For example, letters in 1959[76] indicate that there was some unhappiness on Moe's part with respect to the issuing of Folkways records without having been paid the agreed $50 per recording by Topic. Topic claimed this as a bookkeeping oversight and it did not appear to significantly damage the agreement, but it certainly foreshadowed a relationship that never appeared to be particularly positive.

In terms of documentation, there is very little between 1960 and mid-1965. At that point, the relationship between the two companies was clearly coming to an end. Part of the difficulty appeared to be Topic's conflict with English taxation law and the inability to send Folkways the royalty amounts without having deducted English tax. The double taxation dilemma undoubtedly tied up a considerable amount of money (perhaps over £1,000).[77] At about the same time, however, Topic announced that it had picked up Caedmon Record's *Folk Songs of Britain* series and had begun to clear out their remaining Folkways titles at discounted prices. This clearly upset Moe, who was always sensitive about the diluting of the value of Folkways's product and resisted discounting his material. At the conclusion of a letter 16 December 1965,[78] Gary Sharp of Topic wrote, "I don't think you can complain about us selling off at a cheap rate as this is the normal trade practice. Furthermore, I understand that this is what you did with the Topic records you had in stock when you wanted to clear them."

Earlier in the letter, however, Sharp tried to explain the situation and express his confusion about the whole matter:

> With the easy availability of Folkways recordings in England[79] now it did appear that we were no longer fulfilling a useful function in this direction as we had so little of it, and consequently we decided to delete the material which was in the Topic catalog. . . .
>
> I have been trying to understand what you mean when you speak of a "personal vendetta." On reading some of the correspondence which has taken place between us, I can only think that you are referring to your previous misunderstandings which I have attempted to correct. . . . I regret that you have never troubled to call on me on your last two occasions in England so that we could have a talk together to clear any such misunderstandings. . . .
>
> As I look through the old correspondence I think of how much help you could have been to Topic in its early struggles instead of leaving us to pull ourselves up by our own shoe-strings. There was of course no obligation on your part to do so but when I read some of your early sentiments on the identity of interests between the two labels, I feel rather sad about it.

Regrettably, it seems that Topic fell victim to the same difficulties as many domestic distributors: inadvertent neglect. It is certainly impossible to say at this point what might have driven Moe to spend considerable time developing one set of distribution relationships and to neglect others. Perhaps it was the nature of the personal relationships behind the business that made the effort worthwhile. It might also have been Moe's perception of the value of the relationship of the distributor to Folkways Records: the more the distributor did for Folkways, the better the relationship, while those distributors that did not work as hard for the label were somewhat neglected.

Other Foreign Markets

Folkways' reputation was starting to spread globally, and this reputation was having an impact on the interest expressed by various companies to distribute Folkways. The first are documents from 1957[80] that quite clearly see Folkways as a useful ally in the global dissemination of folk music. The first, a letter of 14 January 1957 from Rose Records of Gand, Belgium, begins:

> We take pleasure in establishing contact between our two firms. In view of a possible business cooperation.
>
> Your company is known as the only great company which distributes folk music throughout the world. On account of this we

wish to get into touch with you because we have released a sort of record you might be able to use on a large basis: a typical old Flemish carnival medley with numbers at least 50 years old . . .

We send you a sample of this record under separate cover. If you are interested, kindly advise us and we shall send you the mother matrices or tapes for you to lease and issue under your label, providing a royalty agreement.

The second letter (7 August 1957) was a follow-up to a meeting between Moe and L.P. Mabel of Henry M. Snyder and Co., Inc.—"Export representatives for American book publishers"—regarding other possible export markets. Interestingly, Mabel notes in the letter that though they had done a little work with recordings, "we do not know just what we could do with your excellent records." Importantly, Mabel points to the "possibility of our representing you in countries in the export market other than Mexico, Belgium,[81] Holland,[82] and Switzerland, where you already have other contractual arrangements."

The final letter is from Mike Glasser at Transglobal Music Co., Inc. of New York. Dated much later (12 October 1965[83]), Glasser was pretty blunt:

I have spoken to you several times by phone in regard to acquiring your product for the Scandinavian area. I would like to know what price your product is available for per album and the shipping cost to Sweden.

The Scandinavian territory includes Sweden, Finland, Norway, Iceland, and Greenland. If Denmark is available, we would also be interested in acquiring rights for your product in Denmark. . . .

By the 1960s, a couple of deals had also been pursued with Italian companies. The first was the collaboration in the release of an Italian edition of "The Epic of the Far West" by Mondadori Publishing of New York and Milan. In appreciation for the efforts of Folkways, the company even presented Folkways with a parchment scroll that read:

To Folkways Records and Service Corporation of New York who with constant and disinterested action and dedicated effort collaborates to spread in the world the culture, ideas and civilization of America. Arnoldo Mondadori publisher expresses his grateful thanks for its contribution to the success of the work by Piero Pieroni "The Epic of the West" published in Milan the 7 of December 1961.

Moe responded by acknowledging the award: "It is gestures such as yours that make it worthwhile to issue the type of material we do. We really appreciate it."[84]

An interesting subtext to this exchange is the addition of a request following the announcement of the award for a licensing agreement from Folkways to publish an edition in French and German, with the same fee—$100 per edition—"for the use of the same record." After gracefully acknowledging the award, Moe gives permission for the licenses. While the award was undoubtedly well intended, pairing it with the licensing request likely did not hurt Mondadori's chances of getting the Folkways license.

The second Italian company, Fratelli Fabbri Editori, was interested in licensing Folkways material for release on 7-inch EPs that would be included in "magazine-type publications" sold either door to door or through mail order. There is not a lot of information rounding out the details of this deal, or even if it was ever finalized,[85] but a letter addressed "Dear Sirs" closes with a thank-you "for the cooperation you will give to Mr. Prosperio who plans to reach a definitive agreement with you during his visit in the States in the next few days."[86]

Relationships with companies in France appeared to have been more extensive, and according to form, quite confusing. By the late 1950s, Folkways had been importing and distributing the Encyclopedia Sonore line of the Hachette Company.[87] However, in a letter to Hachette, Moe was pointed about the problems:

> In recent months there has been a decided change in our attitude for handling your records in this country. We have found that the Federal Government is taxing us for the importation of the records and this excise tax of 10% of whatever monies we get is in addition to the duty that we have to pay as well as other such expenses. It becomes impossible for us to break even with imported records.
>
> Since, if we were to continue selling Encyclopedia Sonore records in America, we have to publish textual material to accompany the records, it would be more feasible if we were to make our own masters and press records here in the States. If you will let me know in what areas you have little or no sales, we could consider working with you as we have just outlined.[88]

An exchange with Hugus Panassie of the Hot Club de France (Paris) in 1960 outlines other difficulties concerning distribution of records in France. The initial request from Panassie to Folkways was for records to be reviewed in the "Bulletin du hot club de France."[89] However, Panassie claimed the problem was that "your records are never issued in France despite their interest."[90] Shortly after, Moe sent the records, but noted to

Panassie that "Perhaps it would be of interest to you to know that Ricordi has contracted with us for records to be released in France, but so far they have not shown any interest in Jazz. You might be able to persuade them along these lines."[91]

A reply by Panassie soon after indicated that not only did Panassie not know about the Ricordi deal,[92] but that Panassie had thought a deal had been made between Folkways and the "President" label: "At least, that's what one of the heads of the 'President' told me, and I even remember telling him to hurry and release one of your BIG BILL LP's for the first anniversary of Bill's death. But nothing materialized. Funny people, those 'President' guys . . . "[93]

Likely the largest cross-licensing deal that Folkways entered into in France was with Chant du Monde. There is not much in the way of existing documentation, but the existence of release lists and a number of recordings in the Folkways Archive supports significant, although finite, activity. Beginning with an agreement from 31 December 1964, Folkways and Chant du Monde continued their relationship into the late 1970s. According to an application that Folkways made for a reduction on the payment of French royalty taxes, "Le Chant du Monde produces phonograph records and tapes from master tapes supplied by Folkways Records and pays Folkways Records royalties on sales of these."[94] Despite the intention, one of the largest problems seemed to be getting Chant du Monde to pay the royalties at all. As late as June 1978, Moe was writing to Jean Miailhe, Director General of Chant du Monde that:

> I cannot wait for our money this long. You notice that the American dollar is down our inflation is high and I cannot get records from our pressing plants unless Folkways pays them in 90 days. Yet Chant du Monde owes a large sum of money for 11 months.
>
> Please let me know immediately how we can do business in regard to payments. I cannot go on with Chant du Monde anymore this way.[95]

Apparently, neither could Chant du Monde. Not long after this exchange, Chant du Monde went bankrupt and, according to Marilyn Averett, Folkways' office manager/bookkeeper at the time, sent Folkways a large number of recordings and various pressings.[96] This would likely have been as part of the disbursement of assets to outstanding creditors including Folkways. The disbursement also explains why there is a relatively significant number of Chant du Monde items in the archive itself.

Marketing and Sales

As a businessman, Moe obviously had little option but to distribute recordings through the more traditional distributor/dealer/retailer routes.

Table 6 Genre Categories of Folkways Records, c. 1961

FA—Americana	FC—Children	FD—Dances	FE—Ethnic
FJ—Jazz	FI—Instruction	FT—Special (Music)	FG—Personality
FH—Historical	FL—Literature	FM—Monograph	FN—Topical
FQ—Instruction (Language)	FR—Religious	FS—Specialty	FSS—Stereo
FW—International	FX—Science		

The mechanisms were well in place for Folkways to exploit, and with the help of Larry Sockell, subtle variations in the distribution networks could pay off. Along with distribution, the complementary process of promoting new recordings was also crucially important, but still fraught with economic danger. If Moe spent too much on the promotion of some recordings, he would not have the budget to put out other, equally important recordings. If, on the other hand, he did no promotion at all, Moe ran the risk of not selling enough recordings to support the enterprise as it existed. However, the truth of the matter is that, from the beginning, Moe was creative in focusing on his marketing activities, using a variety of means to inform the public about the Folkways catalog.

One of the most important organizational moves to help people understand the catalog was a systematic change in the numbering of recordings.[97] The 1957 listing makes changes to 357 recordings with the proviso that any numbers that do not appear remain the same. This listing makes at least an attempt to systematize the numbering system. The end result was a category structure that was largely maintained throughout the rest of Folkways' life. The coding structure was outlined to the Federal Trade Commission in 1961[98] (see Table 6).

It is important to note that this range of categories came to be identified with Folkways. Although more categories could be added, the sheer mass of recordings would undoubtedly continue to exert considerable momentum on the direction of Folkways. Although Moe was quick to capitalize on any opportunity that might present itself, he would not take a risk with Folkways that could be better handled with a more appropriate business arrangement. This was largely the case with Record Book and Film (RBF), Broadside, and the second incarnation of DISC in the 1960s. Any of the releases on these labels could potentially have been lumped into the Folkways catalog. However, with such ventures, Moe's strategies strongly suggest that he was not interested in risking either the financial status of Folkways (which was precarious anyway), or Folkways' ever-increasing cultural status as a leader in alternative recordings.

Early evidence shows that Moe was clearly concerned about how to market the types of recordings that Folkways produced. In what is literally the most calculating manner, Moe was actively involved in 1948 with a written analysis[99] of the potential first-year sales success of the Ethnic Folkways[100] series. Further insight into the early promotion of Folkways Records comes from an outline made on Eastern Airlines stationery in 1952.[101] This is an important document as it closely reflects the course Folkways was to take in the decades that followed.

As an early and relatively complete marketing strategy, the Eastern Airlines document indicates that Moe basically envisioned Folkways recordings being used in three areas: museums, libraries, and schools. Under museums, he thought his recordings could find a place in aquariums, natural history, sciences, art, Hall of Man, and music. Similarly, libraries for children, music, and languages would find Folkways records useful. Most importantly, at least according to his outline were schools: from elementary to university. Indeed, he saw Folkways recordings as part of school exhibitions in musical instruments, social studies, anthropology, and language. As important, however, would be Folkways' role in teacher training and for teachers' use in social studies, music, and curriculum developments through literature, conventions, demonstrations, and workshops.[102]

This particular document disputes something of a popular myth about the operation of Folkways Records. Moe himself would often suggest that he would not spend a dime on advertising; that there were enough people out there to find his records and who would support Folkways. Furthermore, he could use the money spent on advertising to produce more records, which was the whole point of the enterprise. However, this was not entirely true. Outside of the distribution relationships central to the basic survival of Folkways, there was, in fact, a consistent effort on Moe's part to make sure that Folkways and its artists were promoted above and beyond basic distribution. Although this seems self-evident, it is an important aspect of the Folkways budget that is largely ignored.

Although Moe used a number of different means of promotion, the aspect that was most surprising was his utilization of an advertising agency. Typically, Moe used industry papers, catalogs, and the like to list the records that were released in any given year. Nonetheless, Moe enlisted New York advertising firm Lee-Myles Associates to promote Folkways in the mainstream media. In fact, Folkways advertised quite extensively, with a notable proportion of Folkways' budget spent on the Lee-Myles account (at least during the period from the mid-'50s through the mid-'60s).

Two account lists from Lee-Myles give a good indication of the scope of Folkways advertising. Unfortunately, neither list is dated, but based on some of the accounts mentioned (*Billboard*, for example) the first "regular ac-

Table 7 Advertising Account Expense List

Publication	Cost
American Sociological Review	Nov.—$30
Catholic Education Review	Nov.—$25
Childhood Education	Dec.—$38.50
Billboard	1 per month—$23
Film News	Fall—$27
Grade Teacher	Dec.—$70
Hi Fi[a]	Nov.—$195
Horn Book	Dec.—$33
Parents Magazine	Nov. and Dec.—$518
New York Post	Oct.—$20
New York Times	Page 1, 4X in Oct.—$160
Scholastic Teacher	Dec.—$68.40
This Mos [Month's] Records	Dec.—$75
Trains	Nov.—$40

[a]A proof sheet exists for an ad in *High Fidelity* in 1960. *Proof sheets for Folkways Records advertisement in High Fidelity magazine. Proof deadline 22 April 1960.*

counts" list (Table 7) is likely the earlier of the two. It is likely that they date from between 1958 and 1962. One list summarizes Folkways ads that were running on a regular schedule.[103] The other list (Table 8) gives further evidence of the types of directed advertising that Moe wanted for Folkways.[104]

One indication of the degree of interaction between Moe and Lee-Myles Associates is a letter, again undated, to Moe from "Bob."[105] The document itself illustrates the personal interactions that were working "behind the scenes" to plan the success of Folkways:

> Moe—
>
> As I was trying to go to sleep a thought hit me that I couldn't get out of my mind, the more I thought about it, the more I decided it was "right" so decided to take my typewriter into the bathroom and get my thoughts down on paper before I got to the office in the morning and get bogged down in details.
>
> Folkways has reached the point, and the Folk & Hoot. [enanny] craze has reached the point where I feel you should run some large, well designed ads showing many of your albums (& maybe listing additional ones) in some top publications.
>
> What I have in mind is a ⅓ page in Playboy, maybe a full color full page in NY Times magazine section, maybe a column in the N.Y. or

Table 8 Review List of Publications for Advertising (information in parentheses is on the original document)[a]

- *Downbeat*
- *FM & Fine Arts* (Every other month 4 more ads to go)
- *State Teachers Magazine* (Not published over summer—1 more issue to go before fall)
- *Explorers Journal* (Only 4 or 5 times per year)
- *Instructor*
- *New York Times* book exchange
- *Variety* (Cancel)
- *Cashbox* canceled
- *Billboard* canceled
- *WFMT Perspective* (cancel)
- WDTM FM
- *Schwann* (CANNOT CANCEL)
- *Evergreen Review* (5 times a year)
- *American Record Guide* (CANNOT CANCEL)
- *Natural History* (5 times a year) (cancel)
- New York Times bottom of page 1
- *FM & The Arts*
- *WFLM Program Guide* (*Can* be canceled if you wish) (cancel)
- *Forecast FM* (Wrote them awaiting reply)

---

[a]*List of adds running on a regular schedule, from Lee-Myles Associates.*

Eastern edition of Life or Look. At same time a full page in Billboard & Cashbox (maybe Schwann, maybe High Fidelity).

This would establish you more firmly as the leader in the folk field (which of course you are). I think the time is ripe for you to do this now and I think its something you should do. Of course this would be expensive, and by expensive I don't mean $3,000 to $5,000 added to your regular ad budget, but more like $10,000 to $20,000 (although I'm just guessing at this point as I have no rate books here at home). You would know whether this is something you could afford, but at this point it would seem to me that you could, and if so I feel you might be making a mistake not to do this at this time.

As soon as I get to the office I'll start working on a layout to show you the type of ad I have in mind and hope I can have it ready to show you Friday or Monday. let me know if you agree with me, or if you feel I'm way off base—

Obviously Bob had enough experience in handling the Folkways account to have the inclination to write out an advertising plan in his bathroom. Bob also had several existing accounts already in his head concerning where Folkways was being advertised, as well as the knowledge of the Folkways material to make some suggestions regarding further efforts at advertising placement; *Playboy* would indeed be an interesting choice. Finally, he had a dollar-figure awareness of the Folkways account and what Moe might normally spend on advertising, as well as having a sense of how much Moe might either want, or be able, to spend on pushing an advertising campaign.

The ongoing difficulty for Moe was to be able to consistently get Folkways recordings into the media without a great deal of expense. One of the more cost-effective ways of doing this was to list Folkways in many of the national record catalogs that are central to many retailing and institutional organizations. The Schwann catalog[106] and Phonolog Publishing[107] were but two of the listings that Moe used to promote Folkways. Unfortunately, Moe seemed to have had trouble with Phonolog, but it is not clear why. In a very short letter in 1963, Moe states—perhaps with some exaggeration: "I am very grieved and very disturbed that Pete Seeger and many of our Folkways artists are listed in the Phonolog catalog, while we, who outsells Columbia in Pete Seeger and many other companies listed in Phonolog, as yet are not listed. What does it take to be listed in the Phonolog?"

The problem facing Moe with many of these types of outlets was the sheer volume of his releases and the difficulty in getting review copies and information of new releases sent out.[108] This is the case with the documentation for Schwann, as well as with another trade magazine, *Record and Sound Retailing*. In fact, in the latter case, Moe was soundly reprimanded for the lack of consistency in getting copies of Folkways records to the reviewing staff in time for review columns. The publisher of *Record and Sound Retailing*, Molly Harrison, began a two-page 1960 letter[109] to Moe with the pointed, "In answer to your recent complaint about omitting some of your recordings from our holiday roundup, I can only say, and quite firmly, 'Penny-wise and pound foolish.'" She closes the letter by again reminding Moe that "You are always welcome to this review coverage, and I can sincerely assure you of the attention your recordings are worthy of, but we must get the recordings if we are to be intelligent about our recommendations."

One of the better relationships Moe seemed to have was with *Notes*, the quarterly journal of the Music Library Association. Certainly the choice would have been a good one for Moe to pursue. As a letter from Richard Hill of *Notes* magazine[110] points out to Moe:

... the time has come for deciding what to do about the March [1957] issue. You've sunk so much into publicizing the Folkway releases already in Notes, that I shall quite understand if you decide to let things ride for a time. On the other hand, if the little record[111] has the effect we are all counting upon and produces a lot of new buyers among the librarians, perhaps this is just the time to strike while the fire is burning brightly.

Indeed, the manner in which the layout was set in the journal served a double purpose: first to advertise the new releases of Folkways, but also to act as a reference list for music librarians. As Moe suggested in a response to a lengthy letter from Hill some time later, "The type, therefore, can be set up and used for reproduction and the libraries would have a listing from Notes."[112]

Promoting Folkways Records on radio presented itself as another option and was largely based on three approaches. The first was the promotion of Folkways recordings in conjunction with some type of music programming. In exchange for the use of Folkways recordings on the air, Folkways would provide promotional copies to the station to use for the program. A good example of this was the agreement made with WSEL-FM in Chicago in 1960.[113] Part of a request letter for recordings reads:

As per your agreement with ... our station manager, to furnish WSEL with ten to twelve FOLKWAYS Recordings per month for promotional usage on the air on our FOLKWAYS AND FOLK SONGS and ODDBALL CORNER, we submit the following list. . . . You may be sure that we give full credit—label and number—to FOLKWAYS.

The second approach that Folkways used in this area was to assist local dealers in the promotion of themselves in conjunction with Folkways Records. In a letter to The Music Box in Charleston, W. Virginia from Marian Distler,[114] she states that:

We are interested in pursuing further the possibilities of developing sales through radio. Our regular radio fee is $2.00 per record. These of course are for promotional purposes, and we will be glad to send those records requested by the station on their letterhead. And if the records are used in conjunction with retail outlets such as yours we will be able to give you an additional discount—at 50%—for this direct tie-up.

This is an important letter in that it shows an interest in the more systematic management of this type of promotion. With the work of Larry Sockell as national sales representative for Folkways, a more generalized approach was needed. The more developed criteria were outlined in a letter prompted by a request from the Rebel Recording Co. of Mt. Ranier, Maryland.[115] Sockell responded that:

> Folkways Records can always be counted upon to cooperate in the promotion of folk music, provided the cooperation requested is reasonable.
>
> In view of this I suggest you compile a list of stations and addresses, noting the program directors who can be counted upon to feature our records. In addition, you can request the program directors to choose a reasonable quantity of records that can be scheduled over a 60 day period.
>
> Immediately upon receipt of this information we shall see that your stations are serviced directly from New York.
>
> We would appreciate being kept informed of the progress made by the programs, and the effect in your territory.
>
> Under separate cover Folkways Records will send you the supply of catalogs noted in your letter.
>
> I would assume that your organization will be placing an order to cover the records which will be featured by the local station. . . .

The third approach was the promotion of a particular performance event by a Folkways artist. Although Folkways was open to supporting virtually all of its artists in some fashion (free slicks, catalogs, some promotional recordings), this particular approach really only applied to a few of the working artists that recorded on Folkways. Furthermore, as Moe pointed out in a letter in 1961[116]:

> One of the problems that we are now facing is that many of the artists appear on a number of labels and we have no desire to promote our competitors' records. Therefore, we are limiting our participation with dealers only to artists and recordings associated with our firm. So far we have five exclusive Folkways artists, and you'll have 100% cooperation. They are: New Lost City Ramblers, Jean Ritchie, Sam Hinton, Bill McAdoo and Alan Mills.

One of the significant exceptions to this rule were the Seeger family: Pete, Peggy, and her husband, Ewan MacColl. Moe did a great deal to help promote their endeavors, particularly for Pete Seeger.[117] Moe provided sponsors of concerts with an assortment of promotional material, including interviews with Pete, flyers, bulletins, recordings, or funds up to 10 percent of the total cost of the advertising program that the sponsor undertook.[118] There is little doubt that much of Moe's additional support of Pete in particular (aside from his sales volumes) came from the long and personal relationship that joined Moe and the Seeger family.

Moe himself did his fair share of travelling and promotion in aid of Folkways. The convention circuit was one of the most important information outlets for Folkways. In large part, this was due to the particular kind of exposure that could be gained by participating in very specialized conventions. With such a broad range of material available in the catalog (even early on), a convention would allow Moe or, occasionally a Folkways representative, to target the convention with only a few, highly pertinent titles. Of course, for this strategy to prevail, a wide variety of conventions would have to be attended. This was exactly the approach that Moe took.

A specific example of this strategy could be found in a folder held in the Archive called "Conventions '59." The contents of the folder are of interest, but not nearly to the extent of the itinerary listed on the inside of the folder itself. Table 9 roughly approximates the layout and markings of the itinerary.[119] This itinerary is particularly impressive given these convention appearances were done for promotion and sales, a practice unusual for a record company. In a financial summary sheet for 1957, the following figures were recorded for the accounting of Moe's convention year (Table 10).

Judging by the summary, especially of the profit–cost ratio, conventions were a relatively profitable enterprise. It is unclear whether the "Folkways Gross Sales" column refers to sales generated at the convention, resulting from the convention, or in general. If it does represent sales directly in association with the conventions (which is the logical conclusion), it represents something on the order of 25 to 35 percent of the total gross sales for the year.

Although it was most common for Moe to attend conventions and conferences himself, he often worked out deals with other companies to represent Folkways when he was unable to attend. A 1957[120] cost breakdown from Robert Coles of the Book-of-the-Month Club lists the cost items that they had agreed to share for participation in four Music Educators National Conferences that year. There is ample evidence, however, that many of these conferences were attended by Folkways' representatives and that considerable effort and cost were undertaken to ensure a good presentation.

A variety of invoices from companies like Brede (Convention Services) Inc.[121] and United Convention Services[122] also illustrate the costs for simply setting up a booth: approximately $40 to $50 a day for materials. This does not include the applications made directly to the conference organizers for the space and appropriate materials,[123] which could potentially run the costs into the hundreds of dollars per convention.

Tables 11 and 12 also illustrate how important the "Combined Book" account was to the convention success of Folkways. The information for the tables were taken from account books that reflect Moe's personal ac-

Table 9 Convention and Conference Itinerary, 1959[a]

Month	Dates	Conference and Location
January	23–27*	Eastern MENC[b], Buffalo
	25–28	National School Boards, San Francisco
February	7–11	Secondary School Principals, Philadelphia, PA
	14–18*	School Administrators, Atlantic City
	22–25	Southwest MENC, Wichita, Kansas
	24–28	Music Teachers National Association, Kansas City, Missouri
March	1–5*	Association of Supervision (?) and Curriculum (?), Cincinnati, OH
	4–7	Northwest MENC, Seattle
	22–25	Western MENC, Salt Lake City
	29–April 3	Childhood Educators International, St. Louis, Missouri.
	31–April 3*	National Catholic Educators Association, Atlantic City.
	28–April 12	International (?) Children's Fair, Roosevelt Raceway, Long Island (?)
	31–April 4*	National Science Teachers, Atlantic City
April	3–7*	Southern MENC, Roanoke, Virginia
	13–16*	DAVI[c], Seattle
	17–18*	Teachers of Foreign Language, Washington, D.C.
May	1–2	Central States Modern Language Teachers, St. Louis
	7–10*	North Central MENC, Chicago
June[d]	21–27*	ALA[e], Washington, DC
	22–25*	NAMM[f], New York City
	28–July 3*	NEA, St. Louis
September	3–5	American Sociology, Chicago

[a]Note that dates marked with an * are those circled on the original list. These seem to indicate a desire to participate in these conventions in some manner. It is unclear what (?) means, but are included from original.
[b]Music Educators National Conference. A department of the National Education Association. Moe also advertised in their official magazine, The Music Educators Journal.
[c]Department of Audio-Visual Instruction of the National Education Association.
[d]Missing from this itinerary is the American Book Association, 14–17 June 1959, as evidenced by a United Convention Services invoice. *Invoice to Folkways Records from United Convention Services, Inc. 25 June 1959.*
[e]American Library Association.
[f]National Association of Music Manufacturers.

Table 10 Moses Asch: Convention Summary, 1957[a]

Month	Convention Purchases	C d[b]	Folkways Gross Sales	Cash Record Book Cost	Profit
Jan.				$400.00	$100.00
Feb.				400.00	100.00
Mar.				1,600.00	400.00
Apr.				—	—
May				853.80	213.45
June				400.00	100.00
July	$325.03	$237.75	$14,121.36	—	—
Aug.	118.75	160.53	16,487.00	—	—
Sept.	56.50	157.00	22,153.05	—	—
Oct.	—	71.80	17,899.86	—	—
Nov.	227.65	666.17	23,818.42	1,200.00	300.00
Dec.	141.25	284.28	16,777.18	—	—
	869.18	1,577.53	111,256.91	4,853.80	1,213.45

February—Atlantic City—Schl Adm. Profit $ 1,213.45
March—   "   "   —Music Ed. Comm.   11,125.69
      St. Louis—Curriculum   [Ray/Roy][c]   1,215.10
Apr.—Milwaukee—Nat'l. Catholic   13,554.24
June—Kansas City—ALA   Conv. Booth Rental and   2,446.71
                                     Supplies
      Philadelphia—Nat'l. Educ.
July—Music Merchants—Chicago   11,107.53
Aug.—Washington, D.C.—Sociologists
Sept.—Madison, Wisc.—Modern Lang.
Oct.—Albany—N.Y. Libraries
Nov.—Pittsburgh—Soc. Studies   (Costs: Out-of-town travel and
                                    expenses, plus NYC expenses,
                                    including rent and taxes)   6,365.16
Dec.—Indianapolis—Scientists   4,742.37
                                   Salary [presumed to be Moe's] 1,000.00
                                                                5,742.37
                                   (Other assorted costs)   1,425.31
                                                                5,317.06

[a]From *Moses Asch: Convention Summary 1957*. Note that this document is reproduced here approximately as it is in the original. Not all entries are clearly marked. In those cases, the items are summarized as well as possible and included into the calculations.
[b]Based on other accounting entries, I would assume this to be Credit and Debit. However, this is as they are originally marked.
[c]It is completely unclear what this is in reference to.

Table 11 Summary of Information from Moses Asch's Purchase Book,
Mar. 1958—Nov.1959

Date	"Combined Book" Account	Total Convention Expenses	Total Account Payable	Membership Dues	"Brede Inc." Account
Mar. 1958	$229.00	$996.90	$1,543.84	—	—
Apr. 1958	242.00	274.04	274.04	—	—
May 1958	37.50	242.50	280.00	$36.00[a]	—
June 1958	109.25	399.25	399.25	—	$233.00
July 1958	63.75	296.77	306.75	10.00[b]	—
Aug. 1958	—	13.00	13.00	—	—
Sept. 1958	—	—	105.19	30.00[c]	—
Oct. 1958	—	100.00	100.00	—	—
Nov. 1958	111.25	—	437.60	—	—
Dec. 1958	323.00	665.11	665.11	—	—
Jan. 1959	—	24.42	33.69	—	—
Feb. 1959	—	325.00	325.00	—	—
Mar. 1959	204.75	—	204.75	—	—
Apr./May 1959					
June 1959	102.50	429.72	690.17	—	179.10
July 1959	89.25	603.40	816.27	—	—
Aug. 1959	—	—	114.44	—	—
Nov. 1959	32.50	—	32.50	—	—

[a]Museum of Modern Art, $18.00, NEA-DAVI, $10.00 and $8.00.
[b]Association of American Indian Affairs.
[c]Educators Film Library [Librarian] Association.

counts. Importantly, these accounts reflect almost entirely the expenses for conventions generally, with only a small percentage of other, nonconvention expenses (the amount being the difference between total convention expenses and total accounts payable).

It is clear from these summaries that convention activity was very important to Folkways.[124] In many respects, convention attendance likely proved to be one of the most effective means of communicating the importance and value of Folkways recordings to the most appropriate consumers. Because Moe only required a few hundred sales per title for a recording to break even, this type of direct sales was undoubtedly a major contributor to the success of a vast array of recordings.

Aside from conventions, Moe used other means of reaching the educational market. For example, a couple of particularly interesting promotional flyers were released in 1956 and 1957, respectively.[125] The first item was a flyer sent out to music librarians by the Educational Department of

Table 12 Moses Asch: Accounts Payable[a]

Date	Total Payable[b]	"Combined Book" Payable
31 Mar. 1958	$866.60	$270.25
30 Apr. 1958	992.64	512.25
31 May 1958	1,169.64	549.75
30 June 1958	1,464.89	584.00
30 July 1958[c]	1,764.10	647.75
31 Aug. 1958	1,459.75	587.75
30 Sept. 1958	1,532.95	536.25
31 Oct. 1958	1,472.00	495.00
30 Nov. 1958	1,567.10	548.75
31 Dec. 1958	2,050.10	871.75
31 Jan. 1959	1,969.13	751.75
28 Feb. 1959	1,944.13	701.75
31 Mar. 1959	1,287.27	604.00
31 May 1959[d]	2,584.18	866.50
30 June 1959	2,964.96	847.00
31 July 1959[e]	2,832.96	797.00
18 Aug. 1959	3,435.03	886.25

[a]Accounts overlap with those in Table 11.
[b]These accounts are predominantly convention-related accounts. Unfortunately, there is no summary column for "convention expenses" as there is in the purchase books entries. However, most of the accounts include accounts like AAAS, EAC, MLA, NAVA, NEA, NYSSMA, Rowan, Combined Book, plus miscellaneous hotels.
[c]Information taken from summary on 31 August 1958 entry.
[d]31 May 1959 includes two months—31 April 1959 is not missing, it had not been entered.
[e]Information taken from summary on 18 August 1959.

Sam Goody Records. It consisted of two parts: a promotion of Folkways Records in which Goody notes that Folkways Records are:

> preeminent in their field. They are on-the-spot recordings, authentic in every way. Technically, these records employ the latest developments both at the source and playback. The complete Folkways library is available at our Educational discount of 30% below list price.[126]

The second part of the flyer is a promotion for a product called PHONOTAPES. These were reel-to-reel tapes that were marketed as, in part, an alternative to LPs. These, too, were offered by Sam Goody at a 30 percent educational discount. The combination of Folkways and PHONOTAPES as part of the same promotion is notable in large part because of the degree of cross-licensing that occurred between the two companies. Folkways used several of their language titles in exchange for more contemporary titles that were released by PHONOTAPES, in addition to the sale of the Speak English series to Folkways for approximately $1,670 plus royalties.[127]

The second promotional flyer[128] was one released from Folkways and directed to primary and secondary school principals. It included a list of thirty-one recordings that had either been approved or had been recommended for approval by the Board of Education of New York City (see Appendix 10). The flyer prefaces this list by stating that these recordings:

> are listed in "List of Approved Instructional Recordings and Transcriptions for use in Elementary Schools and Junior and High Schools" published by the Board of Education of the City of New York. You may purchase these records from us at 30 percent discount from prices listed in the enclosed catalog. Your net prices, therefore, are: 10"—$3.00, 12"—$3.95. There is no delivery charge.

After all this discussion of marketing and distribution of records, the sales figures themselves are notoriously difficult to track. Sales of Folkways recordings were usually only tracked internally to calculate royalties or sales commissions, and were typically recorded in 11" by 17" tally books. Unfortunately, only a few of the recordings in the catalog seemed to be noted with any degree of consistency, although not enough to track individual sales trends. Furthermore, there seemed to be separate books kept for Folkways tallies and Pioneer Record Sales tallies, although few of the Pioneer books seemed to have survived. Nonetheless, the overall domestic (Table 13) and foreign (Table 14) sales trends of the catalog are interesting. The H1 and H2 designation with the years indicate the first half of the sales year (January to June) and the second half of the sales year (July to August), respectively.

As is clear, the total number of titles varies considerably from period to period. During the investigation of the tally books, it was initially thought that when the recording number was omitted, there were no sales during the period for that recording. However, this proved not to be the case, so the summaries are presented to give a sense of the minimum and maximum sales of any recording noted during the period, and the average sales for all the titles recorded. Unfortunately, as the actual recordings noted often changed from period to period, it proved virtually impossible to accurately track a single recording over several years.

The minimum, maximum, and average sales figures, however, clearly illustrate that Folkways simply did not sell a lot of any individual title, as

Table 13 Domestic Sales

	Number of Titles	Minimum	Maximum	Total Sold	Average Sold per Title
1959: H1	178	1	893	11,831	66.47
1960: H2	211	1	967	11,760	55.73
1961: H1	260	1	1,350	20,366	78.33
1961: H2	302	1	1,247	33,832	112.03
1963: H1	66	2	780	3,820	57.88
1963: H2	307	2	3,912	52,576	171.26
1964: H1	414	1	2,713	55,913	135.06
1964: H2	172	1	130	2,594	15.08
1965: H1 (Pioneer)	407	0	1,243	28,658	70.41
1965: H1	22	3	39	438	19.91
1965: H2 (Pioneer)	405	0	760	12,155	30.01
1965: H2	395	1	245	8,150	20.63
1966: H1	27	1	122	750	27.78
1966: H2	28	3	398	1,981	70.75
1967: H1	38	1	259	2,153	56.66
1967: H2	41	8	543	4,082	99.56
1968: H1	49	1	664	3,230	65.92
1968: H2	54	1	921	3,816	70.67
1969: H1	57	0	635	4,954	86.91
1969: H2	60	0	361	2,821	47.02
1970: H1	135	0	335	5,308	39.32
1970: H2	116	1	749	6,820	58.79
1972: H2	441	0	205	13,379	30.34
1973: H1	446	0	244	10,770	24.15
1973: H2	448	0	414	13,685	30.55
1974: H1	447	0	238	14,717	32.92
1974: H2	464	0	180	10,947	23.59
1975: H1	456	0	138	7,106	15.58
1975: H2	437	0	228	7,976	18.25
1976: H1	449	1	137	10,086	22.46
1976: H2	457	0	145	7,349	16.08
1977: H1	435	0	147	6,498	14.94
1977: H2	463	0	148	7,366	15.91
1978: H1	501	0	127	6,608	13.19
1978: H2	495	0	200	6,235	12.60
				406,326	**50.87**

Table 14 Foreign Sales

	Number of Titles	Minimum	Maximum	Total Sold	Average Sold per Title
1963: H2	280	2	450	9,428	33.67
1966: H1	21	4	94	482	22.95
1966: H2	25	2	172	1,061	42.44
1967: H1	29	2	123	1,098	37.86
1967: H2	35	1	55	417	11.91
1968: H1	47	1	761	1,875	39.89
1968: H2	27	5	85	769	28.48
1969: H1	34	1	270	2,338	68.76
1969: H2	55	1	409	2,353	42.78
1970: H1	67	1	285	1,599	23.87
1970: H2	63	1	200	936	14.86
1972: H2	409	1	157	8,034	19.64
1973: H1	423	1	171	8,390	19.83
1973: H2	445	0	210	12,273	27.58
1974: H1	435	0	113	8,123	18.67
1974: H2	463	0	168	10,022	21.65
1975: H1	422	0	103	4,992	11.83
1975: H2	453	0	206	12,985	28.66
1976: H1	450	0	326	14,501	32.22
1976: H2	448	0	417	12,223	27.28
1977: H1	444	0	319	11,323	25.50
1977: H2	465	0	331	14,665	31.54
1978: H1	479	0	256	16,248	33.92
1978: H2	480	0	320	9,945	20.72
				165,563	**29.14**

popular as some recordings might have seemed. A domestic sales high-water mark of 3,912 for a single title in the second half of 1963 and a foreign maximum of 450 during the same period, are definitely top numbers for Folkways. However, it was the consistency of sales that kept Folkways going, for as small as the numbers might seem, they are persistent enough over time to realize a modest return. In the end, a foreign average of less that 60 units a year per title and a domestic average of just over 100 units a year per title, speaks volumes for the necessity of a large catalog to push sales. That said, Folkways sold well over 500,000 recordings during this period, with similar sales continuing into the mid-1980s, just prior to the sale of Folkways to the Smithsonian (Table 15).

Table 15 Domestic and Foreign Sales Summary, 1984–1986

		Domestic Sales			
Year	Number of Titles	Minimum	Maximum	Total Sold	Average Sold per Title
1984	692	0	236	10,924	15.79
1985	710	0	2,518	17,345	24.43
1986	719	0	176	7,683	10.69

		Foreign Sales			
Year	Number of Titles	Minimum	Maximum	Total Sold	Average Sold per Title
1984	693	−5	309	11,655	16.82
1985	710	−1	2,559	14,171	19.96
1986	719	−27	1,010	5,306	7.38

Exploiting the Catalog: Licensing and Contracts

The issue of contracts was also an important one for Folkways and one that, to some degree, has been somewhat misrepresented. Very often when an accusation of either failing to issue a contract or failing to uphold a contract was made against Moe or Folkways, there was the implicit suggestion of calculated illegality, intentional misrepresentation, or bad-faith dealing with respect to the partners of the contract. There have been a variety of accusations that have circulated around Folkways, suggesting that Moe routinely disregarded the terms of contracts on one hand, but aggressively pursued others when he felt he had been taken advantage of, on the other.

The information in the archive, however, suggests that Moe was in fact quite diligent concerning the creation of contracts with performers or with other companies. Without doubt, many of the documents illustrate that Moe was careful about the terms of a variety of contracts and would take care to ensure that he was being represented correctly. Nonetheless, although many of Folkways's licensing deals—and other agreements that Moe made—were executed in the technical sense, Moe sometimes assumed rights that perhaps were never explicitly contracted. He often felt it was more important for recordings to be heard than adhering exactly to specific terms, particularly if he had the chance to sell a few albums in the process. In one case, Moe obtained tapes from recording engineer ("toningenieur") Walter Hennig, working for Tondienst Hamburg,[129] who supplied material for what became the 2–12 inch set FE 4520, *Music from Italy*.[130] Hennig then discovered that his material was being distributed beyond the boundaries of the original licensing agreement that he had made with Folkways. In a letter from Hennig's lawyers of 10 January 1963,[131] they point out that in a 1955 agreement, Folkways had the right to distribute Hennig's material only in North America and Japan.[132] The letter states in part:

> As you have no right according to the agreement to import to Germany and to sell here the above mentioned record No. FE 4520, you are violating the contract. By your attitude the contract has been so heavily offensed that my client sees himself forced to cancel immediately for this most important reason the whole contract. As you know quite well, even in the past you did not respect the agreement, so that my client has no more confidence in you and that he must cancel the contract. Therefore you have no longer a right to produce and sell any longer in any country of the world my client's reproductions and I ask you herewith to stop production and selling immediately.

Moe's response to this was to state that a mutual verbal amendment had been made of the contract and that he would wait and talk to Hennig himself on Hennig's next trip to New York. In a letter of 17 January 1963[133] to Hennig, Moe points out that "please be advised that there was a mutual understanding on the version of the contract with Mr. Paul Lazare[134] when he was here in our office." In a letter to one of his German distributors, Electrola Gesellschaft m.b.H.,[135] he also expressed the same belief that the contract had been amended and that a meeting with Hennig would "clarify the situation."[136] In what could be taken to be something of an act of good faith, Moe did ask Electrola to cease sale of the album until the matter could be settled. He did add, however, that "since you bought only about 10 records in the last year or so, there is really no damage as far as monetary matters are concerned." As an aside, Folkways and Electrola Gesellschaft m.b.H. had related difficulties in 1966–1967. Electrola Gesellschaft was concerned that Folkways did not have permission to release material by Ernst Busch contained in Folkways' *Songs of the Spanish Civil War, Vols. I and II* (FH 5436 and 5437). The details of the exchanges among the several parties will not be detailed here. Suffice it to say that is stands as a prime example of the difficulties that can occur with even the best intentioned use of material, even going back as far as Asch's difficulties with Stinson in the 1940s.[137]

The letters from Moe on the Hennig matter do suggest that it was all just a misunderstanding and that in fact, there was no reason to think that there was any deliberate violation of the terms of the contract.[138] Nevertheless, Hennig's lawyers reinforced the termination of the contract between Hennig and Folkways in 1965. Moe argued in response that "it would be a real shame to take these records off the market, even though so few records are sold each year, as they represent music of both Italy and Spain which are unusual and which are needed by anthropologists and scientists for study purposes."[139] Unfortunately, the final outcome is unclear. Given that by this point the varying conflicts in this interaction were almost eight years old, and the dollar amounts insignificant, it may have just fallen to the bottom of the priority list.

Paying Artist Royalties

In dealing with artists as well as licensees, Asch endeavored to reduce Folkways's overall financial obligation—a not-unreasonable tactic—and to also reduce the overall paperwork involved with maintaining the agreement. One of the best examples of a simple artist's contract, and one that was probably the most satisfactory in Moe's eyes, was a contract made between Folkways Records and the performer Hsin Lee in October 1958.[140] The contract itself is short and to the point with a minimum of legalese. The contract reads in total:

> This is a Letter Agreement between us in consideration of the mutual covenants herein contained and of the payments herein provided for services rendered by you of performances for phonograph records and/or tape recording albums of "The Saying of Confucius." You hereby give us the exclusive right to manufacture, advertise, sell, lease, license or otherwise use, control or dispose of in any fields of use throughout the world, phonograph records, tapes and matrices embodying said performances; to license or permit said records and/or tapes and matrices to be publicly played by others (including radio, television, motion pictures, concerts and places of amusement or entertainment) or re-transcribed in other mechanical forms. To use and publish and permit others to use and publish your name and picture in connection herewith and to write and publish and to permit others to write and publish articles concerning you for advertising and trade purposes in connection herewith. In consideration of the above Folkways Records will pay you a fee of $100.00 representing total and complete payment and releasing us from further obligations to you.

The reasons such a contract would be preferred are obvious. It clearly favors Moe in that it grants him total control of the finished product, while at the same time releasing him from further financial obligation to the signee. This may have been a very beneficial contract for Mr. Lee as well, as $100 in 1955 was rather more substantial than it is now. Nonetheless, it does favor Folkways—increasingly so based on sales volume.

This is perhaps an appropriate place to deal with a recurring myth concerning Moe Asch and Folkways. A number of published sources over the years have suggested that Moe often did not pay royalties that were owed to particular artists, and consequently lined his own pockets. Truth be told, it is clear that he did not pay royalties with any regularity and, in the process, likely did not pay royalties to some artists that legitimately have a claim to some compensation. That said, it is also clear that there are comparatively few artists that sold enough recordings to actually earn royalties in the first place. Moe's practice of typically paying between $50 and $100 as advances against royalties would cover the sale of the first few hundred recordings, depending on the rate. By the 1970s, this amount was typically up to a $200 advance, with a few artists receiving up to $500 total payment in lieu of royalties. Obviously, Moe would pay what he had to and negotiated freely with each producer/artist.

As the sales figures suggest, not that many artists sold more than a couple hundred recordings in total. As a result, it simply was not worth the time to spend calculating the royalties on a semiannual basis as per normal practice. With a relatively young catalog of 1,000 to 1,500 titles in the 1950s and 1960s, it still would have meant at least one full-time staff member to do the calculations—a cost that Folkways simply could not afford. Instead, Moe generally waited until an artist felt compelled to ask for the royalties. At that point, Moe would check the sales, calculated the royalties, and write the artist a check. As for the suggestion that Moe lined his pockets with the unpaid royalties: there is ample evidence that this simply was not the case. Indeed, Pete Seeger—who probably earned more in royalties than any other Folkways artist—suggested that if Moe did keep royalties from his artists, it was understood that Moe would use the money to put out another recording anyway.[141]

It must also be noted that it was common practice in the pre-World War II period for record companies to pay a flat amount to an artist for all rights to his or her recordings. Small labels in the 1950s continued this practice, and many were notoriously lax in paying royalties. Others would deduct recording or touring expenses from royalties owed. Sometimes, a label owner would take a paternalistic interest in his acts; Leonard Chess of Chess Records, for example, guaranteed loans and provided fancy cars to some of his artists in lieu of royalties. By these standards, Asch was hardly the most flagrant abuser of his acts. At least he had a higher purpose—beyond making a profit—and in his own thinking was consistent in how he dealt with royalties.

It is also interesting to note that Moe was basically not interested at all in acquiring the copyrights for a piece of material, even though that might have been more economically valuable in the long run. Many other record companies insisted on owning publishing rights to the music that they re-corded, and were able to profit from these rights.[142] Moe took advantage of the copyright laws of the time and purchased all rights to the reproduction of a recording, not to the material itself. As Moe put it[143]:

> I have the same agreement with everyone—Pete Seeger, whoever it is . . . in which we mention they turn over the recording rights to their material. And that's all I want. I don't ever ask them for copy-right material, that's their own. I have right to license for record use. My record, not their compositions. So if a motion picture company wants a right to one of the records, they have to clear with the artist for the copyright, then they have to clear with me to copy the record.

Given that in the latter decades of Folkways' operation virtually all of the material came to Moe already recorded, this process of purchasing the reproduction rights played a very important role in Folkways success. With very few exceptions, Moe was only interested in exclusive reproduction rights, which would guarantee that what came out on Folkways could not be found somewhere else. This exclusivity, combined with the single, lump-sum payment for all royalties or licenses in the material for an album, gave Moe enormous autonomy in developing other licensing agreements. The absence of monthly royalty or licensing payments based on sales also saved a fortune in administrative costs, cutting overhead quite dramatically. Thus, even though Moe could have made more money by being more ruthless about the purchase or control over the copyright of the material, the additional headache would not have been worth it finan-cially or otherwise.

As Tables 13 and 14 illustrate, paying up front for royalties would likely have been more generous than actual royalty payments on a per sale basis. At something averaging 24 cents to 30 cents per album for someone who had the rights for all the tracks, it would take between 330 and 415 records sold to make $100 in royalties. Very few Folkways recordings would sell that many copies within the first few years of release. Although Moe likely got the better end of the royalty calculation in the long run, artists proba-bly did better getting the money up front, rather than a few dollars at a time over the next two or three decades. Of course, as mentioned earlier, Moe was quick to calculate royalties when asked, but the administrative costs of calculating royalties would have been so much more expensive than occasionally overpaying someone. Again, in both the short and long term, Moe's unorthodox payments strategies and licensing helped keep Folkways viable.

As time progressed, the nature of the contracts entered into by Folkways with artists and licensees became increasingly complicated. In general, however, Moe was quick to add a consistent set of conditions to Folkways' contracts. Beyond the flat-rate payment that Moe preferred, the conditions and stipulations below came to be typical additions to the general contracts:

- royalties calculated on a per unit basis with or without conditions or additional calculations (e.g., 25 cents per copy sold domestically; half that rate for foreign sales);
- outlining geographical limitations for distribution (where the recording can be sold or not sold);
- stating who has control of the material being brought into the contract (i.e., whether it is the performer's own material or is owned by someone else and requires previous agreement);
- stating who has control of the material during the tenure of the contract and to what extent (i.e., does Folkways have exclusive rights to the material or can the artist continue to use the material?);
- noting the time duration of the agreement and under what circumstances the contract could be terminated.

Of course, it would be naive to think that, on a day-to-day basis, the intention at Folkways was not to make the greatest profit with the least investment. However, in many respects, if control of the material—and the profits derived from such control—was the true priority within the Folkways business environment, one would expect to find certain things that do not seem to be in evidence. First, one would expect much greater attention to the maintenance of the contracts within the everyday paperwork of the office. Some effort had been spent to maintain the contracts that existed, but given the potential profit at stake with ownership, the level of attention focused on contracts and licenses as a whole is simply not what would be necessary to extract from them the maximum financial dividends.

Second, in the examination of many of the contracts that span several years, there is a startling variety of forms and conditions that are used to create the contracts. Some of the contracts are clearly forms that were used on a regular basis. However, the range of contracts, from simple letter agreements to elaborate corporate contracts, would suggest once again that the attention to such details was not driven by a pure profit motive. Indeed, such inattention to what some would suggest are the most crucial details of music production might lead to the opposite conclusion: that Moe entered into contracts more for a sense of security for himself and his artists than as an exploitative arrangement that would most benefit Folkways.

IN THE RECORDING BOOTH. MOE ASCH
OPERATES HIS RECORD MAKER —

Caricature of Moses Asch operating his recording machine, early 1940s, by Don Freeman.

Disc label, c. 1945. Courtesy David A. Jasen.

Asch label, c. 1943. Note that this release has no catalog or matrix number, and is not listed in Asch's catalogs of the period. Courtesy David A. Jasen.

Moses Asch (left) and Harold Courlander (right), editor of the "Folkways Ethnic Series," in the Folkways office, c. mid-1950s. Photograph © David Gahr; used by permission.

All illustrations courtesy Smithsonian/Folkways Archives except as noted.

Charles Edward Smith, Moses Asch, and Big Bill Broonzy during a recording session, c. mid-1950s. Photograph © David Gahr; used by permission.

Marion Distler in the Folkways office, c. 1950s. Photograph © David Gahr; used by permission.

Front cover of the booklet for Harry Smith's *Anthology of American Folk Music*.

Leadbelly's Last Sessions album cover.

Album cover for Frederic Ramsey, Jr.'s *Jazz* series.

Pete Seeger's *Goofing-Off Suite* cover, 1954.

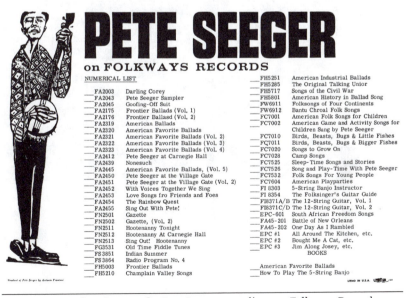

1960s era advertisement for Pete Seeger recordings on Folkways Records.

Moses Asch in the Folkways offices, c. 1960.

Broadside label, 1966. Courtesy
Richard Carlin.

RBF label, 1974. Courtesy David A.
Jasen.

Folkways records & service corp.

FOLKWAYS — ASCH — RBF / PIONEER RECORD SALES, INC.

43 West 61st Street ● **New York, New York 10023** ● **212-586-7260**

David & Josen   *7/15/77*

This is to confirm our agreement on the sole and exclusive production
of phonograph records and/or tapes and other mechanical and/or elect-
rical means by Folkways Records from material selected from your
recordings and performances of:

Rip - Roomy Ragtime will Dave Josen

It is understood that, in so far as your rights and interests are concerned, you give us the perpetual and exclusive right, title and
interest to our manufacturing, advertising, selling, licensing, or
otherwise using, controlling or disposing of in any fields of use
throughout the world, any transcriptions made from these recordings,
including phonograph records, tapes, matrices and any kind of reproduction; nor to our having such transcription played by others
in various fields including radio, motion pictures, concerts, television or other places of amusement and entertainment; to our using
and publishing and permitting others to write and publish articles
concerning you and/or the performers for advertising and trade
purposes in connection herewith. We agree that such income as shall
be derived from sources other than by the sale of phonograph records
and/or tapes, etc., shall be divided equally between us.
Paragraph 3:
In consideration of the above Folkways Records & Service Corp. will
pay *300.00 and   5% ?* per ablum sold.*

½ of this amount of foreign sales.*

½ of this amount on records sold at special discount prices (Clubs,etc.)*

We agree to make royalty payments within thirty days after the expiration
of each (fiscal June - December) semi-annual year from and after the date
of insurance of records and/or tapes, and other mechanical means.

Our agreement provides that you make available to us, in addition to the
recordings, pamphlet notes to accompany the album, and photographs if
possible.

This agreement shall benefit and be binding upon us and our respective
heirs, personal representatives, successors and assings.

If you own or control any copyrighted work that is embodied in this
recording, then you grant Folkways a royalty free license and no other
compensation will have to be paid except for the "consideration" listed
in paragraph 3.

Your signature below will signify your acceptance of the above terms and
conditions. Please sign and return one copy to us. Thank you.

Pd 300.00 7/11/77
    FC 8841

                                          Yours very truly,
                                          FOLKWAYS RECORDS & SERVICE CORP.

ACCEPTED AND AGREED TO: By: _____
    Li N . X

Typical 1970s era Folkways Records contract. Courtesy David A. Jasen.

Folkways Records label, 1983.

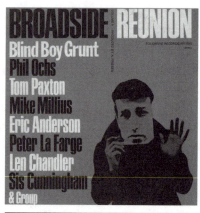

Broadside Reunion cover, 1973.

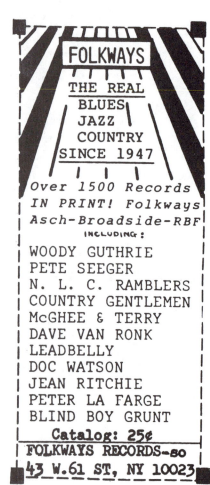

Folkways Records advertisement that appeared in *Sing Out!* magazine, 1978.

Moses Asch on the street in front of the W. 61st Street Folkways offices, c. 1980.
Photograph © David Gahr; used by permission.

6
Finances

As we have seen, the topic of Folkways's finances is a tantalizing one. On one hand, it would seem an obvious place to start any discussion about production and distribution within a business. However, in the case of Folkways, the financial information is also the most difficult to trace, when it exists at all. Even though much of the financial information is spotty, it is truly incredible that some sense of the financial life of Folkways is available at all. There are various points in time where a brief, but surprisingly complete, financial picture is available. Better still, in addition to the Folkways data, documentation also exists for much of Moe's own business finances, as well as the closely related distribution company, Pioneer Record Sales. The existence of financial data on these three areas at the same point in time provides a virtually unprecedented look at the interplay between two associated businesses and the man who ran them.

That said, it is still a fragmented set of documentation to say the least. Before the discussion of this information begins in earnest, a few cautionary comments need to be made about this documentation.[1] By all appearances, the accountant who prepared most of the financial statements and did the nuts and bolts accounting from the mid-1950s to the mid-1960s was Abe Wasserman. According to the Pioneer Record Sales ledgers beginning in late 1961, Abe was paid amounts that seemed to average about $125 biweekly. According to the books, Abe's pay would vary more often in frequency than in amount, although neither was particularly consistent. The entries are also listed as a single payment, not as payroll with the appropriate tax and social security deductions as were listed for some of the other employees. This would indicate that Abe was working on a piecemeal or

hourly basis and was likely operating as something of an independent con-
tractor as opposed to a regular employee.

Abe was, by all accounts, a good and fair bookkeeper for Moe. The difficulty from the point of view of analysis is the unfortunate fact that Abe did
not have the most legible penmanship, nor did he label all of the entries as
clearly as might have been hoped. Some of the entries, particularly for accounts receivable, were entered on a per-order basis and thus have a hur-
ried and inconsistent presentation that makes them difficult to decipher.
Furthermore, in a few cases, totals that would be expected to match do not,
presenting additional difficulties in making some sense of the money flow
throughout the various organizations. All of the entries for all of the accounts had been hand-entered in 11" by 17" ledger books. Unfortunately,
the binding has failed in some of the volumes and many of the pages are
loose or in collections that are not complete. Thus, much of the information is presented in summary form, which has either been drawn directly
from summaries provided by Abe, or were compiled through analysis.
However, despite all the difficulties just mentioned, for the most part, the
figures presented should be read with a high degree of confidence in their
accuracy and legitimacy.

In the end, although some of the accounting is confusing and perhaps
raises more questions than it answers, there is little cause to believe that
there was any "funny stuff" going on with the books. Besides, it is most unlikely that if some activity were occurring that contravened the laws of the
time, it would not have been recorded and evidence for such activity would
be nonexistent. Nonetheless, I do not believe that such manipulation of the
accounts was occurring—in spirit at least. Ultimately, the books as they
exist are a relatively accurate representation of the activity of Folkways, Pioneer Record Sales, and perhaps most interesting, Moe's own income during the periods available, as the following sections will illustrate.

Folkways

The first set of ledgers outline the structuring of the amounts owed (accounts receivable) to Folkways. The format of Table 16 is similar to that of
the original ledgers.

The entries provide information for the date of the amount due (left
column) and the dates that the amounts were originally owing (reading
from left to right in the top row), and the total owing for all accounts due.
Reading across the table from the "month ending," the first amount is the
total amount owing. Further to the right are, first, the amount owing from
the current month, then follow the amounts owing from the second, third,
and fourth months, and finally an amount with "prior" marked above. The

Table 16 Accounts Due Summaries from Folkways Accounts/Receivable: 31 July 1958–30 June 1959

Month Ending	Total Receivable	Dec. 1958	Nov. 1958	Oct. 1958	Sept. 1958	Aug. 1958	July 1958	June 1958	May 1958	Apr. 1958	(Prior)
31 July 1958	$25,137.24						$14,444.39	$4,743.97	$2,137.97	$1,033.39 (Prior)	$1,975.58
30 Aug. 1958	$23,194.10					$11,824.39	5,439.74	$3,243.51	853.75 (Prior)	2,380.56	
30 Sept. 1958	22,671.19				$14,546.69	1,469.67	2,018.96	2,491.58 (Prior)	2,535.24		
31 Oct. 1958	25,350.34			$18,237.35	3,021.87	576.86	916.41 (Prior)	1,495.03			
30 Nov. 1958	23,395.12		$15,468.65	3,496.44	1,891.50	543.38 (Prior)	2,509.90				
30 Dec. 1958	25,111.34	$16,313.43	3,394.46	2,162.25	1,385.17	2,433.25					

Month Ending	Total Receivable	June 1959	May 1959	Apr. 1959	Mar. 1959	Feb. 1959	Jan. 1959	Dec. 1958	Nov. 1958	Oct. 1958	Sept. 1958
30 Dec. 1958	$25,111.34							$16,313.43	$3,394.46	$2,162.25	$1,385.17 (Prior)
31 Jan. 1959	25,308.14						$15,736.04	2,409.14	970.86	782.90 (Prior)	
28 Feb. 1959	27,989.54					$15,958.30	4,477.47	809.52	645.56 (Prior)	1,431.84	
31 Mar. 1959	25,990.47				$12,817.63	4,199.53	2,013.95	300.13 (Prior)	932.72		
30 Apr. 1959	26,673.12			$10,959.06	3,086.28	1,202.26	1,049.90 (Prior)	1,072.46			
31 May 1959	27,803.56		$11,995.85	3,254.98	1,076.06	415.12 (Prior)	832.28				
30 June 1959	33,501.88	$15,208.02	3,498.01	1,175.43	639.20	1,225.61					

Table 17 Folkways Accounts Receivable Monthly Summaries:
July 1958–June 1959

	July–December 1958					
	31 July 1958 (378 Accts)	30 Aug. 1958 (375 Accts)	30 Sept. 1958 (353 Accts)	31 Oct. 1958 (349 Accts)	30 Nov. 1958 (344 Accts)	31 Dec. 1958 (378 Accts)
First of the month:	$−25,137.24	$−23,537.74	$−23,194.10	$−22,673.69	$−25,360.76	$−23,410.72
Amount received:	(No other	+18,526.53	+24,805.39	+23,126.44	+22,973.76	+19,427.83
Amount still owed:	information	−5,011.21	+1,611.29	+502.75	−2,387.00	−3,482.89
Sales for the month:	available)	−18,182.89	−24,282.48	−25,853.09	−21,008.12	−21,128.45
End of the Month:		−23,194.10	−22,671.19	−25.350.34	−23,395.12	−24,111.34
(amount credited back to some accounts):[a]	(799.68)	(647.85)	(391.15)	(418.98)	(514.75)	(577.72)

	January–June 1959					
	31 Jan. 1959 (375 Accts)	28 Feb. 1959 (386 Accts)	31 Mar. 1959 (370 Accts)	30 Apr. 1959 (360 Accts)	31 May 1959 (355 Accts)	30 June 1959 (368 Accts)
First of the month:	$−25,112.74	$−25,314.09	$−27,990.40	$−25,979.57	$−26,676.82	$−27,819.16
Amount received:	+21,146.76	+20,390.98	+25,560.17	+19,912.54	+18,770.97	+16,335.10
Amount still owed:	−3,965.98	−4,923.11	−2,430.23	−6,066.98	−7,905.97	−11,484.06
Sales for the month:	−21,342.16	−23,066.43	−23,560.24	−20,606.14	−19,897.71	−22,017.82
End of the month:	−25,308.14	−27,989.54	−25,990.47	−26,673.12	−27,803.56	−33,501.88
(amount credited back to some accounts):	(551.38)	(688.30)	(1008.24)	(812.63)	(539.38)	(854.80)

[a]Added to the accounts receivable lists were a list of (presumably) dealers that, for one reason or another, were to have a certain amount of money credited back onto their accounts. This amount represents the total amount owing to all those entitled (usually twenty to thirty). This amount has already been added into the total amounts owing.

"prior" amount represents money owing for more than four months. In the case of the month ending 31 July 1958, the total amount owing at the end of that month was $25,137.24: $14,444.39 was owing at the end of July 1958, $4,743.97 was still owing from the end of June, $2,137.97 was owing from the end of May, $1,033.39 owing from the end of April, and $1,975.58 owing from due dates prior to April. Interestingly, there are slight discrepancies between the sum of the individual accounts receivable and the total receivable. Clearly there are some accounts that were not recorded in this running tally that are included in the total accounts receivable. Perhaps what is most notable about the numbers presented in Table 17 is the consistency of the amounts and degree of credit that was owing to Folkways at any given time. This situation certainly harkens back to the brief discussion concerning the 30-, 60-, 90-day credit periods that all parts of the production chain use to pay amounts owing. Obviously, Folkways did its fair share of waiting for others to pay for their recordings. Table 16 has been split to fit on the page; the lower chart repeats part of the upper chart for continuity in the presentation of the data.

Table 17 represents an expansion of the summaries of the Folkways Accounts Receivable presented in Table 16. Table 17 provides more detail of the month-to-month cash flow for one calendar year: July 1958 to June 1959. As an illustration, the information for 30 August 1958 would be read as follows: At the beginning of the month $23, 537.74 was owing by Folkways (−). The amount of $18,526.53 was paid to Folkways on existing debt (+), resulting in a net difference of $5,011.21 (the " − " indicates the amount is still owed). Folkways then sold $18,182.89 on account, which, added to the $5,011.21 still owing from the previous month's accounts, meaning that at the end of August, Folkways was owed $23,194.10. Each month, dealers and distributors would send back records for refund, the amount of which is listed at the bottom ($688.30).

A couple of parts of this particular table are notable. First, despite the constant, end-of-month debt situation that persisted throughout the period, most of the existing accounts receivable would be paid; in some cases, even more money was received that was currently owed (although it is likely that this is an accounting anomaly and that the "extra" amounts are simply accounted for in a different month's debt calculation). Second, although there were always a certain number of returns that had to be accounted for every month, the amounts were comparatively small: perhaps 300 to 400 units at a time when Folkways was selling several thousand units a month.

Table 18 Folkways Accounts Payable: December 1955–March 1956

Date		Total Payable	Bartok	Cue	Lee-Myles	Plastylite	Prog. Labels	RCA
30 Nov. 1955	Bal.	$−21,814.14	$−488.03	$−761.42	$−2,760.77	$−4,220.55	$−529.93	$−720.04
(1 Dec. 1955)	+	9,746.833	146.10	386.77	634.50	3,348.51	311.20	233.04
	−	11,285.87	201.20	319.41	1,069.77	5,366.20	249.46	0
27 Dec. 1955	Bal.	−23,252.87	−543.13	−694.06	−3,196.04	−6,238.24	−468.19	−487.00
31 Dec. 1955	Bal.	−23,927.38	−543.03	−541.10	−3,196.04	−6609.39	−468.19	−587.00
	+	10,466.07	75.00	451.49	1,826.02	3,269.00	296.01	313.50
	−	10,995.63	0	472.89	2,085.75	3,327.90	376.02	126.00
30 Jan. 1956	Bal.	−23,956.94	−468.93	−562.50	−3,455.77	−6,678.29	−548.20	−388.50
31 Jan. 1956	Bal.	−24,290.01	−468.03	−1,562.50	−3,584.82	−6,678.29	−548.20	−397.50
	+	10,617.59	60.00	171.60	939.06	3,211.19	235.40	173.50
	−	8,812.81	0	251.02	319.88	4,597.20	144.15	0
27 Feb. 1956	Bal.	−22,485.23	−408.03	−641.92	−2,965.64	−8,064.30	−456.95	−224.00
29 Feb. 1956	Bal.	−25,026.45	−408.03	−552.31	−2,965.64	−9,718.04	−673.83	—
	+	5,711.70	30.00	177.68	713.06	2,184.81	94.79	—
	−	2,809.08	0	264.71	0	963.53	0	—
12 Mar. 1956	Bal.	−22.123.83	−378.03	−639.34	−2,252.58	−8,496.76	−579.04	—

Table 19 Folkways Accounts Payable July 1958–June 1959

Date		Total Payable	Bartok	Cue	Lee-Myles	Plastylite	Prog. Labels
1 July 1958	Bal.	$−36,339.74	$−943.77	$−1,401.05	$−4,771.16	$−7,832.15	$−870.03
	+	2,511.78	50.44	172.32	217.50	467.50	46.90
	−	1,280.55	0	0	354.55	174.00	139.30
22 July 1958	Bal.	−35,108.51	−893.33	−1,228.73	−4,914.21	−7,538.65	−962.43
	+	2,353.20	60.00	110.47	240.00	497.00	49.32
	−	2,826.75	0	150.69	276.00	336.90	16.44
29 July 1958	Bal.	−35,582.06	−833.33	−1,268.95	−4,850.21	−7,378.55	−929.55
	+	3,056.02	41.45	0	235.83	1,167.60	0
	−	2,528.31	86.49	89.37	0	903.40	108.05
5 Aug. 1958	Bal.	−35,052.35	−878.37	−1,358.32	−4,614.38	−7,114.35	−1,037.60
	+	2,242.72	41.45	227.53	226.61	444.10	0
	−	1,262.98	100.94	0	61.25	648.60	31.69
12 Aug. 1958	Bal.	−34,173.61	−937.86	−1,130.79	−4,449.02	−7,318.85	−1,069.29
	+	3,180.94	100.00	0	292.50	1,500.00	175.00
	−	2,325.71	0	247.82	0	1,181.00	31.69
19 Aug. 1958	Bal.	−33,318.38	−837.86	−1,378.61	−4,156.52	−6,999.85	−925.98
	+	2,837.57	128.84	137.57	249.34	445.65	55.02
	−	2,802.79	0	0	0	474.40	0
26 Aug. 1958	Bal.	−33,283.60	−709.02	−1,241.04	−3,904.18	−7,028.60	−870.16
	+	2,119.13	60.75	0	265.80	565.00	0
	−	3,247.77	51.00	150.13	700.81	698.50	78.59

Date		1	2	3	4	5	6
31 Aug. 1958	Bal.	−34,412.24	−699.77	−1,391.17	−4,339.19	−7,162.10	−948.75
(1 Sept. 1958)	+	2,253.21	75.00	170.12	469.00	0	87.09
	−	2,926.29	128.75	581.20	251.86	453.20	16.44
9 Sept. 1958	Bal.	−35,085.32	−753.52	−1,802.25	−4,122.05	−7,615.30	−878.10
	+	4,424.74	75.84	168.57	488.83	1,388.50	92.68
	−	3,411.19	0	0	0	1,793.30	0
17 Sept. 1958	Bal.	−34,071.77	−677.68	−1,633.68	−3,683.22	−8,020.10	−785.42
	+	2,750.74	80.00	113.56	438.82	727.40	95.03
	−	2,127.80	0	0	0	927.80	95.03
23 Sept. 1958	Bal.	−33,448.83	−597.68	−1,520.12	−3,244.40	−8,220.50	−785.42
	+	3,009.11	50.00	0	264.87	741.60	73.48
	−	2,443.38	0	217.44	0	738.20	237.00
30 Sept. 1958	Bal.	−32,883.10	−547.68	−710.06[a]	−2,979.53	−8,217.10	−948.94
(1 Oct. 1958)	+	2,841.70	75.00	115.37	280.30	756.30	79.82
	−	3,872.59	99.43	387.99	454.36	1,153.20	0
7 Oct. 1958	Bal.	−33,913.99	−572.11	−982.68	−3,153.54	−8,614.00	−869.12
	+	3,910.03	75.00	158.03	348.98	1,606.60	100.14
	−	2,758.49	0	0	0	1,199.40	219.38
14 Oct. 1958	Bal.	−32,762.45	−497.11	−824.65	−2,804.61	−8,206.80	−988.36
	+	3,584.64	86.49	0[b]	390.80	768.90	108.84
	−	3,362.50	0	0	0	1,840.10	0
21 Oct. 1958	Bal.	−32,540.31	−410.62	−824.65	−2,413.81	−9,278.00	−879.52
	+	2,908.73	50.00	135.35	283.21	643.90	139.74
	−	6,466.48	0	0	2,017.62	1,068.80	126.77
28 Oct. 1958	Bal.	−36,098.06	−360.62	−689.30	−4,148.22	−9,702.90	−866.55
	+	2,963.98	50.94	0	277.50	529.00	78.59
	−	4,467.81	0	576.50	451.00	400.29	188.92
4 Nov. 1958	Bal.	−37,601.89	−309.68	−1,265.80	−4,321.72	−9,574.10	−976.88
	+	2,458.38	51.50	100.00	251.51	492.00	95.03
	−	1,167.94	0	0	0	819.40	0

Date		Total Payable	Bartok	Cue	Lee-Myles	Plastylite	Prog. Labels
11 Nov. 1958	Bal.	$−36,311.45	−258.18	−1,165.80	−4,070.21	−9,901.50	−881.85
	+	2,879.84	50.00	131.50c	290.00	575.00	125.49
	−	2,036.65	0	31.68	0	200.10	48.13
18 Nov. 1958	Bal.	−35,468.26	−208.18	−1,065.98	−3,780.21	−9,526.60	−804.49
	+	3,803.05	50.00	0	298.56	1,662.60	127.91
	−	2,442.24	0	0	0	747.20	344.02
29 Nov. 1958	Bal.	−34,107.45	−158.18	−1,065.98	−3,481.65	−8,611.10	−1,020.60
	+	3,490.86	28.25	222.95	298.00	746.30	110.28
	−	6,905.31	114.01	13.22	538.94	740.20	49.32
30 Nov. 1958 (1 Dec. 1958)	Bal.	−37,521.90	−243.44	−1,456.25	−3,722.59	−8,605.00	−959.64
	+	2,779.86	25.00	114.85	278.36	617.50	109.74
	−	3,564.28	0	228.10	100.80	1,251.50	63.13
10 Dec. 1958	Bal.	−38,305.72	−218.44	−1,569.50	−3,545.03	−9,239.00	−913.03
	+	2,773.60	24.43	157.64	273.86	758.00	140.79
	−	2,300.36	0	0	0	1,368.00	0
16 Dec. 1958	Bal.	−37,813.08	−194.01	−1,411.86	−3,271.17	−9,849.60	−772.24
	+	3,130.55	25.00	92.50d	462.70	656.30	113.89
	−	3,462.81	112.40	145.95	647.73	255.00	328.45
23 Dec. 1958	Bal.	−38,145.34	−281.41	−1,465.91	−3,456.40	−9,448.30	−987.40
	+	2,696.74	34.01	101.98	298.00	757.30	124.35
	−	4,479.74	332.63	450.17	858.00	1,214.90	46.90
31 Dec. 1958 (1 Jan. 1959)	Bal.	−40,025.34	−580.03	−1,813.50	−4,116.40	−9,905.90	−909.95
	+	2,620.93	25.00	0	281.00	644.00	154.13
	−	172.91	0	0	0	0	0

Date							
6 Jan. 1959	Bal.	−37,590.32	−555.03	−1,813.50	−3,835.40	−9,261.90	−755.82
	+	2,618.56	40.00	243.44	292.00	621.40	0
	−	2,185.42		95.23	427.19	358.00	0
13 Jan. 1959	Bal.	−37,147.18	−515.03	−1,665.29	−3,970.59	−8,998.50	−755.82
	+	2,998.35	40	170.26[e]	242.00	754.50	109.12
	−	2,535.79	0	219.92	0	725.90	31.69
20 Jan. 1959	Bal.	−36,684.62	−475.03	−1,714.95	−3,728.59	−8,969.90	−678.39
	+	2,890.53	30.00	0	270.86	680.50	82.00
	−	1,942.89	0	23.69	0	812.10	0
27 Jan. 1959	Bal.	−35,736.88	−445.03	−1,738.64	−3,457.73	−9,101.50	−596.39
	+	2,962.78	32.40	91.16	244.76	831.60	46.22
	−	5,274.35	0	442.70	299.51	683.80	191.25
31 Jan. 1959 (1 Feb. 1959)	Bal.	−38,048.55	−412.63	−2,090.18	−3,512.48	−8,953.70	−691.42
	+	5,589.29	95.47	442.06	487.50	1,297.40	141.72
	−	4,581.78	51.50	0	170.00	2,357.80	93.34
17 Feb. 1959	Bal.	−37,041.04	−368.66	−1,668.12	−3,194.98	−10,014.10	−643.04
	+	3,174.63	50.00	100.00[f]	298.50	599.20	78.59
	−	4,172.33	0	322.51	0	1,254.10	0
25 Feb. 1959	Bal.	−38,038.74	−318.66	−1,890.63	−2,896.48	−10,669.00	−564.45
	+	3,302.39	51.50	0	234.18	1,638.90	46.90
	−	3,732.62	0	0	563.21	849.20	187.71
28 Feb. 1959 (1 Mar. 1959)	Bal.	−38,468.97	−267.16	−1,890.63	−3,225.51	−9,879.30	−705.26
	+	3,101.50	51.50	137.77	229.00	589.20	92.68
	−	1,117.63	0	0	0	0	62.18
9 Mar. 1959	Bal.	−36,485.10	−215.66	−1,752.86	−2,996.51	−9,290.10	−674.76
	+	3,448.70	51.50	686.45	249.00	654.30	78.59
	−	3,044.40	211.54	556.89	0	214.00	64.57
17 Mar. 1959	Bal.	−36,080.44	−375.70	−1,623.30	−2,747.51	−8,849.80	−660.74
	+	3,333.28	50.00	196.95[g]	244.00	669.30	78.59
	−	4,520.58	0	328.53	0	1,168.00	157.24

Date		Total Payable	Bartok	Cue	Lee-Myles	Plastylite	Prog. Labels
27 Mar. 1959	Bal.	$ -37,267.74	-327.70	-1,754.88	-2,503.51	-9,848.50	-739.39
	+	5,015.43	34.16	246.38	412.41	1,383.70	78.59
	-	5,182.18	496.61	895.02	650.33	823.60	49.32
7 Apr. 1959	Bal.	-37,434.49	-788.15	-2,403.52	-2,741.43	-9,288.40	-710.12
	+	3,409.08	50.00	118.97	216.95	638.50	65.76
	-	1,848.94	0	0	0	1,000.50	0
14 Apr. 1959	Bal.	-35,874.35	-738.15	-2,284.55	-2,524.48	-9,650.40	-644.36
	+	5,986.26	50.00	222.85[h]	404.00	1,483.30	93.36
	-	7,837.55		977.83	0	2,462.40	248.93
28 Apr. 1959	Bal.	-37,725.64	-688.15	-3,039.53	-2,120.48	-10,629.50	-799.93
	+	2,496.51	0	101.97	231.93	611.80	0
	-	4,678.45	0	383.52	967.87	1,320.70	64.57
5 May 1959	Bal.	-39,907.28	-688.15	-3,321.08	-2,856.42	-11,338.40	-864.50
	+	2,713.40	30.90	0	213.19	639.70	124.37
	-	2,999.40	0	0	0	1,084.20	95.06
12 May 1959	Bal.	-40,193.28	-657.25	-3,321.08	-2,643.23	-11,782.90	-835.19
	+	3,000.27	31.54	216.93[i]	211.00	650.90	63.34
	-	2,454.01	0	133.80	0	737.80	0
19 May 1959	Bal.	-39,622.03	-625.71	-3,237.95	-2,432.23	-11,869.80	-771.85
	+	2,293.06	0	120.00	202.80	647.00	62.18
	-	2,287.54	0	0	0	1,143.40	16.44
26 May 1959	Bal.	-39,616.51	-625.71	-3,117.95	-2,229.43	-12,366.20	-726.11
	+	2,601.59	30.00	138.28	209.72	626.70	64.57
	-	7,346.98	0	466.09	1,326.90	642.80	173.58

Date						
3 June 1959	Bal.	−44,361.90	−595.71	−3,445.76	−3,346.61	−12,382.20	−835.12
	+	2,591.96	30.00	119.48	198.00	648.30	78.62
	−	1,742.62	123.60	0	0	431.20	0
9 June 1959	Bal.	−43,512.56	−689.31	−3,326.28	−3,148.61	−12,665.20	−756.50
	+	3,953.19	35.00	125.15	203.70	1,635.70	78.62
	−	4,065.71	0	275.27	0	735.10	16.44
16 June 1959	Bal.	−43,625.08	−654.31	−3,467.40	−2,944.91	−11,764.60	−694.32
	+	3,079.82	35.00	120.61[i]	219.00	614.80	65.76
	−	2,668.42	92.70	136.12	229.16	435.10	0
23 June 1959	Bal.	−43,214.28	−712.01	−3,491.91	−2,955.07	−11,584.90	−628.56
	+	3,079.78	35.00	97.08	−187.00	635.20	64.57
	−	4,465.70	0	173.50	−669.29	1,387.60	280.06
30 June 1959	Bal.	−44,600.20	−677.01	−3,568.33	−3,437.36	−12,337.30	−844.05

[a] This amount represents the remainder after Folkways took out a credit note with Cue for $1,027.50. Payments made against this credit note will be marked.
[b] Payment of $102.50 made against the credit note. $927.00 owing.
[c] An additional payment of $101.00 made against the credit note. $826.00 owing.
[d] An additional payment of $101.50 made against the credit note. $724.50 owing.
[e] An additional payment of $102.00 made against the credit note. $622.50 owing.
[f] An additional payment of $102.50 made against the credit note. $520.00 owing.
[g] An additional payment of $103.00 made against the credit note. $417.00 owing.
[h] An additional payment of $103.50 made against the credit note. $313.50 owing.
[i] An additional payment of $104.00 made against the credit note. $209.50 owing.
[j] An additional payment of $104.50 made against the credit note. $105.00 owing.

By the late 1950s, Folkways was already operating at better than $300,000 a year in sales—a considerable amount at that time. Furthermore, Folkways was receiving on average 70 percent of the total amount owing within 60 days of billing. This ranged from receiving a low of 49 percent of money due in August 1958 to a high of 80 percent in May and June 1959. This is one of the more crucial statistics with respect to the company operation: without a large percentage of accounts paying in a timely fashion, the ability of Folkways to continue to produce recordings and manage debt would have been severely hampered.

As interesting and important as these figures are, they are quite literally only half the story. The other half of the story is the amount of money that Folkways had to pay out in order to maintain production, distribution, and advertising. The accounts payable listed in the following table contains some of the most telling financial information concerning the operation of Folkways. Table 18 represents the earliest of the Accounts Payable records for Folkways dating from December 1955 to March 1956. The second set of data (Table 19) is listed chronologically by date from July 1958 to the end of June 1959 in weekly or biweekly increments. Table 19 also provides an excellent picture of the operations of Folkways over an entire year with accounting in very small increments—often just a few days.

The column categories have been taken from a much larger set of owing accounts, many of which, due to abbreviations and lack of supporting documentation, were not identifiable. The columns, however, represent the three phases that appeared to be most important with respect to the production of Folkways records: *Bartok* is Peter Bartok who ran a studio that Moe used quite extensively for preproduction work, while *Cue* is a studio where Moe sent artists to get material recorded, or on occasion recorded himself with their facilities; *Plastylite* and *Progressive Labels*, as noted earlier, were Moe's main pressing plant and label supplier, respectively (notwithstanding his limited use of RCA). The *Lee-Myles* category is particularly interesting; this was the advertising agency that Asch employed to promote Folkways releases. Although Asch made many statements through his career denouncing the need for advertising Folkways releases, we shall see that he wasn't against using an ad agency when necessary. These accounts not only provide further support for the use of an advertising agency to promote Folkways, but indicate the striking amount of money spent on the account itself. Note that the "+" indicates money paid by Folkways toward the amount owing on the account; the "−" indicates the amount charged against the account by Folkways during the same period. The accounts payable for 1955–1956, based on the above accounts are listed in Table 18.

It is also important to note that the RCA account seems to have been taken off the books at the end of February 1956. Even though the account

Table 20 Summary and Comparison of Tables 18 and 19

	Total Payable	Bartok	Cue	Lee-Myles	Plastylite	Prog. Labels
Net difference from 1 July 1958 to 30 June 1959	$−8,260.46	$+266.76	$−2,272.28 (inc. credit note)	+1,333.80	$−4,505.15	$+25.98
Net difference from 12 Mar. 1956 to 30 July 1959	−22,476.37	−298.98	−3,078.99 (inc.credit note)	−1,184.78	−3,804.54	−265.01

does not appear to have been paid out, it is likely that Moe had simply begun to use Plastylite as his main presser. It is also interesting to note that Moe was not averse to using a plant run by one of the major record companies. Indeed, it would be fair and entirely accurate to assume that Moe was using whichever facility was giving him the best rates for his needs. The accounts continue from July 1958 in Table 19, while a brief comparison of Tables 18 and 19 is shown in Table 20.

The data in Table 19 do not show any expenditures that would be unexpected for a small company whose business clearly increases over the December holidays and eases considerably over the summer months. In particular, the peak in spending on advertising during the 21 October 1958 period would be fully expected given holiday anticipation. However, the figure of $2,017 charged to Lee-Myles represents almost 100 percent of both Folkways standing debt with Lee-Myles and of the total debt payments made by Folkways to all accounts in that period. This is a clear illustration of the importance of getting sufficient advertising out during the holiday period and the financial support that Moe was willing to put behind such an effort.

A good example of the difficult financial environment within which Folkways operated can be seen in a brief comparison of the data in Table 17 with that in Tables 18 and 19, particularly the comparison of the money owed to Folkways against money owed by Folkways. Comparing three data points (end of August 1958, end of December 1958, and end of June 1959) it is clear that although Folkways appears to be in serious financial straits with respect to the amounts owing in Table 19, the net amounts actually owed by Folkways were not as serious as it would first appear (see Table 21).

Nonetheless, the fact that Folkways Records was managing to continue to operate quite successfully carrying between $10,000 and $15,000 in debt during this period is commendable. It is also likely reflective of the operating practices of the industry as a whole. Payment schedules of 30–60–90 days, or 90–120–150 days meant that most companies in the recording industry were likely operating in a chronic debt condition, much in the way that Folkways appeared to be doing during this time.

Table 21 Comparison of Accounts Receivable and Accounts Payable, August 1958–June 1959

	End August 1958	End December 1958	End June 1959
Amount owed to Folkways	$23,194.10	$24,111.34	$33,501.88
Amount owed by Folkways	$34,412.24	$40,025.34	$44,600.20
Net difference	$−11,218.14	$−15,914.00	$−11,098.32

The extent to which the general financial health of Folkways can truly be evaluated during the 1950s and into the 1960s is quite limited. One might say that we know Moe survived this period so it must have been manageable. Nonetheless, it would have been helpful to have financial reports similar to those that were prepared on Folkways in 1964 and 1965 to compare to the 1950s data. These reports are extraordinarily valuable in giving an accurate, professional assessment of the Folkways books. Of course, they may not necessarily reflect the actual state of affairs on a day-to-day basis, but they are invaluable nonetheless.

The two sets of financial reports for 1964 and 1965 (Tables 22 and 25 for 1964; Tables 23 and 26 for 1965) give an unusual amount of information about Folkways. The first comparison are the balance sheets for 1964 and 1965 (Tables 22 and 23). Typically, there would be nothing as organized as a financial statement coming out of the Folkways offices, so the reasons that such audits might have been done are unclear. However, one might speculate that these audits were done was in response to financial questions from Scholastic Magazine or MGM regarding the licensing arrangements, particularly if the negotiations had begun as early as 1962–1963.

Another possibility might be that Moe was preparing Folkways for some type of larger arrangement of the sort eventually seen between Folkways and Scholastic Magazine or Folkways and MGM. In that case, such summaries would have to have been available in order to proceed with negotiations. Thus it makes sense to have some information regarding the performance of the company. It has also been suggested that concerns over taxation were partly behind these summaries, but given that two different sets of certified public accountants compiled the reports (Orenstein and Orenstein for the 1964 reports; Becker and Becker for the 1965 reports), these actions were probably not part of a larger organized tax plan.

Whatever the motivation to have these summaries done, it most likely came from within Folkways, because both sets of summaries note that all

Table 22 Folkways Records Balance Sheet: 30 June 1964[a]

Assets		
Accounts Receivable	$112,473.13	
Merchandise inventory—submitted by management	76,350.70	
Security and deposits	1,482.00	
Prepaid expenses	571.50	
Furniture and Fixtures–net after depreciation	2,274.51	
Other assets	252.90	
Total Assets		$193,404.74
Liabilities and Capital		
Trade accounts and notes payable	125,523.42	
Bank overdraft	6,256.02	
Taxes payable	17,769.25	
Total current liabilities	149,548.69	
Debts payable—officers	79,030.24	
Total liabilities		228,578.93
Capital stock issued	10,150.00	
Capital surplus	3,000.00	
Deficit—June 30, 1964	(48,324.19)	
Capital—June 30, 1964		(35,174.74)
Total liabilities and capital		193,404.74

[a]*Financial statements from Orenstein and Orenstein, CPA. 30 June 1964.*

the information was submitted by management and thus was not independently verified. It would be most logical that if the summaries were requested by outside sources that such financial information would, if at all possible, be independently verified.[2] Some interesting observations and conclusions can be drawn by comparing Tables 22 and 23. A brief summary of the reports shows some interesting trends (Table 24).

Overall, the adjusted net assets of the company did not substantially change from 1964 to 1965. However, all of the other indicators show that Folkways was starting to slide financially in 1965, particularly if royalty income is factored out. Royalty income is a very fickle income: compare $3,595 in 1964 to $28,964 in 1965. Profits minus royalty income give a more accurate picture of the sales income of Folkways specifically, not just of the licensed product. If the royalty incomes are included for both years, there is an approximately equal gross profit against a substantially lower nets sales that would indicate better economic performance, with gross profit representing 24.5 percent of net sales in 1965 compared to 19.1 per-

Table 23 Folkways Records Balance Sheet: 30 June 1965[a]

Assets			
Current Assets			
Cash		$4,050	
Notes receivable—customers	$7,587		
Less—notes receivable discounted	7,269	318	
Accounts receivable—customers		33,315	
Merchandise inventory—submitted		52,950	
Excise tax refund receivable[b]		36,926	
Total Current Assets			**$127,559**
Accounts receivable—affiliated company			57,786
Furniture and equipment		$5,800	
Less—accumulated depreciation		4,105	1,695
Master records[c]			50,000
Other assets			1,922
Total			$238,962
Liabilities and capital			
Current liabilities			
Notes payable—trade		$36,734	
Accounts payable—trade		49,600	
Taxes payable		9,886	
Excise tax payable—trade—note 2 (see above)		25,601	
Total Current Liabilities			**$121,821**
Loans Payable			92,005
Capital stock		$10,150	
Capital surplus		53,000	
Deficit—July 1, 1964	$(48,324)		
Net profit—for the year ended June 30, 1965	10,310		
Deficit—June 30 1965		(38,014)	25,136
Total			$238,962

[a]*Financial statements from Becker and Becker, CPA. 30 June 1965.*

[b]"Note 2—The 10% federal excise tax on phonograph records was repealed on June 22, 1965. As a result, the Company has applied for a refund of excise taxes on customers' inventory as of that date."

[c]"Note 4—The company always followed a practice of expensing all phonograph record production costs, in the year incurred. Accordingly, the value of the entire catalog is not shown on its balance sheet. However, as a result of this licensing agreement, management has decided to place a value of $50,000 on these master tapes."

Table 24 Comparison of Data from Table 23

	Year Ending 30 June 1964[a]	Year Ending 30 June 1965
Net assets	$193,405	$238,962 [152,036][b]
Taxes payable (including excise)	17,769	35,487
Gross profit	84,588	86,718
Gross profit (less declared royalties)	80,993	57,754
Net profit	6,570	10,310
Net sales	443,445	354,202
Debts owed by officers of the company	79,030	92,005

[a]Numbers have been rounded up or down to the nearest dollar for comparison. See tables for the figures as they were given on the original documents.
[b]The bracketed value is the adjusted value. In the 1964 report, the estimated value of the master recordings ($50,000) was not included in the asset calculation. Furthermore, in 1965, a projected excise tax rebate of $36,926 was included because of the repeal of the excise tax. This would have been a liability in 1964.

cent in 1964. However, if the royalty incomes are removed from the gross profit calculations, the performance of Folkways falls substantially in 1965 to 16.3 percent compared to 18.3 percent in 1964.

Furthermore, if the royalty income is removed from the income statements of each year, the net profits also drop substantially. In 1964 net profit drops to $2,974; In 1965, however, it is a drastic change: $10,310 to $−18,654. This is quite a precipitous drop for Folkways and may well have been part of the push from Moe to solidify licensing income from some source—in this case, Scholastic. A note on the 1965 statement concerning the inclusion of the Master Records line item adds the following:

> In May 1965, the company [Folkways] concluded an agreement with a major record company [it is not stated, but it is assumed to be MGM] for the licensing of a certain group of masters. The company [Folkways] is to receive the following: $35,000 the first year, $45,000 for the second and third year and $50,000 for the fourth and fifth year.

A second and very important feature of these statements is the line regarding the debts owed to officers of the company. One can reasonably assume that the debt was incurred by Moe for himself, as a note regarding the 1965 statement indicates that:

> The amount shown as loans payable [$92,005] represents balances accumulated principally in prior years, as due to a director of the company. Management has advised us that this indebtedness is to be

treated as a non-current liability, as the company does not intend to repay any part thereof during the ensuing twelve month period.

The exact purpose for the loan(s) are unclear; they may or may not have been for personal use or a way of deferring taxes on salary. However, there may be a potential link here with Moe's other company, Pioneer Record Sales. Not much has been said to this point about this company, but the inclusion of transferred accounts receivable makes its participation in this case notable. On an asset line item on the 1965 balance sheets is included "Accounts Receivable—Affiliated Company—$57,786." A note to this line explains that:

> Pioneer Record Sales, Inc. is the exclusive distributor of the company's records to commercial sources. In addition, the company and "Pioneer" share personnel and other operating costs. The allocation of such costs are based on an arbitrary percentage decided upon by Management. The balance in this receivable reflects the net balance of various charges and offsets.

The importance of this item is demonstrated primarily in two ways. First, in the absence of the transferred receivable, Folkways would have shown a net loss of almost $58,000, which in the context of balancing the books would make accounting much more difficult. However, this very difficulty leads to the second point. The presence of Pioneer seemed to be in part—perhaps a substantial part—an initiative by Moe in response to the pressures of the recording industry against Folkways. For Folkways to have existed as a lone company, the pressures against it would be very pointed, and would have been—although there is no direct evidence of this—very likely fatal to Folkways early in its life. The presence of Pioneer in particular, appears to be the buffer that Folkways needed to protect it from the occasional slump in the market. Both the selective nature of sales—whether a sale is "commercial" or not and whose books reflect the sale—and the discretionary interchange of assets between the two companies acts almost as an internal credit agency for Moe. Such maneuvering might also account for the final accountant's note on the 1965 report: "The company has not provided for any federal income taxes on the current year's net profit, as there is an operating loss carryover from prior years available to offset any tax liability."

Paired with each of the Table 22 and Table 23 income statements were more detailed statements of profit and loss for both 1964 (Table 25) and 1965 (Table 26). These statements provide a much more detailed breakdown of the basic costs involved in the Folkways operation during these periods. It is unfortunate that the statements were prepared by two different accounting agencies. After attempting to compare many of the line

Table 25 Statement of Profit and Loss for Year Ended 30 June 1964

Sales	**$448,455.42**	
Less discounts	5,010.59	
Net sales		$443,444.83
Cost of Goods Sold		
Merchandise inventory July 1, 1963	117,250.00	
Purchases—direct production costs	321,552.61	
		438,802.61
Less: merchandise inventory—June 30, 1964	76,350.70	
Cost of goods sold		362,451.91
Gross Profit		80,992.92
Operational Expenses		
Salaries	8,911.90	
Advertising and promotion	30,955.27	
Rent	2,998.00	
Taxes	1,520.48	
Interest	3,868.14	
Freight and postage	4,939.35	
Telephone	2,385.38	
Professional and Secretarial	6,623.80	
Insurance	768.39	
Stationery and office supplies	3,393.20	
Repairs and Maintenance	308.30	
Traveling and Entertaining	612.01	
Legal	358.61	
General expenses	9,882.35	
Depreciation	493.34	
Total operating expenses		78,018.52
Operating income	2,974.40	
Other income—royalties	3,595.29	
Net profit for year ending June 30, 1964		6,596.69

items between the two statements, it becomes clear that many of the income or cost categories have been defined in different ways and money appears to have been allocated to different categories in each statement.

There are several observations that can be made that may shed more light on the financial activity of Folkways. It appears that the production costs fell quite substantially from 1964 to 1965. However, the degree to which such costs fell is not clear. If both "production costs" and "salaries and handling" are included in the 1965 calculation, the drop is $ 48,506 (15

Table 26 Folkways Records Income Statement for Year Ended
30 June 1965

Sales—Net		**$354,202**
Costs of Goods		
Merchandise inventory—July 1	$ 76,351	
Production costs	171,424	
Salaries and handling	101,623	
Total	$349,398	
Merchandise inventory	52,950	
Cost of goods sold		296,448
Gross profit		$ 57,754
Royalty income		28,964
Total gross profit		$ 86,718
Other Costs		
Convention and traveling	$ 17,378	
Professional and legal	6,846	
Royalties	14,629	
Salaries	8,703	
Warehouse costs	6,055	
Clerical	3,330	
Interest	3,306	
New York City Taxes	2,868	
Rent	2,373	
Postage	2,319	
Telephone	2,068	
Stationery and supplies	2,455	
Miscellaneous	1,698	
Depreciation—office equipment	580	
Insurance	493	
Payroll taxes	1,307	
Total other costs		76,408
Net profit		$ 10,310

percent). If, on the other hand, the 1965 statement is read literally, the impression is that the production costs fell off by $150,129 (47 percent). It seems most likely the actual figure is somewhere in between 15 percent and 47 percent. Similarly, the inclusion of "purchases" with "direct production costs" in 1964 is vague enough to include or exclude a number of figures that might substantially alter the 1964 figure in comparison to 1965. The conclusion must be, however, that there was indeed a drop in production costs and the drop was substantial. With the accounting covering only two to three months of the Scholastic and MGM agreements, it is hard to imagine such a dramatic impact in such a short period.

On a more mundane level, a consideration of base costs also provides some interesting figures, virtually all of which support the slowing production (and thus sales volumes) of Folkways in 1965. Salaries dropped by a bit more than 2 percent (though these salary figures almost certainly did not include Moe's salary as a separate item). Rent dropped almost 21 percent, which likely indicated some type of consolidation of warehouse and office space. In line with a loss of office space is the 27 percent drop in costs for office supplies, although it must be said that this is a vague category to begin with, so its accuracy may be questioned (particularly since other office supplies—postage and telephone, for instance—are not included). The curious item is the "miscellaneous/general expenses" category. Given that there is such a drastic difference between the two entries ($9,882 in 1964, $1,698 in 1965), the interest in discovering what is included or excluded is certainly piqued. Unfortunately, such information, once again, is frustratingly not available.

However, the question of warehouse costs is an important one. With such a large catalog and a correspondingly large inventory, warehousing likely contributed the most to rental expenditures. For example, when Moe opened a wholesale sales office and showroom at 121 W. 47th Street in New York, his rental agreement stated a rate of $200 a month from 1 May to 31 October 1957.[3] Across the street at #304, 117 W. 46th Street, Asch Recordings was paying a little less at $125 a month in 1965.[4]

A receipt dated 12 December 1958 for "rent of stockroom plus services rendered" from Sam Goody (235 49th W. Street, New York) shows that Moe paid $4000 per year for both 1957 and 1958. This is the earliest reference in the documentation to costs for storage space, although clearly Moe needed such space twenty years earlier. In 1970, Folkways was paying $575 a month ($6,900 annually)[5] plus taxes for space at 701 7th Avenue, New York. Other locations include the entire second floor of 17–23 West 60th Street, New York, where Folkways held much of its stock for filling shipping orders. In 1975, rent was $2111.23 a month[6] (something over $25,000 a year) plus various taxes assessed by the landlord for the property, then absorbed by the tenants according to terms in the lease agreements. By 1980–1983, rent for this space alone was $45,000 a year[7] plus taxes.

It is difficult to establish the burden of renting multiple locations for office, shipping, and inventory. The amounts above provide a tantalizing, and somewhat startling, suggestion of the basic infrastructure costs that Folkways was bearing during the 1970s and 1980s. However, an additional cost that is virtually never mentioned in any discussion of independent re-

Table 27 Location and Insurance Coverage Rates of Folkways Assets, 1978[a]

Location	Existing Coverage
609 W. 51st Street, NYC.	$20,000 contents
1290 Avenue of the Americas, NYC	$20,000 contents
3011 S. Fulton Avenue, Mt. Vernon, NY	$5,000 contents
925 N. 3rd Street, Philadelphia, PA	$10,000 contents
449 W. 49th Street, NYC.	$100,000 contents
1449 37th Street, Brooklyn, NY	$40,000 contents plus $10,000 extra expenses
333 N. Drive, Plainfield, NJ	$50,000 contents plus $10,000 extra expenses
17 W. 60th Street, NYC	$215,000 contents plus $10,000 extra expenses
8th and 13th Floors, 43 W. 61st Street, NYC	$30,000 contents plus $20 000 extra expenses plus $5,000 Mercantile Open Stock Burglary on office
Gilpin Ave. (Cardinal Industrial Park), Hauppauge, NY	$20,000 contents plus $10,000 extra expenses
Cook Records, 375 Ely Avenue, S. Norwalk, CT	$5,000 contents
$500,000 Liability including personal injury covering 17 W. 60th Street and 43 W. 61st Street NYC	
$25,000 Accounts receivable	

[a]Listed in an insurance summary letter to *Folkways Records and Service Corp. from Princeton Brokerage Corporation, Great Neck, NY, 15 December 1978.*

cord companies is insurance. Folkways, in particular, would have been extremely foolish to avoid insurance with such an enormous inventory. In fact, the distribution of Folkways' assets in 1978 was best illustrated by a compilation of existing insurance coverage (Table 27). It is very likely that some of these locations are other businesses, like pressers or printers, where Folkways assets were held. Although it is not entirely clear, 333 North Drive, Plainfield, New Jersey, is the address of Faculty Press, a company that Moe had used for many years to print the booklets and other materials that he needed.

Based on Table 27, coverage in 1978 totalled more than a half million dollars in inventory alone. The cost of such a policy, in addition to covering the half million for liability, $60,000 for expenses, and $5,000 for theft, would be considerable. An invoice from the Princeton Brokerage Corp.—the same company that produced the list in Table 27 in 1978—for a "Special Multi Peril Policy," billed Folkways for $8,345 per year for premiums.[8] During the same year, Folkways had additional Workers' Compensation and Employer Liability coverage for an annual premium of nearly $1,300 per year.[9] The evidence suggests that Moe never cut corners with insurance, obviously feeling that it provided an important sense of security and made good sense. In addition to personal policies, Moe also held group life policies for himself and employees through Folkways and Pioneer Record Sales.[10] Nonetheless, insurance premiums exceeding $10,000 per year would add a considerable cost to absorb into the production expenses year after year of operation.

It is obvious that while certain entries are represented in one year and not the other, it does not indicate that these expenses were not present. Moe's "convention and traveling" expenses, for example, were almost certainly part of the accounting for almost every year of the life of Folkways (although Moe, himself, did less traveling from the mid-1970s because of his age). Therefore, differences in line items are much more a testament to different accounting procedures, and perhaps a degree of forethought to the taxation guidelines of the year, than to the presence or absence of certain types of expenditures or income sources. It should also be said that the inclusion of certain figures—particularly the royalty income discussed earlier—makes Folkways appear much stronger financially than might otherwise be the case. Given the proximity of the accounting to the Scholastic and MGM agreements, this fact should not be overlooked. This is not to suggest that improper reporting is involved. Instead, it makes sense to use a reporting method that showed Folkways on its best financial footing.

In closing, what is most striking is the overall net profit/net sales ratio. In 1964, the net profit represented only 1.49 percent of the net sales, indicating an extremely thin profit margin in both relative percentage terms and dollar terms ($6,597). In 1965, this ratio nearly doubles to 2.91 percent on profit of $10,310. Although it would be fair to place much of the credit for this improvement on the apparent drop in production costs, I would still be more inclined to credit the inclusion of royalty income as the saving grace in both years. As mentioned, factoring out the royalty income for each year leaves a net profit of $3,002 in 1964 and $−18,654 in 1965. This translates in net profit/net sales percentages of 0.67 percent and −5.23 percent, respectively. Though it may not have been representative of other years, the importance of royalty income in 1964 and, particularly, 1965 is yet another demonstration of the fine balance that Moe was able to manage to keep Folkways alive.

Pioneer Record Sales

There also exists a fair amount of information concerning the operation of Pioneer Record Sales during the 1960s. The difficulty has come in attempting to decipher the details of the relationship between Folkways and Pioneer beyond simply suggesting that Pioneer sold Folkways records. The financial records themselves do little to help clarify this situation, given that the accounting in the Pioneer books are equally difficult to read, let alone to interpret.

Table 28 shows a summary of accounts receivable and accounts payable on a monthly basis from October 1961 to December 1963. Although the various account columns are relatively straightforward, the relationships between one category and another are not made clear at all in the original documents. Further investigation would be necessary to establish the correct relationships between many of the summary figures.

There are a number of interesting items in Table 28 that should be noted. The first is the relationship between the Net Accounts Receivable "Banked," Total Sales and the Net Payable owed by Pioneer. Table 29 offers some summary figures for comparison.

A quick examination of the summary figures would suggest that Pioneer was doing exactly what it was supposed to do: sell Folkways records and draw a small profit in the process. The comparison of net receivables and net payables indicate that there was just a little bit of profit to be drawn from the difference (1.0 percent in 1962, 1.7 percent in 1963). In fact, the margin appears to be so slim that for the last three months of 1961, Pioneer appears to have run a deficit of $232.95.

It is interesting to note that the months ending 1961 do not actually represent the high-sales period of the calendar year. These three months, which would be expected to be a good time for seasonal sales, only represents 27.4 percent of sales in 1963 and only 18.8 percent of sales in 1962—hardly the spike that such a gift-giving rush would generate. Indeed, the peak sales months in Table 28 are September 1963 ($95,855.52), June 1962 ($69,030.20), and August 1963 ($57,086.53), respectively. This is clearly suggestive of the academic school year, with sales peaking at the beginning and at the end of the school year. This also supports the contention that Moe focused heavily on the academic market.

The emphasis on the academic aspect of sales is perhaps most intriguing when compared with many of the figures already discussed on Folkways. Much of the Folkways accounting suggests quite strongly that efforts were, in fact, directed to the December gift-giving period. This is confirmed by the considerable sums spent through Lee-Myles directly or the $30,955.27 cost for "Advertising and Promotion" in Table 25. However, the

Pioneer accounts reflect the academic/institutional sales market: Folkways' "commercial" markets. Indeed, the majority of funds spent on attending conferences and exhibitions were a means of reaching the academic market. It would then make good business sense to hire a specialist in retail advertising like Lee-Myles, as well as continuing to support the efforts of Larry Sockell to keep retail outlets informed and stocked with current releases, to augment Pioneer's efforts.

A critical category is the net payable figure for Folkways. Such a category should naturally be expected given that Pioneer is the exclusive distributor of Folkways and as such would be expected to owe Folkways a certain percentage of the net sales. In this case, the figures account for about 45 percent of sales in 1962 and slightly more than 46 percent in 1963. However, what is missing is the matching accounting in the Folkways books. With growth in Pioneer from 1962 to 1963 of 15.9 percent in total sales and a growth of 19.1 percent in the payments to Folkways, it would be a reasonable assumption to make that such payments should continue at least within the same degree of magnitude in 1964 and 1965. An examination of the Folkways statements (Tables 22 and 23), however, show no evidence of such an income stream. The only possible entries that might account for this transfer are found in the undisclosed 1964 "Accounts Receivable" line item for $112,473.13 and the 1965 item "Accounts Receivable—Affiliated Company" for $57,786. Neither amount comes even close to the amounts suggested in the Pioneer accounting.

The likely explanation for this discrepancy seems to be an accounting method that draws figures for both companies from a single cash-flow stream. This is strongly suggested by the fact that in Table 30 (paired with Table 31), the "Accounts Receivable—Affiliated Company" line item has Folkways owing Pioneer $22,839. An additional liability is listed as the "Loans Payable" line item of $52,624.

In their comments at the end of the report, the accountants identify this amount as:

> a net total of various unrelated loans from several sources, including loans from related companies, in which the Company's sole stockholder has a substantial interest. Management advised us that this indebtedness is to be treated as a non-current liability since the company does not intend to repay any part thereof in the next twelve month period.

Even though Pioneer does indeed owe to a variety of companies, it is most likely owing money to Folkways. Perhaps the best explanation for

Table 28 Pioneer Record Sales Accounts Receivable and Payable: October 1961–December 1963

Month End	Net A/C Receivable "Banked"[a]	Total Sales[b]	Net Payable	Moe's Pay	General Labor[c]	Total Labor (incl. Moe's salary)	Net Payable to Folkways
Oct. 1961	$25,388.10	$24,419.19	$27,042.47	$510.00	$2,020.27	$2,530.27	$12,158.81
Nov. 1961	32,772.49	38,380.58	30,475.84	720.00	2,366.01	3,056.01	10,919.17
Dec. 1961	24,117.94	25,630.25	24,993.17	360.00	1,967.03	2,327.03	10,715.87
Jan. 1962	26,939.31	35,703.10	25,234.87	1,080.00	2,558.88	3,638.88	18,429.87
Feb. 1962	42,025.64	33,698.52	34,709.87	1,955.00	2,147.47	4,102.47	16,943.07
Mar. 1962	41,524.71	40,441.84	36,840.11	1,430.00	2,168.17	3,598.17	21,802.66
Apr. 1962	22,038.21	29,073.62	16,183.73	510.00	2,162.33	2,672.33	16,183.73
May 1962	28,376.00	24,570.95	35,760.11	565.00	2,531.90	3,096.90	11,395.34
June 1962	25,483.51	69,030.20	25,055.79	670.49	2,386.53	3,057.02	9,530.42
July 1962	23,856.43	22,623.21	24,475.72	1,255.00	2,313.80	3,568.80	11,906.95
Aug. 1962	16,319.84	30,703.67	20,486.79	380.00	1,943.55	2,323.55	15,924.04
Sept. 1962	24,755.23	27,589.86	19,004.53	825.00	1,654.37	2,479.37	14,172.84
Oct. 1962	20,439.54	25,238.22	21,232.90	770.00	2,532.25	3,302.25	12,322.75
Nov. 1962	22,060.62	29,132.07	24,552.70	840.00	2,117.14	2,957.14	14,715.80
Dec. 1962	13,381.71	18,261.24	20,488.79	465.00	2,872.45	3,351.45	10,881.64

					General	Clerical[d]		
Jan. 1963	29,964.56	27,330.00	32,308.76	856.00	1,796.60	235.00	2,887.60	14,205.84
Feb. 1963	18,265.86	22,906.66	18,884.32	1,056.00	1,931.00	200.00	3,187.00	11,838.30
Mar. 1963	23,562.86	17,854.25	24,101.53	1,103.23	1,592.13	500.00	3,195.36	9,006.58
Apr. 1963	21,119.65	21,391.29	20,149.72	706.00	1,906.76	1,620.00	4,232.76	10,669.68
May 1963	21,439.28	29,902.94	18,020.93	1,190.00	1,425.85	1,110.00	3,725.85	16,655.30
June 1963	26,220.47	15,436.35	29,059.51	910.00	1,781.45	640.00	3,331.45	7,753.98
July 1963	35,266.79	37,213.51	31,030.25	1,510.00	2,369.15	1,420.00	5,299.15	20,077.42
Aug. 1963	38,957.27	57,086.53	34,442.09	2,205.09	1,769.54	1,525.00	5,499.63	38,446.45
Sept. 1963	48,888.09	95,855.52	46,576.70	1,821.23	2,605.54	1,340.00	5,766.77	19,933.37[e]
Oct. 1963	39,025.37	49,939.87	40,663.15	2,843.52	3,421.97	1,340.00	7,605.49	25,037.33
Nov. 1963	47,969.76	44,434.44	38,221.50[f]	1,851.17	2,695.80	1,685.00	6,231.97	20,159.04
Dec. 1963	35,657.64	28,228.36	46,505.61	1634.46	3,987.46	1,675.00	7,296.92	13,718.30

[a]This total is taken from a book total that appears to represent the amount actually received and "banked" against previous accounts owing, for the month listed.

[b]Total sales figures are taken from a single figure labeled as such on the summary sheets of the account books. The total accounts receivable owing is consistently the same as the total sales given. Therefore, the total accounts receivable is the same for each month as the total sales for that month.

[c]As noted below, "general help" appears to mainly refer to warehouse-type labor. Typically, this payroll amount was for five employees.

[d]The payroll summary does not include an entry for "clerical" until this point. It is an important separation as it appears that "general help" is basically warehouse work—inventory, filling orders, shipping, and receiving. The inclusion of a "clerical" category suggests that the office work was becoming increasing pressing on Moe and the rest of the staff.

[e]This particular amount is taken from the column total, as there was no summary total available in the summary for this month.

[f]This is an estimated amount based on the amounts given on the summary sheets.

Table 29 Comparison Data from Table 28

	Net A/C Receivable "Banked"	Net Payable Total Sales	Net Payable	to Folkways
Oct. 1961–Dec. 1961	$82,278.53	$88,430.02	$82,511.48	$33,793.85
Jan. 1962–Dec. 1962	307,150.75	386,066.41	304,025.91	174,209.11
Jan. 1963–Dec. 1963	386,337.60	447,579.72	379,964.07	207,501.59

Table 30 Pioneer Record Sales, Inc. Balance Sheet 31 December 1964[a]

Assets			
Current assets			
Cash overdraft		(3,620)	
Notes receivable—customers	$14,215		
Less—notes receivable discounted	14,215		
Accounts receivable—customers		58,479	
Merchandise inventory—submitted		63,929	
Total current assets			118,788
Accounts receivable—affiliated company (note 1)			22,839
Furniture and equipment		$ 5,874	
Less—accumulated depreciation		2,958	2,916
Other assets			125
Total			$144,668
Liabilities and Capital			
Current liabilities			
Notes payable—bank (note 2)[b]		$21,000	
Notes payable—trade		23,611	
Accounts payable—trade		15,771	
Taxes payable		5,626	
Total current liabilities			$ 66,008
Loans payable (note 3)			52,624
Capital stock		$ 2,606	
Retained earnings—January 1, 1964	$22,569		
Net profit—for the year ended December 31, 1964	861		
Retained earnings—December 31, 1964		23,430	26,036
Total			$144,668

[a]*Balance Sheet and Income Statement for Pioneer Record Sales, Inc. for year ending 31 December 1964. Prepared by Becker and Becker. 14 May 1965: Exhibit A.*
[b]Note 2—The Company is indebted to the Franklin National Bank in the amount of $21,000.00 repayable in equal monthly installments.

Table 31 Pioneer Record Sales, Inc. Income Statement for Year Ended
31 December 1964[a,b]

Sales—Net			**$325,413**
Cost of Goods			
Merchandise inventory—January 1		$ 52,650	
Purchases		216,560	
Total		$269,210	
Merchandise inventory—December 31		63,929	
Cost of goods sold			205,281
Gross profit			$120,132
Selling Expenses			
Salesman's salary	$ 2,000		
Commissions	14,005		
Shipping salaries	24,244		
Payroll taxes	4,322		
Traveling and convention expenses	13,141		
Bad debts	2,767		
Union welfare	877		
Christmas expenses	1,330		
Total		$ 62,686	
Administration Expenses			
Officer's salary	$ 12,123		
Office salaries	14,098		
Rent	2,076		
Miscellaneous	5,732		
Telephone	3,919		
Professional and legal	6,329		
Office expenses	1,548		
Interest	5,825		
Insurance ·	2,420		
Depreciation—office equipment	821		
Collection charges	478		
Other taxes	973		
Total		56,342	
Total Expenses			**119,028**

[a]There is an attached "Note 4" that does not have a specific reference to a line-item on either statement, but that reads: "In May 1965, Folkways Records and Service Corp. entered into two contracts, which may materially affect the operation of the Company. One contract provides that Pioneer will receive no less than $15,000.00 for the first year, and $20,000.00 annually for the following four years for relinquishing exclusive distribution rights to the 'Folkways' catalog. The effect of the second contract cannot be determined at this time."

[b]*Balance Sheet and Income Statement for Pioneer Record Sales, Inc. for year ending 31 December 1964. Prepared by Becker and Becker. 14 May 1965: Exhibit B.*

such intertwined accounting is the note attached to the "Accounts Receivable—Affiliated Company" item: "Folkways Records Service Corp., and the Company [Pioneer] share personnel, and other operating costs. The allocation of such costs are based on an arbitrary percentage decided upon by management."[11] Thus, the interrelationship of the two companies has clearly become pivotal in maintaining a more resilient financial foundation from which to continue to produce and sell recordings.

Examination of these financial statements in many ways raises more questions than answers. For example, it is not clear whether the labor costs listed in Table 28 are separately listed between Folkways and Pioneer. As they shared office space and personnel, they likely had the same employees as well. Yet, their wages were listed as specific costs on Tables 25 and 26 for Folkways, as well as Table 31 for Pioneer. Furthermore, most of the basic expenses listed in Tables 25 and 31 are repeated for the same year: rent, telephone, professional and legal, interest, office expenses, cost and depreciation of office equipment, and office salaries. If such an arrangement was acceptable to the authorities (especially the tax authorities), then Moe was very clever to organize his business affairs the way he did. By all appearances, he was listing, and presumeably deducting from his taxable income, the same values under two different companies. This would appear to allow Moe to deduct his staff, office, and rental expenses twice, giving him a considerable tax break. As there is no evidence that any of the declared information is incorrect for either Pioneer or Folkways, and two sets of certified public accountants were involved in organizing the financial material, this would appear to be a very useful loophole that Moe exploited to the greatest extent possible.

Moe's Money

One of the central questions that has circulated throughout investigations of Folkways is that of Moe's income. There have often been accusations of the exploitation of artists based primarily on the failure of Folkways to pay appropriate royalties to artists. However, the books indicate that Moe was not attempting to squeeze excessive amounts of income out of artists, Folkways, or any of the other enterprises that he controlled. Indeed, one comes away being somewhat surprised that, as the sole proprietor in many of his projects, he did not assign himself a more generous salary package.

The salary that Moe was drawing from Pioneer was very reasonable in comparison to that of his other employees. In fact, a number of observations are worth making about the Pioneer entries, but that are not shown on the summary presented here. First, Moe very rarely took his salary at the same time as the rest of his regular employees. This was sensible from the point of view that to take such a large sum out of a fragile cash-flow situation would be dangerous. His regular employees were normally paid weekly, whereas Moe typically drew a single paycheck, usually toward the end of the month. Moe also enforced all of the normal payroll deductions that were due to himself and his other regular employees. Furthermore, Moe submitted his payroll taxes with surprising consistency, given the disarray of the rest of the office.

Finally, Moe let his pay float with the level of income for each month. If there was not much left after paying accounts and employees, Moe's pay would often drop. Similarly, if the month had particularly good cash flow, he might pay himself a little more. Examination of the Pioneer accounts (Table 28) show that Moe's salary could change more than $900 in a single month: from March 1962 to April 1962 his salary changed from $1,430 to $510—a drop of $920. Not only does this change reflect Moe's changing income, but it also highlights how variable the cash flow could be on a monthly basis.

That is not to say, of course, that Moe did not do well for himself. The most interesting observation is that Moe appeared to receive pay according to his activities. The Commissions list (Table 32) appeared as a summary document among the financial records. It is important because it quite clearly demonstrates that Moe was taking quite a healthy paycheck for sales commissions, apparently separate from his Pioneer salary. The amounts vary, of course, but on average it appears that Moe was averaging between $1,500 and $2,500 a month in commission income in the late 1950s.

It is not clear, however, if this income continued for Moe when Larry Sockell became Moe's sales manager at about this time. As Larry recalled, by the mid-1960s he was making about $25,000 a year from Moe.[12] Thus, it can be assumed that the commission income that Moe was enjoying in the late 1950s began to go to Larry after 1960; certainly the amounts listed in Tables 31 and 32 would support such an annual income.

Twenty years later, wages and income were still concerns for Folkways. Tax records and wage calculations offer some insight into some of the employment expenses that Moe had to deal with, not the least of which was the complication of filing quarterly withholding tax forms for the prepayment of taxes throughout the year. Based on these forms and the calculations done by an accountant (by hand in sometimes indecipherable penmanship), the following wage figures can be summarized for Folkways through the latter 1970s (Table 33).

What is telling about these figures (and from the quarterly breakdown not shown), is that Moe kept to his patterns from twenty years before. He

Table 32 Commissions Due Moe Asch, 1958

Date	Amount	Total Paid
15 Mar. 1958	$579.99	
29 Mar. 1958	468.92	
5 Apr. 1958	351.58	
1–7 May 1958	—	
12 May 1958	462.03	
24 May 1958	322.30	
7 June 1958	270.65	
14 June 1958	353.84	
21 June 1958	346.67	
28 June 1958	243.78	
	3,399.76	[pd. 9.3.58]
14 July 1958	659.86	
19 July 1958	299.46	
26 July 1958	605.83	$1,559.35
1 Aug. 1958	373.67	
8 Aug. 1958	441.42	
15 Aug. 1958	424.00	
23 Aug. 1958	463.29	
30 Aug. 1958	393.94	2,096.32
6 Sept. 1958	503.26	
13 Sept. 1958	571.11	
20 Sept. 1958	571.55	
27 Sept. 1958	502.25	
3 Oct. 1958	545.36	
11 Oct. 1958	545.87	
18 Oct. 1958	313.76	
25 Oct. 1958	431.14	1,836.13
1 Nov. 1958	764.23	
8 Nov. 1958	470.01	
15 Nov. 1958	423.24	
22 Nov. 1958	435.63	
29 Nov. 1958	692.11	2,785.22
6 Dec. 1958	607.20	
13 Dec. 1958	626.44	
20 Dec. 1958	436.80	
30 Dec. 1958	341.07	[2,011.51]
		12,437.70[a]

[a]This is the year-end total, not including the initial $3,399.76 already paid. The section total above was not in the original, but is included here for reference.

Table 33 Folkways Wages Paid 1976–1980

Year	Total Annual Wages	Moe Asch Income
1976	$114,173	$15,300
1977	163,844	25,000
1978	Not enough information	
1979	133,229	25,000
1980	Approx. 125,000	Approx. 10,000

did not draw a salary that was consistent in either timing or amount. However, at this time, Folkways was likely Moe's primary income source. A tax document filed for Pioneer at the end of May 1976 contains a note stating "This company has been inactive for the past six years and had no assets or liabilities and has ceased filing returns."[13] A later notice from the New York Department of Taxation and Finance indicated that Pioneer Record Sales was slated for dissolution by proclamation for its tax delinquency. It is not clear when Pioneer officially ceased to function, but it is likely that this notice marked the official end of business for one of the key components in the success of Folkways.

At around the same time that Pioneer was no longer operating, Folkways would have been coming back into operation after the end of the Scholastic agreement. Although Folkways was dormant at this time (there is a copy of a quarterly tax return from the first quarter of 1971 indicating that there were no employees at Folkways and thus no tax was due), it is a little curious that Moe was not listed as an employee as he had been on other returns. The cessation of Pioneer's operation also coincides with the time that the documentation indicates business was returning to Folkways.

There is no question that much of the financial data presented here are unique in the investigation of recording companies. However, along with its revelation comes much frustration. The data raise issues that at this point must simply be left for the time being. Whether additional financial records were generated or whether the documents held by the archive are the only sets that exist may never be known. Either scenario raises questions about Moe's actual financial situation.

7
Easing the Burden
Folkways in the 1960s

As Moe and Folkways entered the 1960s, his thoughts began to turn toward succession and the disposition of Folkways. Because Moe was unable (or unwilling) to finally sell Folkways until 1986, other solutions had to be found to reduce some of the workload and secure Folkways' continuance. Moe was nearing his golden years and was rightfully entitled to lighten his workload (although ultimately that didn't really happen). In the end, he ended up entering into a variety of comprehensive licensing agreements that moved much of the responsibility of producing and marketing/distributing the material to someone else while he retained ownership of the Folkways catalog.

Over the years, licensing deals had provided Folkways with a variety of opportunities to obtain material for release, or to get its own material released elsewhere. In the mid-1960s, other companies seized the opportunity to exploit Folkways' vast and unique catalog. Although there have been a number of licensing agreements that used Folkways' material, the reason for focusing on the Scholastic and MGM agreements is largely because of their size. These two agreements very likely represent the largest licensing deals ever entered into by Folkways. Furthermore, they are interesting because both organizations wanted access to the considerable Folkways catalog of the mid-1960s. For this access, both Scholastic and MGM were willing to pay handsomely.

Reaching the Educational Market

There has been a substantial amount of confusion regarding the status of Folkways Records in the mid- to late-1960s. This was primarily due to a very large licensing/production/distribution deal that Moe made with Scholastic Magazines. This particular deal was a strange one for a couple of reasons. First, the sheer quantity of the material involved (despite the educational context of the agreement, there was certainly an appearance that the entire Folkways catalog was available to Scholastic) made the arrangement unusual. Moe had never made a deal of that magnitude before. Second, the degree of access that Scholastic was granted to the Folkways catalog was unusually broad. Although there had been other licensing arrangements that Moe had entered into, the access that Scholastic had into Folkways' inventory was so deep that Moe was ultimately hired by Scholastic as a consultant to oversee the educational and licensing issues.

The contract between Folkways and Scholastic Magazines was formally implemented in April of 1965.[1] Surprisingly, given the scope of the contract, the terms of the contract are less than clear. However, a question-and-answer release to Scholastic representatives announcing the agreement helped to answer some of the more practical implementation steps for the agreement.[2] According to the introductory statement of the release, "In the spring of 1965, Scholastic entered into an agreement to be the exclusive educational sales representative for Folkways Records. This fact sheet is intended to provide Scholastic Representatives with information about this exploratory program, information which is not available elsewhere."

The release goes on to note that Scholastic will be selling "that part of the Folkways library that is in most demand in schools and colleges. This consists of some 700 records chosen by Scholastic editors." It is revealing, to say the least, that nearly 60 percent of the Folkways catalog (at the time Folkways had about 1,200 titles in its inventory) is deemed to be "in demand" in educational institutions. Furthermore, Scholastic will be focusing their sales on "a very broad range of institutions," which include "kindergartens to colleges, from Sunday schools to museums and hospitals and schools for the deaf—any non-profit educational institution." It certainly seems that the Scholastic sales strategy should be put in some doubt, given their enthusiasm for targeting schools for the deaf for an LP record sales campaign! The release goes on to note that the initial contract was for eighteen months, with an option to continue to be exercised by Scholastic. Certainly, a provision for terminating the contract was also available to Folkways, but considering the advantage that the agreement seemed to provide for Folkways, Moe likely would not have invoked it.

A final point of interest in these dealings was the parallel agreement between Scholastic and Pioneer Record Sales, signed in May 1965. It is a statement of assignment directing that all payments due to Folkways will instead be paid to Pioneer Record Sales, Inc. Furthermore:

any advances, discounts, credits, payments, offsets, claims, refunds in favor of Scholastic Magazines, Inc. under said agreement may be claimed and collected by Scholastic Magazines, Inc. from Folkways Records and Service Corp. or may be offset against monies to be paid under this Assignment to Pioneer Record Sales, Inc.

This particular assignment is important because it again highlights the central role of Pioneer Record Sales in the management of Folkways accounts.[3]

The biggest question about this particular arrangement was why Moe would put Folkways on the line in the way that he did. There was a provision in which Scholastic had an option to purchase any of the masters that Folkways owned. In May 1968, Scholastic exercised this option for fifty-three recordings (see Appendix 11), which, as the letter states, "does not necessarily represent all of the Schedule A Masters which Scholastic may elect to purchase."[4] Interestingly, Moe suggested they use only the Ella Jenkins recordings as a test case to see what sort of difficulties they might encounter in transferring rights from Folkways to Scholastic.[5] In a comment to his lawyer after apprising him of the situation, Moe wrote that " . . . we discussed the fact that the record once purchased should not be a Folkways/Scholastic product or label. I said that I want it to be a Scholastic."[6]

Confirmation of this process is reflected in a note attached to a financial statement of the year ending 30 June 1965. Assumed to be based on information from "management" (i.e., Moe), the note indicates that:

After the close of the fiscal year, the company negotiated a contract with an educational publishing house, to handle all of its educational sales. Further negotiations are in process between the two parties whereby the entire catalog will either be sold or licensed for both commercial and educational distribution in return for "Folkways" relinquishment of all of its activities. In this event Folkways would receive royalties on record quantities sold. The sale includes existing inventories and mothers and stampers for a substantial sum, but will however materially restrict the company's future operations.

Almost immediately word started to get around about the Folkways/Scholastic agreement. In a particularly detailed letter to V. C. Clinton-Baddeley of Jupiter Records in London, Moe goes to great lengths to explain the relationship that exists between Folkways, Scholastic, and Jupiter[7]:

. . . starting in the early spring and continuing till last month, I have not been able to have any clear positive indication as to where Folkways stood in relationship to schools. Now it has become more clarified, although new concepts occur every day. First of all, none of the Jupiter records have appeared on any list other than the Folkways catalog, as I have no rights to cross license. Scholastic Magazines is negotiating and has a temporary arrangement with me to be the exclusive distributor of Folkways Records all over the world for educational purposes. They have negotiated with me first for all the recordings which I have all rights to, which are called "Schedules A," and which they contemplate purchasing eventually. Naturally, the Jupiter licensed recordings do not fall in this category. Recently Scholastic Magazines asked me to act as a consultant in relationship to the exploitation of phonograph records in education, with an emphasis on the college and higher education market. Naturally, Jupiter Recordings fit right into this area.

It is my thought that we should have a permanent arrangement as we have now, and you would be getting the same royalties and authors' fees as you are now. Also, the name Jupiter-Folkways would be used on the label. In this way, Scholastic, through its arrangement with Folkways, would naturally include these within the catalog of Folkways records and be able to merchandise and exploit Jupiter-Folkways in the same manner as it does Folkways records. . . .

Business in education for English recordings, especially at the college level during the last year, has been very poor. First Caedmon controlled the field and second, Columbia Records, MGM, London and Argo have pressured the area of college English and I did not have sufficient finances to counteract this pressure. Now with Scholastic Magazines being interested in exploiting this market, if the same arrangement that you and I have had before continues, they will be in a position to exploit to our mutual benefit the recordings you so well put together. Also, I would be in a better situation to issue more of your catalogs than I have in the last year. . . .

In a second letter to V. C. Clinton-Baddeley about eighteen months later, Moe continues[8]:

The agreement with Scholastic and Folkways is for a 5 year period. Folkways leases to Scholastic its catalog-name and agreements (contracts). Scholastic must maintain the same items that Folkways did in the same manner and pay Folkways for this right and also pay Folkways the royalty due as per contract with Folkways licensees. Scholastic pays Folkways all moneys (sic), then Folkways distributes.

Scholastic will be issuing its own records too. I am hired as a consultant in the audio-visual area. Primarily to oversee the Folkways operation to be sure that the items issued are as I want them. Part of the time will be devoted to help them in production and promotion of their own product. Meanwhile I have still three labels of my own that do not come under their agreement: Asch, RBF, and Broadside. And I wanted to take life easy.

It is interesting to note that Moe maintained his independence, even while trying to "take life easy" by keeping separate the three subsidiary labels of Asch, RBF, and Broadside. Whether or not Scholastic was aware of these labels when making the deal with Folkways is not known, but they were likely ignored by Scholastic because of their comparatively small size and catalog.

With such a large agreement in place for the requisite first five years, it is not surprising that there was some difficulty in getting things "back to normal" at the expiration of the agreement. However, there is considerable disagreement over when exactly Folkways regained control over its catalog from Scholastic. The original agreement held for five years with the possibility of extension. By most accounts, that option was not exercised due to the inability of Scholastic to market Folkways with any great success. Larry Sockell, who was also kept on as a consultant, recounted that even with all the salesmen that Scholastic had at the time, they would spend all their time marketing to schools. Although schools were part of the Folkways target market, they would only order one or two of any title.[9] Scholastic ended up ignoring most of the retailers and distributors that Larry knew so well.

The end result was that although Folkways helped get Scholastic into the audio/visual arena in the school system, they really had no idea how to merchandise the range of the catalog they were handling. Furthermore, according to reports at the time, the costs of inventory for such a large collection of recordings, along with the administration and sales force needed to sell them, quickly turned Scholastic sour on the agreement. Reports that the deal failed at the five-year mark support the general sentiment that Scholastic could not or would not continue with Folkways. However, the five-year mark would be April/May 1970. In a letter of agreement from Scholastic Magazines dated 4 June 1970, Scholastic licensed five Folkways titles (6804, 8712, 4251, 4439, and 4539) to Nippon Columbia of Japan. In the first clause of the agreement, Scholastic refers to "the Asch/Scholastic distribution agreement which expires on August 31, 1971."[10]

The correspondence that follows this agreement is rife with confusion about who is actually responsible for the terms with Nippon Columbia. Eventually it appears as though Scholastic handed the agreement back to Moe. Even though Moe did not sign the agreement, he seemed to agree to go along with it. As late as February 1972, checks were being paid to

Scholastic for agreements already transferred back to Folkways and Pioneer, with numerous memos and calls back and forth to track payments.[11] Finally in May 1972, Carl Sandberg from Scholastic attempted to clear up the mess with Nippon Columbia in particular by writing that "Moses Asch is the owner of both the Folkways and Pioneer Record Companies, and is no longer associated with Scholastic International."[12]

However, in the 1983 interviews between Moe and Smithsonian representatives concerning the possible sale of Folkways, Moe maintained that the Scholastic agreement tied up Folkways for ten years, not five as some of the documentation indicates. Moe explained that[13]:

> I had a deal with Scholastic Magazine—a ten year deal—in which they paid me dollar for dollar for the stock. I have about a 300K record stock. Then they gave me money for supervising the thing on top of it. Then they operated it. It didn't come out though because they were really not interested. They used Folkways in order to get into the audio/visual with the schools. . . . They took over the producing, the selling and everything. I got a royalty for every record sold and I got a weekly stipend, for hanging around doing whatever they wanted me to do.
>
> [In the end, the Scholastic arrangement] had been a disaster. Although I made a lot of money, . . . it doesn't enhance Folkways in any way. When you went to a convention, all you saw was Scholastic, they forgot there was a Folkways. I lost ten years of exposure. All they did was make a catalog they sent out.

There are a lot of discrepancies between Moe's account and the documentation at the time. Perhaps one explanation was that Moe continued with Scholastic domestically while exercising his option to terminate the agreement for international distribution. However, although the agreement itself does appear to allow a provision to split distribution like that, it would not make much sense for Scholastic to terminate part of the agreement that was so closely tied to what was happening domestically. The second possibility was that it simply took ten years for Moe to get out from under such an enormous agreement. In the end, the Scholastic Magazines/Folkways Records agreement was ultimately a big mistake from both sides, despite the fact that Moe made a lot of money. Little exposure and poor management came close to crippling Folkways, and in large part explains why there is not much documentation of Folkways' activities through the period. Another side to the story might be that, as Moe's appeal for a loan from K. O. Asher in 1964 indicated, things were looking pretty bleak for sales in the early to mid-1960s. Moe could easily have seen the Scholastic and MGM agreements as a solution to a cash-flow problem while letting other people do most of the work. In the end, it did not work out that way, but in the beginning, these agreements were likely seen as a golden opportunity.

After regaining Folkways's back catalog from Scholastic, Asch was again faced with the problem of distributing his product. Apparently, by the early 1970s, Pioneer was moribund, so a second distribution company was developed. The reasons it was developed are not clear at all, but with an endearing name like The Blue Giraffe, Ltd., it warrants at least a mention. Very little documentation exists for the company, but a very interesting unsigned agreement outlining the purpose of Blue Giraffe is worth investigation. Dated 7 February 1972, the document[14] outlines an agreement between Moe Asch and Dr. Barry Lew, giving each man 50 percent ownership in Blue Giraffe. The contract sets out that Blue Giraffe Ltd. "is to be the national distributor of Folkways Records with the exception of its educational business and those trade accounts which cannot be economically handled." Moe was also agreeing to take on quite a bit of the risk of the enterprise. The agreement sets out that "The books and records of Blue Giraffe are to be kept at the offices of Moses Asch, whose address shall also be used for billing and receipt of funds," and Moe agreed to put up a $7,000 loan to get the Blue Giraffe off the ground. It is interesting that the contract is dated 7 February 1972, but the agreement as it is set out, expired on 30 April 1972–not much time at all.

A catalog release from 1971—predating the agreement—describes Blue Giraffe as a "Distributor of High Performance Recordings" doing business out of the 701 7th Avenue location in New York City. In the catalog, titles from other companies are also available, including Arhoolie, Delmark, Orion Records, and also Scholastic. Unfortunately, it appeared as though such a distribution plan was not very successful. A wage statement from 1973[15] indicates that Moe only grossed $4,800—not a stellar income. In fact, by spring of 1974, an income tax extension request[16] indicates that "the company has ceased operation and has no employees any longer. To date, the books of the company have not been closed for the year and therefore the company is unable to file its return by the due date"—all in all, a short-lived but illustrative company. Moe was still keeping his eyes open for additional ways to diversify his cash flow. In this case, not much came of it, but Blue Giraffe does not appear to have cost Moe much capital over the three years of its existence.

A third and equally mystical company (from a documentary point of view) can be found in Aschco Records Inc. Operating out of 43 West 61st Street, New York City, the life span of Aschco was a bit longer than Blue Giraffe, if not any more active. A notice from the Internal Revenue Service assigning a new employer number starts the clock on 9 August 1977.[17] Very little other information is available, other than some banking information that indicates quite active deposits and withdrawals[18] in early 1981. A pair of corporate resolutions confirm a relationship between Folkways Records and Aschco Records at the same time:

> At a meeting of the Board of Directors, of the Aschco Records, Inc., this 17th day of February 1981, it is resolved by a unanimous vote, that checks made payable to the Folkways Records and Service Corp., may be deposited into the bank account of the corporation. Folkways Records and Service Corp. being a related and parent company of Aschco Records, Inc.[19]

A virtually identical resolution was written up to reflect the agreement of the Folkways Board of Directors to this arrangement.[20] Both copies have signing spaces for Moses Asch, President and Marilyn Conklin (nee Averett), Secretary. One suspects that they comprised the board of directors of both organizations. Although the purpose and function of the company is unclear, the company was writing checks up to the final year of Folkways Records. A check was written to cover what appear to be Folkways invoices on 19 February 1986. Perhaps this is the clue to the function of the company: to provide an additional conduit to move funds about in the most economical and strategic fashion.

Reaching the Popular Market

On a similar, but slightly smaller scale, the MGM/Folkways agreement was concluded at virtually the same time as the Scholastic/Folkways agreement. Signed on 1 April 1965,[21] it gave MGM the right to manufacture, release, and distribute recordings from masters owned by Folkways, and to be released on the label Verve-Folkways for two years with a three-year renewal clause. The main recordings of interest are the masters listed on the attached Schedule A of the agreement (Appendix 12). MGM also had an interest in a second set of Schedule B masters (Appendix 13) that were subject to additional conditions of access. These conditions allowed Folkways to release Schedule B masters for an additional six months after notification from MGM that they wished to release a particular title in either the United States or Canada. Further, if MGM ceased to release a schedule B master in both the United States and Canada, the master automatically reverted back to Folkways. If MGM wished to rerelease a schedule B master, it could give the six-month notice as stated in the first condition.

Also mentioned in the agreement was a set of schedule C masters (a listing or further mention of these masters outside of the agreement has not been found) subject to a similar set of conditions to the schedule B masters. An additional proviso was put in place, however, that demanded that all schedule A and schedule B masters must be in current release prior to the release of any schedule C masters. Furthermore, if any schedule A or B masters were to cease being released by MGM, then all schedule C masters would revert back to Folkways. Although a bit complicated, it would be reasonable speculation that this addition to the contract was only a protective clause that allowed further expansion of the terms of the contract without having to reexecute the contract. However, given the size of the schedule B masters list, it is not surprising that MGM never released all of the schedule A and B masters.

In terms of control, MGM was granted by Folkways nonexclusive use of the name "Folkways" in connection to the A, B, and C masters, of course with final approval by Folkways. Interestingly, Folkways granted MGM the right to use "Verve-Folkways" on all labels, packaging, etc., of releases not covered under the A, B, or C schedules on a consent basis, possibly to cover material originating from MGM. The agreement was also geographically limited in the first year to distribution within the United States and Canada. After 31 March 1966, the rights became worldwide, subject to the limitations in place from prior agreements.

A list of short conditions then followed in the agreement:

- MGM was allowed to sublicense material to Canada only through Capri Productions, Inc. Any other sublicense agreements require written consent from Folkways.
- Folkways could order from MGM recordings made from schedules A, B, or C at MGM's cost for Folkways to sell to educational institutions.
- Folkways could license schedule A, B, or C masters to educational institutions during contract with MGM, as long as such institutions do not sell below Folkways' present effective wholesale price.
- Folkways had sole control over the order of presentation of material on individual recordings made from schedule A, B, or C masters.
- All schedule A, B, and C masters released by MGM shall be solely Verve-Folkways.

The issue of payment was naturally at the center of such an agreement. In this case, MGM agreed to pay reasonably well under the terms of the contract. For brevity's sake, the terms are listed in point form below:

- Folkways received 8.5 percent of the retail selling price[22] on 90 percent of recordings that contain schedule A, B, or C masters and that have not been returned.

- If not all releases are from schedule A, B, or C masters, then the above royalty will be paid according to the fraction of [number of Folkways masters] ÷ [total number of masters on the recordings].
- MGM will pay 35 percent of 90 percent of sales not returned (or a fraction as defined above) of records sold by MGM through record clubs other than a record club owned and operated by MGM.
- MGM will pay 35 percent of all gross sums on sales of A, B, or C masters outside the U.S.
- MGM will pay 35 percent or all money received by MGM through public performance of recordings containing A, B, or C masters.
- No payment will be made on promotional copies given away free of charge.
- No royalty will be paid on "cutouts" [deleted records sold at discount] sold below cost by MGM, provided they are not selling the same schedule A, B, or C masters through regular channels, and Folkways receives thirty-day written notice of such a sale.
- Folkways may, within twenty days of receiving MGM's notice of intent to sell recordings as cutouts, may buy the cutouts at the price offered by the purchasing company. Selling cutouts will constitute cessation of production and the rights to such masters will revert back to Folkways.
- Finally, MGM agreed not to sell as scrap any material made from A, B, or C masters.

The importance and scope of this agreement is reflected in the size of the advances paid by MGM to Folkways in each year of the contract. The contract itself was set to expire in two years with options to renew the agreement on a yearly basis for three more years.[23] In each of these years, a nonreturnable advance was paid, to be recouped under certain conditions by MGM through sales throughout the year. Following the contract dates 1 April to 31 March, in the first year (1965), MGM was to advance Folkways $35,000 and $45,000 in 1966. If the option to renew the contract was exercised (and it is not clear if it was—although likely is wasn't), the advances would have been $45,000 in 1967, and $50,000 for the last two years of the agreement.

A second contract was also signed by Moe in connection to the MGM production/distribution agreement. As with Scholastic, the contract was to be a parallel agreement between MGM and Pioneer Record Sales, Inc. The contract,[24] signed 3 May 1965,[25] begins by stating that MGM agrees that Pioneer Record Sales has "a binding arrangement with Folkways whereby you [Pioneer] alone are empowered to distribute within the United States of America all phonograph records embodying the said recorded performance." With this contract, MGM agreed to take over part of the distribution role that Pioneer performed on behalf of Folkways Records while still allowing Pioneer to maintain distribution of Folkways within the limits of the MGM/Folkways agreement. The payment for such an acquisition by MGM amounted to the following:

- MGM will pay Pioneer 4 percent of retail on 90 percent of all non-returned sales of A and B masters[26] within the United States.
- MGM will pay 15 percent of gross sales not returned (or a fraction as defined above) of records sold by MGM through record clubs other than a record club owned and operated by MGM.
- MGM will pay 15 percent of all gross sums on sales of A, B, or C masters outside the U.S.
- MGM will pay 15 percent or all money received by MGM through public performance of recordings containing A, B, or C masters.

The payment schedule for Pioneer was to be $15,000 per year for the first three years (3 May to 2 May of the following year). Again, provided the option to renew was exercised, payments would continue at $15,000 for 1968 and 1969, $20,000 for 1970, and $15,000 for the final two years, 1971 and 1972.[27]

The combination of these two agreements—with Folkways for material, with Pioneer for distribution rights—ties together Moe's two main enterprises. In fact, it is a particularly clever arrangement that, when combined, gave Moe $50,000 for the first year, $60,000 in each of the second and third years, and $65,000 in each of the fourth and fifth years. In addition, Moe would receive:

- 12.5 percent of 90 percent of nonreturned retail sales in the U.S.
- 50 percent of 90 percent of non-MGM record club sales, plus 15 percent of the remaining 10 percent of sales.
- 50 percent on gross sales by MGM licensees outside of the U.S.
- 50 percent on gross sums generated by public performance.

There is little doubt that this was one of the more lucrative contracts that Moe signed. However, what is most interesting is that the MGM/Folkways agreement, the Scholastic/Folkways agreement, the MGM/Pioneer agreement, and the Scholastic/Pioneer assignment agreement all were executed within a month of each other. It seemed, however, that the MGM deal took care of some of the more popular items while the Scholastic agreement took over the educational material. Although there might not have been any conflicting interests, it does have the appearance of a potentially hostile set of arrangements, given the overlap in potential markets that each recording might have.

Apparently, however, it did not seem to Moe that there was a conflict. In fact, it seemed that these arrangements were just the ticket to ease up his schedule. Now in his early sixties, Moe was clearly starting to think about the future. A draft announcement concerning the contracts points out that[28]:

> 1) For general consumer use of Folkways Records, the world's largest producer of authentic Folk Music on records, has made a long term arrangement with MGM Records.
>
> It was mutually agreed that Folkways should maintain its unique ability to create recordings that have lasting value while MGM with its vast facilities of exploitation and merchandising would take the more commercial items and give them the exposure that an independent like Folkways would not be able to do. The first releases will be on a new label called VERVE-FOLKWAYS, dedicated to maintaining the Folkways concept, will consist of five previous Folkways releases and five releases of unissued masters from the vast Folkways archives with such artists as Pete Seeger, Woody Guthrie, Cisco Houston, Lead Belly and The New Lost City Ramblers.
>
> 2) In education, a field that Folkways Records has pioneered in: creating and issuing material especially adapted for school use. Today Folkways Records is one of the leaders in sales and exploitation in the use of recordings for education. With the ever expanding demand for its product, Folkways in order to better serve the school systems and individual teachers has made an exclusive arrangement with Scholastic Magazines, Inc. of 50 West 44th Street, New York City, to distribute and exploit the Educational Folkways Catalog that consists of Ethnic Music, Literature, Music Instruction, Foreign Language, Historic Documentaries in both spoken and folk song, Science and the many children oriented recordings.
>
> With the educational and consumer merchandising taken care of, Moses Asch, the Director of Folkways Records, is now free to pursue the areas most interesting to him and one that he is noted for that of recording and producing material on records that is unique and valid to preserve. Folkways catalog with its 1300 record albums is still available and is still being merchandised by the 20 distributors that is the core of its sales organization. The restrictions are only in the educational field and those masters that MGM Records has made arrangement for and has issued.

Ultimately, however, it does not appear that the MGM/Folkways agreement lasted much beyond the initial two-year period. In fact, the only real evidence that any recordings were actually released under the MGM/Folkways agreement (aside from a few records with the "Verve-Folkways" label on them) is the listing of "Verve/Folkways Releases from FV/FVS 9000" that itemized twenty-five recordings (Appendix 14).

As we have seen, Moe was often quick to license material for release. Through Scholastic, Moe was sure that exploiting such a licensing opportunity would help his expansion in the educational realm. As outlined above, it was a difficult and less than successful undertaking. Given the chance, however, Moe was quick to find other outlets for his catalog: in this instance, using his relationship with CBS Special Products to license additional educational material. Beginning in the late 1960s and lasting more than a decade, CBS licensed a wide variety of material for an array of educational projects. Many of the licenses were single items, but there were, on occasion, quite elaborate contracts that Moe was able to make on a nonexclusive basis. This was important because during much of this time, the Scholastic agreement was in place, which allowed Moe some leeway to negotiate additional agreements for material. Interestingly, in a couple of licensing agreements, there are notations that indicate Scholastic received a portion (usually 50 percent) of the license fee.[29]

The Revival of DISC Records

Following the bankruptcy of DISC Records in the late 1940s, it has often been assumed that the label died once and for all. However, there was quite a concerted effort in the early part of 1964 to get DISC back into action. Although there is no definitive evidence that the promotion of the label was related to the Scholastic and MGM deals with Folkways, the timing is noteworthy. Returning to DISC has every appearance of the reestablishment of a label that Moe had sole control over in the face of reduced input and control within Folkways.

The first step was perhaps a unique one for Moe: he attempted to get a copyright on the name DISC Records. There does not appear to be evidence of Moe attempting to register the names of any of his other enterprises, including Folkways (which caused difficulties with Folkways Music Publishing, an unrelated enterprise). Unfortunately, the attempt failed, in large part because of the commonality of the DISC name itself. A letter to Moe's attorney concerning the trademark search for DISC outlined that there were in fact five closely related trademarks that were already registered[30]: DUODISC, MELODISC, DICTATION DISC, DYNADISC, and THIS IS AMERIDISC.

Based on these findings, the attorneys go on to suggest that in light of the above registrants,

> we cannot recommend the adoption and use of the proposed mark, since obviously any one of the registrants might complain.
>
> Additionally, and also of controlling importance, is the fact that the word "DISC" as applied to records, which are commonly re-

ferred to as "discs", would unquestionably be held to be descriptive. Even if a client has had long use of the "DISC" as a trademark to identify its products, we are of the opinion that the mark would still not be registrable since it would be considered to be virtually impossible to preempt this generic term.

This was then reported through his own attorney to him[31] and, apparently, copyright efforts were abandoned.

However, this was not the end of the effort to reintroduce DISC onto the market. A month after the report on trademark (on 19 June 1964), a letter was sent to Walter Alshuk of RCA to summarize the terms concerning the introduction of DISC into the pressing orders[32]:

As a result of our conversation this morning, the following is, I believe, an accurate resume of our discussion.

Folkways Records is now producing a new label called DISC Records.

It is projected that beginning in July, DISC will issue an average of three new records per month. Opening orders will probably be in the area of 1,000 per record minimum, with actual sales determining re-order quantities. Re-orders plus new releases on DISC will probably average 10,000 plus per month, and possibly much higher.

Estimating the dollar volume which both DISC and Folkways will be doing with RCA as closely as possible we calculate that our billing with you will be $5,000 to $6,000 per month. Further: As this is the nature of the business, as RCA well knows, we must give our distributors the usual 60-90-120 day dating and as a consequence we must anticipate receiving at least the same terms from RCA.

Important:

(a) You will receive weekly payments on account from us.

(b) Folkways as the producer of DISC will be responsible for payment.

Conservatively, we expect to do a sizable volume on DISC and would like to have RCA do all, or the bulk of the catalog for us.

It appears that these terms were satisfactory as the next piece of documentation was a credit guarantee to assure credit for pressings. Interestingly, the guarantor in this case is Pioneer Record Sales, Inc. who backed DISC for $10,000.[33] This is a particularly good example of the importance on Moe's part of having at least two concerns that are financially active (if not necessarily always solvent). It is doubtful whether Folkways would have had the financial resources or have been in the position to back the credit demands covered by Pioneer.

In any event, all things appeared to be ready to go by the time of the press release in January of 1965[34]:

New York, NY (Special)—DISC IS BACK! DISC RECORDS, the leading and influential giant of Folk-Blues-Jazz, which rode the crest of popularity during the mid-forties, thanks to the keen devotion of GI's returning from World War Two, is back on the record scene again!

Ahead of its time in both record content and packaging, two decades ago, DISC's graphic covers were graced with the tasteful and exciting work of many contemporary artists, including David Stone Martin. The DISC packaging concept ultimately became the standard for the entire phonograph record industry. Previously, record jackets contained only the recording artist's name and a group of song titles.

The *new* DISC line is moderately priced and provides excellent Folk and Blues material by top names in attractive packaging that reflects the personalities of its artists. Most of DISC's releases are available in both Mono ($3.98) and Bi-Sonic Stereo ($4.98).

Reappearing for the first time last Fall, the label won immediate renown with its *Sing With Seeger* LP which is still selling well. During the past few months albums by Cisco Houston, The New Lost City Ramblers and a Ghana "High Life" set, have been added to the DISC catalog.

Now the firm is aggressively geared to begin 1965 with a long list of top-drawer releases including a Deluxe Box Set (FF 1) *Favorite Folk Songs,* a 3-12" package that programs the talents of Pete Seeger, Woody Guthrie and Lead Belly. The FF 1 set was shipped to distributors ten days ago.

Other exciting new DISC RECORDS releases (all 12" LP items) are: *Big Bill Broonzy Sings Country Blues*; *Hard Travelin* by Woody Guthrie; *The Friends of Old Time Music* which features Clarence Ashley, Mississippi John Hurt, the Stanley Brothers and other Folk Music All-Stars; *Old Time Music* by the New Lost City Ramblers and *Doc Boggs* a showcase of the famous banjoist-singer of the '20's who was rediscovered by Mike Seeger.

DISC RECORDS are distributed nationally by Pioneer Record Sales, 165 W. 46th St., New York NY 10036.

What is most interesting about this entire project is the timing. Many of these titles are the same titles that appeared to be doing quite well overseas, particularly on the Xtra line by Transatlantic Records in London. The project also appears to coincide with something of a resurgence in the popularity of many of the more traditional artists, including the perennially popular Pete Seeger. However, the fact that it appears to be a "moderately priced" line, compared to the premium prices of Folkways recordings, points to the possibility that Moe was looking for yet another way to capitalize on the situation most efficiently. Obviously rereleasing old material on another, slightly cheaper label not only created another income stream from material already at hand, but it would not distract Folkways from its release schedule of new material, nor would it necessarily interfere with any agreements with Folkways or Pioneer, as DISC would stand as a separate entity selling primarily to the domestic market. DISC records were also more conventionally packaged than Folkways' product; they appeared in regular record sleeves and did not include the inserted booklet that was the Folkways' hallmark.

An added dimension to all of this is the fact that Moe chose to resurrect DISC instead of creating a new label name, which he had done in the past. Perhaps Moe simply had a soft spot for the label and was waiting for a statute of limitations following the bankruptcy to expire. This may have been a very real possibility following the demise of the original incarnation of DISC, but it probably did not have much force the second time around. It appears that Moe was simply trying to capitalize on the former popularity of the DISC in the mid-1940s—which is abundantly clear in the press release. However, the fact that he was releasing primarily folk and blues material certainly changes the complexion of the company compared to the popularity the first company had built on jazz releases.

The final note about timing is related to the fact that both the Scholastic deal and the MGM deal were signed only three and four months, respectively, after the foregoing press release was generated. It would be hard to imagine that Moe did not have any inkling about upcoming agreements with Scholastic and MGM at the time of promoting DISC. Perhaps he thought that there would be no conflict among the various agreements and the operations of any new enterprises that he might engage in (in this case, DISC). Whatever the logic, it certainly has every appearance that any future DISC might have had ceased with this press release. There does not appear to be any other references to DISC activity in the archive, although there may have been a couple of releases after January 1965. Ultimately, the desire to resurrect DISC Records was intense but short lived.

Return to Normal Operations

The 1960s seemed to have ended on a positive note. But by the early 1970s, both the Scholastic and MGM agreements, although apparently lucrative, ultimately ended much more quickly than one would have expected. The only logical conclusion, in line with Larry's perception, was that neither

Scholastic nor MGM really had the knowledge to handle Folkways recordings. Both companies seemed to have the financial resources necessary to support such an endeavor. Certainly both companies were willing to pay for the opportunity to exploit the Folkways catalog. The fact that once the agreements were terminated, Moe went back to his regular routine and continued to release recordings for another fifteen years, would suggest that Moe knew something the others did not. This is certainly further evidence that Moe had Folkways and his sound encyclopedia constructed in a way that seem to confound typical business practices.

The quick demise of the new DISC might also be related to the short tenure of both agreements. This would also support the contention that the reason for reviving DISC was to allow Moe a creative outlet in the absence of control over Folkways. Once Folkways was returned to Moe's complete control, any efforts to maintain DISC might well have appeared superfluous and dropped. This would have allowed all efforts to focus once again on the Folkways project and the maintenance of the Folkways catalog.

8
The Sale of Folkways

In the early 1980s it became clear that Moe needed to return to the issue of succession in a serious way. Moe had long considered options to sell Folkways, beginning in the mid-1960s. One report suggested that one buyer was willing to pay Moe $1 million for the Folkways rights and inventory. However, the sticking point on that deal, as with every effort that followed, was Moe's refusal to sell Folkways to anyone who would not guarantee the integrity of the catalog. As he had maintained from the beginning, the sounds on Folkways were for "the People," and to take any title out of print would be to deny the fundamental right to know under the Constitution. On that basis alone, he refused to sell Folkways in the 1960s, and instead turned to elaborate licensing deals with Scholastic and MGM to lighten his workload. As we have seen, Folkways was returned to him, and Moe continued to work as hard as ever, even as he neared his 80th year.

A number of universities began to see the value in acquiring Folkways.[1] Moe had noted that the University of Washington and Dartmouth (through Jon Appleton)[2] had expressed interest, as well as the University of Maryland at Baltimore. Unfortunately, none of the schools could manage the scope of Folkways' demands. Ultimately, Moe spent considerable time trying to reach an agreement with Rutgers University. In the early 1980s, the jazz archives had become well established at Rutgers and they were consequently very interested in gaining access to the jazz recordings that Moe had done in the 1940s. In particular, they were after his James P. Johnson recordings, in part because he was born in New Brunswick, New Jersey, the home of Rutgers. However, the Rutgers proposal, spearheaded in large part by sociologist Irving Horowitz, would have had Rutgers University Press, which operated at arm's length from the University, take over

Folkways on a royalty or licensing basis, if Moe would donate his archive of material to the University. It seems that this type of arrangement would never suit Moe's demands of both keeping the archival material and the business together, as well as ensuring the ongoing integrity of the catalog. As a result, after much negotiation, Moe backed away from Rutgers' offer.

Moe then used his contact with friend and lawyer Chuck Seaton to help to actively seek out interested parties. One of those that Seaton contacted on Moe's behalf was Ralph Rinzler, then Director of the Smithsonian's International Center and cofounder and Director of the Smithsonian's Festival of American Folklife in Washington, D.C. A noted folk-music collector in his own right, Rinzler was highly placed in the hierarchy of the Smithsonian Institution. More importantly, he was well aware of the cultural value of Folkways and how well it would fit into the mandate of the Smithsonian.

Their first contact concerning a possible sale took place sometime in late 1983 or early 1984. Through a series of meetings and phone discussions that were recorded between Moe Asch, Ralph Rinzler, and Felix Lowe, Director of Smithsonian Institution Press, many of the operating details of Folkways were revealed. Given that so little of the actual operational information about Folkways is available during the last ten or so years prior to its sale, some of the details revealed in these discussions are particularly important.

One of the key elements that comes to the fore is the fact that Moe himself recognized the value of preserving the documents that this book is based on. In all of the documentation reviewed, it is only in these discussions that Moe acknowledges he had actively been keeping documents. As he said during a tour of Folkways, "here are the files from 1947 on, and correspondence. I try to keep the documentation as much as possible because it's of value." It is truly amazing that he had the foresight to see that in fact such documentation would play a key role in understanding the development of his life's work.

Moe also discussed some of the factors that have ultimately played important roles in the longevity and success of Folkways. He noted to Ralph and Felix that he deliberately kept staff at the most basic level of organization, pointing out that "everybody here has a function. One can go into another's. There's no such thing as this is yours, this is not. Everyone knows what goes on and can fill in." Furthermore, based on tax returns and the like, it is also clear that Moe kept employees for long periods, with most of the employees working for Folkways in the 1980s having been there well over ten years. Moe often hired some of the artists that he recorded to give them some income or opportunity. Despite his well-documented temper, Moe was clearly a fair and caring employer, and one who earned the loyalty of his employees.

Even as late as 1984, Folkways was still virtually a manual operation. Filling orders, shipping, packing slips, and all the accounting was still done by hand by one of a half-dozen employees. From such a small administrative base, Folkways was able to handle billing between $700,000 and $1 million a year. Sam Goody, Tower Records, and J&R Distributors were key outlets for Folkways in New York, with Goody carrying at least one of each of the 2000+ Folkways titles. Surprisingly, direct-mail order sales were comparatively small, given the nature of the Folkways' catalog, with billing typically ranging between $300 and $1,000 a week, only about 3 percent to 5 percent of total billing. From a sales point of view, however, it continued to fall to the Children's music to be the consistent moneymaker for Moe, with about 400 titles accounting for 40 percent to 50 percent of total billing—a very significant amount.

Ultimately, an agreement was reached between Moe and the Smithsonian Institution. The final terms of the agreement are not known; however, some of the negotiated terms are close to the purported terms of the final sale. The first document came shortly after the taped discussions previously referred to.[3] Dated 23 July 1984, some of the terms of previous discussions were set out for comment. Most of the provisions have some amendments to them, so it is difficult to say which terms remained in the final agreement and which did not. However, what is clear from this document is the seriousness with which the Smithsonian wanted to acquire Folkways.

The second document is more typically Moe. Unlike the extended legalese of the first draft of terms, the second letter is a single page from Moe to Ralph Rinzler. Dated nearly two years later (9 June 1986), it is clear that Moe wanted to get a deal done, although he was still open to other offers. The 11 points (they are numbered to 12, but Moe skipped number 9) of the letter are worth detailing here, particularly as Moe ends the letter, "This offer must be accepted and agreed to by no later than June 19 1986"—only 10 days from its writing.[4] The terms of the agreement are:

1. You will pay to Moses Asch $800,000, $400,000 now and $400,000 over the next four years.
2. 9% interest on unpaid balance.
3. 10 cents on each record sold over the next 10 years.
4. $200.00 per day for Moses Asch to work on Archives.
5. Reimbursement for lease security deposit and assumption of lease.
6. Current employees are to be retained for at least six months regardless of function.
7. $13,000 for the eight (8) master tapes that Moses Asch is working on.
8. Moses Asch has a right to produce tapes into the future, Smithsonian Institute (sic) will have the first refusal of tapes.

10. Accounts receivables to be discussed and finalized not later than June 19, 1986.
11. This collection is to be known as The Moses Asch, Frances Asch Ethnic Music Collection.
12. Moses Asch has other offers but Smithsonian Institute has first preference.

From my understanding of the eventual adoption of Folkways into the Smithsonian, it does appear that these terms are very close, if not exactly the terms ultimately agreed to. At the end of the day, what mattered most to Moe was that the Folkways catalog remained intact and available, that he received a fair value for the inventory and future earnings of Folkways, and that his employees were looked after. Moe was also able to continue to produce recordings under clause 8, in what seemed to be a standard escape clause. It is interesting to note that in the 1984 outline, the lawyer for the Smithsonian Institution worded the clause, "The Smithsonian Institution would employ for at least one year the existing key employees of Folkways, provided mutually agreeable employment terms can be reached." Beside the clause is a question mark, with the changes indicating that the first clause was not strong enough for Moe. Although employment would be for a shorter period, he wanted *all* his employees employed, period. Its reassuring to see that Moe would make a point of protecting those employees that had worked so long for him.

Clause 12 provides a slightly enigmatic reference to other offers. It is unclear if Moe was actually referring to an offer in particular, or if it was something of a negotiating ploy. There is no question that there were individuals and institutions that would have dearly loved to get their hands on the Folkways inventory, but it is doubtful whether any other offer would have been able to meet Moe's stringent demands. In any event, hindsight tells us that Moe accepted an offer from the Smithsonian either by the 19 June 1986 deadline or shortly thereafter. Interestingly, the first director of Smithsonian Folkways and curator of the Asch Archive was another important member of the Seeger clan, Dr. Anthony Seeger, Pete's nephew and an esteemed ethnomusicologist in his own right.

The timing itself could be considered prophetic. Only a few months after this offer was made, Moses Asch passed away in October 1986. It is certainly reassuring to know that such an important cultural legacy was not only taken in by one of the few organizations that could realistically protect it, but that involvement by Moe's son, Michael Asch, and the Asch family, as well as committed individuals within the Smithsonian Institution, will ensure that the Folkways catalog and archive will continue to grow and enrich the cultural landscape.

Folkways can literally be considered the life work of Moe Asch. His dedication and determination to ensure voices from around the globe are heard in perpetuity has given "the People" a rare gift. With the support of the Smithsonian Institution, The Center for Folklife and Cultural Heritage, Ralph Rinzler Folklife Archives and Collections, and the Moses and Frances Asch (Folkways) Collection, Folkways continues to produce landmark recordings, and to inspire listeners and performers all around the world.

Conclusion

In order to make some sense of the larger processes that Folkways has been subjected to and to better describe the place that Folkways occupies in the history of recording, it is best to take a step or two back from the details of its operation. As the scope of Folkways' history is examined, it becomes clear that the position that Folkways holds in relation to the rest of the recording industry is not what would be considered "typical" of a small, independent recording company. In fact, it becomes quite obvious that the defining features of Folkways are to be found in the foundations of production that Folkways was built on. Many of these issues have been touched on earlier in the book, but it will serve the history well to highlight these issues on their own. There are a number of answers to the question of "How did Folkways survive?" Brief discussion of some of the key elements will help to conclude this particular examination of Folkways, and, with some good fortune, will form the starting point for other works investigating other aspects of Folkways' history.

It is something of an inescapable fact that the identity of Folkways Records was absolutely and irrevocably tied to the identity of Moe Asch. Even now, more than fifteen years after his death in 1986, Folkways is still intimately associated with Moe. Although I have throughout this book attempted to isolate Folkways from Moe Asch, it is here that I must confess that I was not successful. To soften this failure, I must also confess that I do not believe that it is possible to deal with Folkways in the absence of Moe's personality and energies. Although Marian Distler and Marilyn Averett played very important supporting roles in the life of Folkways, it has always been Moe that put his stamp on the personality of Folkways. To put it another way, the business of Folkways is essentially the public persona of Moe Asch. Under different leadership, it would be hard to imagine Folkways maintaining its original mandate of sound collection, or even

183

establishing such a mandate in the first place. We must acknowledge the fortitude of Moe Asch in maintaining such a principled stance against the relentless pressures to generate profit.

Timing must also be considered a major factor in the success of Folkways. Moe came onto the electronics scene in the 1930s when there were significant opportunities in the marketplace for electronic expertise. The formation of Asch Records in 1939/1940 allowed Moe to begin to benefit not only from the dearth of ethnic (particularly Jewish) recordings, but also from the considerable consumer income that was still available prior to the United States' entry into World War II in 1941. Even with the imposition of shellac rations during the war, Moe was still able to connect with Harris and Prosky (Stinson Trading) to continue to produce much of the material that he recorded. The relationship with Stinson did eventually become a very sour one. However, it is doubtful that Moe could have continued recording without the arrangement.

Moe managed to maintain some of his momentum in the recording business by starting DISC Records in late 1945/early 1946. Not only did DISC allow Moe to move away from the entanglement of the Asch/Stinson difficulties, but it also gave him a new banner under which to expand his ideas about the kinds of music that he wanted to release. Asch Records, to some extent, had come to be associated with ethnic and some classical recordings. DISC Records gave Moe an avenue to explore much of the jazz material that he had recorded throughout World War II, but had not had the opportunity to release through Asch Records. Importantly, it was also during the war years that Moe began his associations with Pete Seeger, Woody Guthrie, and Huddie Ledbetter (Lead Belly). Although unknown at the time, the enduring popularity and importance of these three figures alone gave Moe a very solid foundation from which to launch Folkways.

Undoubtedly, lessons were learned in the failures of both Asch and DISC Records. Although these difficulties would be considered by most to be the worst kind of bad luck for Moe, it provided him with two important opportunities. The first was a chance to once again reformulate his vision of what he wanted to accomplish with his recordings. Although his fateful meeting with Albert Einstein is often cited as the seminal moment for the formation of the "sound encyclopedia" concept that he developed throughout his life, I believe the failures of Asch and DISC also played an important part in giving Moe the experience and the perspective necessary to pursue his ultimate goal. It might even be said that DISC would likely have become what Folkways is today, had it been able to survive.

The second bit of good fortune that came along was the chance to form Folkways with the help and dedication of Marian Distler. Were it not for the DISC bankruptcy and the opportunity for Marian to purchase the

DISC assets, Moe might have lost his assets and Folkways might not have been created. Nevertheless, what really propelled Folkways forward very early was the fact that Moe had already amassed a considerable number of titles that could be released on the new label. This gave Moe an important advantage during the creation phase of Folkways. The "recycling" of many titles allowed Moe (and Marian as the *prima facie* owner) to cut costs substantially during the first months and years of Folkways. In some respects, Moe was able to present Folkways as a virtually fully formed concept with a range of titles that immediately reflected his vision.

At the same time, and throughout his life, Moe was able to create value where little or no value seemingly existed. Moe would take a sound object of apparently very limited or marginal value, turn it into a recording, market and distribute the recording, and later generate a greater value for that sound object. This is true for a variety of recordings ranging from the first recordings of Pete Seeger and Woody Guthrie at a time when they might not have been recorded otherwise, to poets, composers, actors, and the array of "nonhuman" sounds. Moe is often given credit for having "discovered" such American musicians as Clarence Ashley, Hazel Dickens, and Doc Watson. To be fair, much of the credit goes to the folklorists who worked for Moe, like Mike Seeger, John Cohen, and Ralph Rinzler, to name just a few. These examples, and an enormous variety of others, demonstrate that despite the apparently "normal" operating practice of Folkways, its position with respect to capitalism was critical to making such a "value translation" a success.

A slightly different angle on the issue of value creation is to see Folkways as a "spatial" translator as well. Much of the material on Folkways came from geographically diverse locations. Folkways provided a repository (and occasionally the funds) to transfer or transport materials to New York at least for evaluation, if not release.[1] In taking recordings from one part of the world and presenting them in a form that could be merchandised in another part of the world, Moe "created" value by providing a type of music that no one had heard before. By using ethnomusicologists, travelers, or professional musicians and recordists to collect this material, Moe was able to transform the geographical differences into value differences within the Folkways sales universe.[2]

In bringing such diverse recordings to the attention of the record-buying public, Moe also managed to develop a label identity that was unusual for the recording industry. Likely started in part as a cost-saving measure, and certainly in response to the huge volume of recordings that Folkways would release, any promotion that was done was largely done from a topical, geographic, or genre approach. Folkways simply could not afford to promote each recording individually as most larger companies do. What was most important was the fact that promotion was always about Folk-ways Records as an entity. This step, a sound one from the point of view of getting the most promotion bang for the buck, grew into an important force in the "alternative" markets for recordings. With a few exceptions, Folkways' customers were drawn to the label out of interest in the content and not necessarily by the identity of the performers. Interest in the products that Folkways had to offer was more often expressed in terms of statements like "Folkways recordings of this type of music" or "recordings of this instrument or from that region of the world" to be able to list the most titles in the smallest printed space.

The timing of Folkways's beginning was also (serendipitously) advantageous, because it corresponded with the beginning of the LP era. LPs—which could hold between forty and sixty minutes of music—were an ideal format for achieving Asch's vision. His earlier 78 rpm albums—often including six to twelve individual records and a booklet—were a far more cumbersome and expensive to package. After the introduction of the LP, there were very few technological changes that Moe had to deal with. The 45 rpm record, introduced within a year of the LP by RCA, failed to challenge the convenience and capacity of the 33⅓ LP. Though the 45 did find a home in the jukeboxes that were increasingly popular at the time, the reasons Moe paid little attention to it are pretty obvious. Little of the material that Moe released would lend itself to single-song play on jukeboxes or within the singles market that grew in the 1950s and 1960s. While a few Folkways recordings are known to have been released on 45, it is clear that the 45 rpm record did not represent a meaningful advance for Moe and was largely ignored.

The introduction of stereo recording, on the other hand, proved to be a slightly more problematic issue for Moe. Although the idea was first developed in the 1930s, the first viable stereo recording and playback systems were not introduced until the mid-1950s, with tape being introduced in 1959.[3] Moe's distaste for the whole concept of stereo, particularly as it represented an alteration of the original sound document, was barely disguised. Although Moe did concede to some pressure with the release of a variety of Folkways titles in stereo, they were often titles that were simply rereleases of existing monaural recordings. Interestingly, Moe eventually regarded stereo recordings not as the ultimate goal of all recordings, but simply as another variety of sound document and assigned it its own prefix: "FSS." Moe even flirted with quadrophonic sound in the 1970s. They were innovations to be taken seriously, but only insofar as it was part of the sound encyclopedia, despite being antithetical to his own recording philosophy.

The introductions of eight-track and cassette tape formats also did not have a significant impact on Folkways production as a whole. Much to Moe's credit, he was always open to exploring new ways of getting his product to those who wanted it, and did actively investigate using tape technologies. Nonetheless, even through the 1970s, eight-track tapes found little footing in the Folkways inventory. Although there is tiny bit of evidence that Moe did attempt to use eight-tracks, on the whole, it likely would not have been a format that appealed to the "typical" Folkways buyer, like libraries, schools, and more conservative listeners. Certainly, the LP format would still have been predominant, and Moe would not have seen much reason to push the change.

Cassettes, on the other hand, did fall within the range of practical formats, particularly with its relatively longer market presence from the late 1960s into the 1980s. That said, there is little evidence that cassettes fared any better as a vehicle for Folkways recordings. One gets the distinct impression that by the late 1960s and early 1970s, major changes in technology as they applied to Folkways would be left to the next caretaker of the enterprise. Moe likely did not see much value in strongly pursuing such technologies as long as LPs continued to be a viable format.

The final note on technology for Folkways pertains to the compact disc and future digital technology. With the introduction of the CD the early 1980s, it would have only been of passing interest to Moe, though I am sure he would have been quick to see its potential value. The CD has proven to have the same technological advantages over an LP as the LP did over the 78, with several additional improvements. Compact discs—and the range of technologies that stem from them—give the longer, uninterrupted playing time that is ideal for the presentation of musics that Folkways continues to be known for. All the other advantages of digital technology—clarity, consistency, portability—have been perfect for the perpetuation of the Folkways mandate. Today, Smithsonian Folkways offers an "on-demand" service, creating the recording as the customer requests it with no standing inventory in a warehouse somewhere—a situation that Moe would have been very happy with.

Perhaps the most important aspect of the relationship between technology and Folkways, however, is the increasing transparency between the artist and the listener that Moe so wanted to achieve. The Internet, digital music formats like streaming audio and MP3, and the proliferation of playback formats give Folkways the means to continue to get the world's music to people in a fashion that really will make Folkways an "invisible conduit from the world to the ears of human beings."

Moe had always been sensitive to the changing demands of the marketplace on the economic stability of all his enterprises, especially Folkways.

From a production and reproduction standpoint, probably the single-most important element in the success of Folkways has been its flexibility. From the very beginning, Moe managed Folkways in such a way as to prevent economic concerns from burdening the production process. Moe was continually trying to keep necessary costs low, from production, salaries (including his own), rent, office expenses, and travel expenses. At the same time, Moe attempted to make as many costs as possible conditional on completed sales, rather than projected sales. As a result, when sales did occur, other costs would come into play—shipping and commissions, for example—but these would only been incurred on the basis of actual sales. Moe could then decide how many recordings he could put into production based on actual cash flow, instead of estimated sales income.

Another area where flexibility has been critical, but largely misunderstood with respect to Folkways, has been the issue of pressing recordings. Much has been made over the fact that Moe was consistently being punished financially for only pressing the absolute minimum numbers of most Folkways titles. In fact, the opposite is true: such minimum pressings were absolutely critical to Folkways' success. The first, and most obvious benefit was that Moe tended to press only as many records as he needed—either to meet the minimum of the pressing plant, or the minimum that he would need to sell to break even—usually no more than 300 to 500 copies. The premium that Moe paid to get so few pressings of a title has often been regarded as a foolish waste of money on Moe's part. However, if Moe had pressed, for example, 1,000 or 5,000 copies of a title in order to save a few cents per copy on the pressing, he would be faced with other astronomical expenses.

The biggest difficulty was that he was required to pay excise taxes on any recordings that he manufactured, not on the quantities that he sold. For an organization like Folkways to unnecessarily commit itself to such an enormous up-front expense would have been disastrous. The second issue that arises from this pressing strategy is storage. For most recording companies, the expected turnover of thousands of copies of a few titles would justify the cost of short-term storage through increased cash flow and (hopefully) profit. However, Folkways was in the opposite position. With several hundreds of titles (culminating in nearly 2,200 in 1986), even 200 or 300 copies of each title would represent considerable storage pressures (see Table 27, for example). In addition, the booklets for all of the records also had to be stored prior to being packaged with the record. Finally, there was a reasonable chance a large percentage of any title pressed might take years to sell out, if ever. Keeping production numbers low simply made much more long-term economic sense.

There is a related point that should also be addressed. There is a commonly held belief that many of Moe's pressings were done out of the goodness and generosity of the printers and pressers involved. Undoubtedly at slow times of the year, or when credit was needed to get some pressings done, Moe would rely on such favors. However, it is misleading to suggest, as Goldsmith somewhat derisively does, that "his production process was only made possible by businessmen who had a soft spot for Asch and his quixotic enterprise. Who else would have been permitted such minuscule production runs and repressings?"[4]

To imagine that Moe only pressed 50 or 100 copies of recordings at a time is to miss the point. He had several hundred titles to press. At the end of the 1960s, the period to which Goldsmith referred above, the Folkways catalog was likely nearing 1,700 or 1,800 titles. Although exact figures are not available, the financial data described earlier would suggest production figures in the region of 125,000 to 200,000 copies a year. This is supported by the correspondence with his pressing company assuring Moe of the capacity for 3,500 to 4,500 copies a week (perhaps 180,000 to 230,000 copies a year).

These numbers are not inconsequential for a company that had already been in business for twenty years and had contracts with smaller custom printing and pressing companies. Although there very well might have been goodwill for Moe's "quixotic enterprise," I would suggest that with respect to production, much of the goodwill was related to Folkways (and Moe) being a long-standing customer with fairly substantial orders. Particularly if Moe was using companies with smaller production ranges, these numbers would form a considerable part of the production process. It is largely a myth that it was simple charity on anyone's part to support Moe. More accurately, many smaller companies needed Moe as much as he needed them, and several smaller pressers and printers would likely be willing to extend some flexibility in part based on the history of Folkways, but also to keep a consistent customer.

It is perhaps appropriate here to consider the catalog more specifically. The ultimate size of the Folkways catalog suggests that Moe did, in fact, come close to achieving his goal of creating the "sound encyclopedia" that he first envisioned as a young man. It is quite a remarkable achievement given that virtually every business person who has expressed an opinion about Folkways, has felt the catalog was the albatross that hung around Folkways' neck. Even Sam Gesser and Larry Sockell, who worked with and respected Folkways have felt this way.[5] However, as I have tried to demonstrate in this work, Moe did not run a typical business in a typical fashion, nor were Folkways' larger goals similar to those of other recording companies.

Perhaps the most important point in understanding the Folkways catalog, and particularly the utility of never deleting a title, is to realize that the
recordings that Moe released had very long sales cycles. Whether explicitly
or not, I believe Moe recognized this. The material that was released would
take a very long time to sell enough copies to break even. The only solution
was to make sure each recording was available long enough ("forever") to
begin to support their own production costs. Although this is not typically
a "smart" business decision, the ideological mandate of the sound encyclopedia and the way it supported such long sales cycles justified the stance of
never deleting a title from the catalog.

Some readers might be tempted to take the view that Moe fabricated the
mandate of Folkways as a justification for his business practices. It is, however, most likely a coincidental convergence. Moe created the Folkways collection from material that he felt should always be available to the public at
large. Coincidentally, this material also had a very small consumer market
and needed additional time in order to meet the necessary sales levels. In
this way, the logic and implementation of the sound encyclopedia happened to fit the organizational structure that was essential to Folkways'
survival. Moe's ideological position also gave him a foundation of moral
strength from which to argue against those who wanted him to cull his catalog down to a manageable size.

Ironically, maintaining such an enormous catalog allowed Moe to
achieve a couple of other important objectives. The first was that the momentum of the catalog allowed Moe to keep recordings available until the
recordings earned back their production costs, despite the possibility of re-
quiring years of single-digit sales to do so. This was extremely significant
for both the material and for Folkways. Although it would be difficult to
demonstrate, I would argue that a much higher percentage of Folkways recordings have broken even than the industry average of about one in ten
recordings released. The combination of low production costs and the
long-term availability of the product clearly gave Folkways an advantage.
Moe did not sell a lot of records, but then he did not need to in order to
break even.

Second, maintaining such a catalog of older material also allowed Moe
to capitalize on the waxing and waning of musical trends. For example,
as interest in the folk revival grew in the latter part of the 1950s and into
the 1960s, Moe's extensive collection of titles by Pete Seeger, Woody
Guthrie, New Lost City Ramblers, and many others were still available and
continued to sell. Even though some of Pete Seeger's recordings were nearing twenty years old by this time, there was still continued interest and
continued sales of his material. The issue of availability thus cast itself not
just in ideological tones, but also as a solid business decision in order to

maximize income (and potentially profit) from products with a long sales life.[6] As Moe put it, "That's the whole trick—if I last long enough, and the album is always in print, in the final analysis I'll sell as many as a commercial company will."[7]

At the same time, Moe was also very sensitive to the risks that were inherent in the industry as a whole, as well as those that impacted directly on Folkways. In a 1973 discussion concerning the hypothetical impact of a hit record on Folkways, Moe made a couple of telling observations.[8] First, Moe pointed out that if he had a "hit" record:

> It would be the end of Folkways. It would be better for me to license a best seller to a company that can merchandise and can fulfill than it is for me, because once you start in that kind of a set-up, you have to have the personnel. To be a million-seller you need promotion men, you need warehouse men, you need a factory of your own, you need everything in a million, people to handle a million, so if you don't have it for the next issue, a million, all these people and all that investment is lost. Meanwhile, unless you can rent the warehouse, and rent people just for that one issue, that one million, you see? If we have six people that operates now—1500 albums, so much dollars per year—the minute I have a million I'd have to have ten people, automated billing, automated warehousing, IBM'd and all that you can't sign for the length of a record, you have to sign for a lengthier period.

The importance of managing the size of the operation, keeping it small and flexible, was clearly the key. If Moe allowed Folkways' infrastructure to grow large enough to handle such high sales figures, then he would be forced to record, produce, and distribute records that sold larger numbers in order to support the organization. This is obviously a very dangerous strategy and one that can very quickly backfire, as he learned with DISC.

Moe suggested that there was another way to handle such events[9]:

> If it is one of those type of records, and I had orders for a million, I would be able to fulfill that. But I wouldn't be able to fulfill it like a big record company, immediately a million copies to go out to the field, because I would have to maintain the rest of the catalog for the people that need it and buy my records regularly, since I know that eventually I won't have this million and I would lose all my customers and all integrity that I built into the company. So I would go to another factory, not the one that supplies me, and I'd make a contract, a deal with them, . . . in other words, I would create another organization in my organization to handle the million copies

so that we as Folkways are not touched by that. But it's a very dangerous thing because you can make a million copies and the next day you're out of business, all these years or not.

Here, Moe most clearly expresses a strategy that he pursued early on: the creation of Pioneer Record Sales and the variety of other concerns to protect Folkways from risk. More specifically, Moe was protecting Folkways from capital risk: risk that grew from capital structures built to extract surplus from product sales in the most efficient way possible. Throughout the life of Folkways, Moe's strategy was not to focus on maximizing profit, but rather to make enough profit to allow him to continue producing records. In this respect, Moe's decisions were based in a solidly grounded personal view that rejected pure profit in favor of his broader mandate that he directed through Folkways. Interestingly, although Moe was quick to take advantage of new situations and opportunities, the fact that he was always sure to insulate Folkways from risk by using other corporate structures speaks volumes about Moe's business acumen and his commitment to the longevity of Folkways and its inventory.

In the end, even though Folkways continues to operate under the auspices of the Smithsonian Institution, it nonetheless has left a legacy that must be recognized. The most obvious component of this legacy is the amazingly varied catalog. The Folkways catalog represents what is possible when vision, ingenuity, and creativity come together. The effort that Folkways represents in terms of the recognition of local sounds and musics and the importance they have to people around the world is staggering. Folkways has set the standard in terms of the range of sounds that it has preserved, as well as recognizing that sound is meaningless in the absence of context. The whole package—sound and explanation—not only defines Folkways, but has set the standards for any other company that might endeavor to preserve some of the world's sounds.

As part of this sound legacy, it is important to point out that many of the sounds on Folkways no longer exist on our planet. For example, *Sounds of an Office* (6142), represents a workplace that, in an increasingly technological world, is no longer reproducible. The soundscapes of New York City recorded by Tony Schwartz (5558–5562, 5580–5583) represent the chatter and hum of a time and place that has passed into history. The recordings that Moe has already made available represent part of a global heritage to peoples who are different now. For many groups, their cultural patterns and musical expressions—their *folkways*—have shifted over time, and they may not remember who or what they were forty or fifty years ago. But for that, we thankfully have Folkways Records to refer to. Like von Horboestel, Moe created his own encyclopedia of sounds that academics can refer to in the search of larger patterns. Like those early ethnomusicological collections, the value of the Folkways collection will continue to grow as new questions are asked of the world's sounds.

Perhaps the most practical lesson that Moe and Folkways have taught the business community is that small can be powerful in the recording world, and perhaps other areas of business as well. Since the founding of Folkways in 1948, many small record companies have since become forces in their own right, specializing in musical niches or genres that are as important to preserve as any popular genre. To name only two companies, Arhoolie Records and Rounder Records have certainly followed in the Folkways tradition with their recordings of the whole gamut of American musics, in addition to a variety of global traditions. What is perhaps more important is to recognize that the drive that kept Moe producing records all his life is alive and well throughout the world in people who just want to collect the sounds around them.

What is doubly exciting is that in the current technological environment, the combination of digital recording and the Internet provide a distribution outlet unheard of only a few years ago. No longer would someone like Larry Sockell need to travel around the country with a case full of the latest record slicks to show distributors. No longer does a company really need to hold a significant inventory of product. With burn-on-demand CD technology, or downloadable MP3 formats, for example, the burden of inventory is no longer borne by the small producer. The production costs continue to drop as the technology drives forward, ultimately making the conduit between the origin of the sound and the listener more invisible than Moe could ever have dreamed.

Appendices

Appendix 1 Material for PERISCOPE[a]

item.

1. Modern art songs
2. Flamenco
3. Swing
4. Calypso
5. Folk
6. Jazz
7. Documentary
8. Negro spirituals
9. Children
10. Ballads—traditional and bardic
20. Opera
21. Solo instrumental
22. Album package sales [crossed off]
23. Poetry
24. Americana—homespun
25. Symphonic
26. Piano
27. Basic classics
29. Love songs
30. Square dances
31. Walk in the sun
32. Social dancing
33. Moldy figs and sour grapes
34. Satire
35. Gypsy songs
36. Ethnic
37. Modern American composition
38. Creole songs
39. Human interest
40. Trade news
41. The role of an artist like Burl Ives
42. Briefs
43. Ethnic
44. John Jacob Niles
45. Universities
46. People's songs
47. Sales and promotion
48. Publicity and advertising
49. Don't miss
50. The month's best
51. People's Songs
52. Juke Box Scoops
53. The role and responsibility of the distributor and dealer to the customer [marked with "#1" and a bracket with "only" written underneath.

[a]Printed on DISC letterhead, this list appears to be a draft list. Numbers are as they are found on the list. *Typed list of Music on DISC—Anthology of DISC Booklets.*

Appendix 2 Music on DISC (Anthology of DISC booklets)[a]

Folkways of the World: USA

Negro Folksongs: Lead Belly	DISC 660
Work Songs of USA: Lead Belly	DISC 735
Songs by Lead Belly—Sonny Terry	DISC 734
Women Blues: Josh White	DISC 661
Spirituals: Thrasher—Gosp. Keys	DISC 658
Creole Songs	DISC 629
America's Favorite Songs	DISC 607
Ballads fr. Dust Bowl: Guthrie	DISC 610
Songs of the Hudson Valley	DISC 611
Eliz. Love Songs	DISC 609
American Legends	DISC 725 RELEASE
Seven Joys of Mary: Niles	DISC 732
Square Dances w. Calls	DISC 630
Square Dances w. Calls	DISC 631
Midnight Special: Lead Belly	DISC 726
Spirituals: Vol. 2	DISC 657
America's Favorite Songs: Vol. 2	DISC 633
John Jacob Niles: Vol. 2	DISC 733
Child Ballads: John Jacob Niles	DISC 665
Ernestine Washington	DISC 712
American Ballads	DISC 663
Cratis Williams	DISC 662
Blue Ridge Ballads: Texas Gladden, H. Smith	DISC 737
Cowboy Songs: Cisco Houston	DISC 608

Folkways of the World: Other Countries

Calypso I	DISC 614
Calypso II	DISC 628
Guitar: Carlos Montoya	DISC 615
Flamenco Songs: Miralles	DISC 721
Songs We Remember: Spanish	DISC 720
Calypso III	DISC 640
Finnish Songs	DISC 750
Choral Music: USSR	DISC 756

Ethnic Series

Amer. Indians Songs & Dances	DISC 161 NO BKLT
Folk Music of Haiti	DISC 142 NO BKLT
Folk Music of Cent. East	DISC 132 NO BKLT
Jewish & Palestinian Folk Songs	DISC 937 NO BKLT
Hebrew Folk Melodies	DISC 902 NO BKLT

Folk Music of Ethiopia	DISC 141
Cuban Cult Music	DISC 131
Cantor Malavsky & Family Choir	DISC 930
High Holidays: Cantor Jonah Binder	DISC 904
Cantor Waldman: Vol. II	DISC 931
Cantor Waldman: Vol. III	DISC 903
Cantor Waldman Vol. I	DISC 900
Sabbath Prayers: Cantor Jonah Binder	DISC 901
Hatikvah	DISC 6100

Children's Albums

Nursery Days: Songs to Grow On	DISC 605
School Days: Songs to Grow On	DISC 604
Folk Songs: Songs to Grow On	DISC 603
Funnybone Alley w. Text of Songs	DISC 606
Animal Jam	DISC 724
Songs to Grow On: Nursery Work Songs	DISC 602
Lullabies and Rounds	DISC 601
City Sings for Michael	DISC 740
Rhythm Band Music	DISC 742
In the Beginning: Sholem ASCH	DISC 1001

Jazz, Blues, Boogie Woogie: Jazzmen Series

Sullivan Jazz Quartet	DISC 701
Pee Wee Russell	DISC 632
Mugsy Spanier	DISC 711
Baby Doods Drum Album	DISC 709
Brownie McGhee	DISC 727
Lonnie Johnston	DISC 710
Doc Evans' Dixieland Five	DISC 714
Doc Evans' Dixieland Five: Vol. II	DISC 715

Blues in Jazz

Stella Brooks w. Orch.	DISC 620
Lonnie Johnson, vc., gt., & pf.	DISC 710

Other Band Groups (or: Misc. Jazz Groups)

Jazz at the Philharmonic Vol. 2	DISC 501
Jazz at the Philharmonic Vol. 3	DISC 503
Jazz at the Philharmonic Vol. 4	DISC 504
Jazz at the Philharmonic Vol. 5	DISC 507
Opera in Vout	DISC 505
Omer Simeon Trio	DISC 708
John Kirby: DISC	DISC 621

King Cole Quintet	DISC 506
Lady Be Good	DISC 2005
Milton Orent: Frank Roth Orchestra	DISC 705
The Four Strings	DISC 707

Jazz Piano

Meade Lux Lewis: Philhar.	DISC 502
Mary Lou Williams	DISC 612
Midnight Piano	DISC 706
Garner-Kyle Album	DISC 622

Music to Dance by
401–406 Include.

Rare Classics: Piano

Erno Balogh	DISC 770–772 INCLUDE.
Josef Lhevinne	DISC 774 NO BKLT
Siegmeister—Amer. Sonata	DISC 773
PF & VC Night without Sleep	DISC 730
Eugene Onegin: Tschaikovsky	DISC 755. 755a, 755b NO BKLT
Romeo & Juliet: Prokofieff	DISC 754 OR 7545
J. S. Bach, Little Preludes	DISC 771
Hovhaness & Cage	DISC 875
Hovhaness Orchestral	DISC 876
Cage	DISC 877
Sextet on Hebrew Themes: Prokofieff	DISC 4020
Khatchaturian: Masquerade Suite	DISC 800
The Bells: Rachmaninoff	DISC 804

Documentary on Following I Have Ramsey's Notes (Prob. Used Inside Covers)

Libration of Paris	DISC 51 RELEASE
L'Honneur des Poetes	DISC 52
Poems: Peguy	DISC 54
Claude Roy: Poems	DISC 55
Claude Roy	DISC 56
Sterling Brown	DISC 39
Alfred Kreymborg	DISC 38
Langston Hughes: Poems	DISC 37
Woody Guthrie	DISC 40
Franklin D. Roosevelt	DISC 201
Franklin D. Roosevelt	DISC 204
Franklin D. Roosevelt	DISC 205
Roll the Union On	DISC 370
Woody Guthrie	DISC 360

---

[a]This list is reproduced as presented on the original. Title is the same as on the original. *Typed list of Music on DISC—Anthology of DISC Booklets.*

Appendix 3 DISC Company production summary list as of
1 February 1948[a]

Unissued Records
26 Sides of Timmie Rosenkranz

Kaufman Represents
Repeggi Sonata
Bennett Sonata
Tchaikovsky Trio
Bach Concerto
Delius Sonata
Bach Partita
Violin Recital

Rachmilovich Represents
Hayden Symphony
Glinka Dances
7 Chamber Works

Disc Owns
Summer Day Suite and Piano Tocata
Slow Waltzes
Tristano Trio Album
Tristano Quartet Album
Sara Gorby Jewish Album
Sholem Secunda Jewish Album
James P. Jonson Piano Album
Hassid Dances Album Jewish
Songs of Louisiana Van Wey
Smokey Mountain Songs Van Wey
Poems by Sterling Brown
Cartis Williams Child Ballads

Indian Medicine Songs
Finnish Ballads
Lead Belly and Sonny Terry Album
In the Beginning
Work Songs of the USA
Choral Music of the USSR

Unissued Masters
DISC owns cont.[b]
Tchaikovsky 2nd Symphony
Bottle and Spoon Calypso
Woody Guthrie Childrens (baby) album
4 sides of childrens Folk Song Album
Cowboy Album
Handy Album
Prince Igor Opera

Paid to Be Recorded
International Dances
Clarence Williams

Have but Need Contracts
India Dances (paid out $400.00)
Chamber Music from Palestine
Charles Ives
Poems by Claude Roy
France in Poems by Claude Roy
Equitorial Africa
Woody Guthrie Noise Album
2 sides for Children's Folk Song Album

[a]Obvious spelling errors were corrected. Alternate spellings were left as in the original document. *Production/inventory list for DISC: 25 April 1948 (as of 1 February 1948).*
[b]There may or may not be at least one page missing from this list. It looks from the document that there is an earlier part to this list of Unissued Masters.

Appendix 4 Licensing Fee Increases on Columbia Recordings Released on Folkways Recordings[a]

Catalog No.	Base Price	Cuts	From	To
RF 1	$7.98	7	14¢	26¢
RF 3	$7.98	1	2¢	2¢
RF 5	$7.98	2	4¢	5¢
RF 6	$7.98	5	10¢	16¢
RF 9	$7.98	8	16¢	32¢
RF 10	$7.98	14	28¢	77¢
RF 12	$7.98	5	10¢	16¢
RF 14	$7.98	4	8¢	12¢
RF 15	$7.98	13	26¢	68¢
RF 18	$7.98	3	6¢	8¢
RF 19	$7.98	2	4¢	5¢
RF 20	$7.98	16	32¢	96¢
2951	$7.98	13	26¢	68¢
2952	$7.98	9	18¢	38¢
2953	$7.98	6	12¢	21¢
3585	$7.98	7	14¢	26¢
FJ 2801	$7.98	3	6¢	8¢
FJ 2802	$7.98	9	18¢	38¢
FJ 2803	$7.98	3	6¢	8¢
FJ 2804	$7.98	8	16¢	32¢
FJ 2805	$7.98	3	6¢	8¢
FJ 2806	$7.98	9	18¢	38¢
FJ 2807	$7.98	7	14¢	26¢
FJ 2808	$7.98	6	12¢	21¢
FJ 2809	$7.98	1	2¢	2¢
FJ 2810	$7.98	4	8¢	12¢
FJ 2811	$7.98	3	6¢	8¢
5525	$7.98	1	2¢	2¢
FE 4504	$8.98	1	2¢	2¢
FE 4505	$8.98	1	2¢	2¢
FE 4510	$8.98	3	6¢	10¢

[a]*Letter from John Franks, General Manager, Columbia Special Products to Moe Asch. 27 September 1978.*

Appendix 5 List of Distributors and Dealers of Folkways Records, 21 May 1959[a]

Name	Address	Territory
Arizona M. B. Krupp Distributors (D)	1919 N. 16 Street Phoenix, AZ	Arizona, New Mexico, West Texas
Bill Lawrence Inc. (D) (Attn: Glenn Miller)	109 5th Ave. Pittsburgh, PA	N/A
Coda Distribution Co. (D) (NL) (Attn: Mr. Bob Dahle)	47 Glenwood Ave. Minneapolis, MN	Minnesota, North Dakota, South Dakota, Nebraska, Wyoming
Crown Distributors (D)	600 15 Street Denver, CO	N/A
Folkways Records (D) (NL)	1827 St. Catherine St. W. Montreal, P.Q. Canada	N/A
Ideal Record Pro. Inc. (D) (NL) (Attn: Al Levine)	549 W. 52 Street New York, NY	New York City
K. O. Asher Inc. (D) (NL)	7818 S. Stony Island Ave. Chicago, IL	Indiana, Michigan, Wisconsin, Illinois, Kansas
Leslie Distributors N.E. (D)	377 Windsor St. Hartford, CT	Connecticut, Western Massachusetts
M. B. Krupp Distributors	PO Box 951 309 S. Santa Fe St. El Paso, TX	Arkansas, Oklahoma, Louisiana, Mississippi, East Texas
Marnell Record Distributors (rep.)	1622 Fairmount Ave. Philadelphia, PA	Eastern Pennsylvania
New Sound (D) (Attn: Mr. Prager)	50 Julian Ave. San Francisco, CA	Northern California, Nevada
Onondaga Supply Co., Inc. (D) (NL) (Attn: Mr. Gerber, Jr.)	344 W. Gennesee St. Syracuse, NY	Syracuse, Albany, Buffalo, Rochester
Peter Fischler (D) (NL)[b]	84 Coolidge St. Brookline, MA	Maine, New Hampshire, Vermont Massachusetts, Rhode Island
Raeburn Flerage (R)	408 S. Austin Blvd. Oak Park, IL	N/A
Stanley Lewis (D)	534 W. 58 Street New York, NY	New Jersey
Sterling Music (rep.) (Attn: Mr. Bowdy)	2928 Prospect Ave. Cleveland, OH	Ohio
Walt Robertson	Seattle, WA	N/A
World Wide Production Inc. (rep.) (Attn: Arthur Cohen)[c]	P.O. Box 154 North Miami Beach, FL	N/A

[a]It is unclear whether this list is meant to be complete, because it very likely is not. There are also two entries that are typed but later scratched out: Sun State Music Distributors of Los Angeles (covering Southern California) and The Children's Music Center of Los Angeles. Note: The presentation of the list here differs slightly from the original. *Distributor/Dealer List. 21 May 1959.*

[b]These letter codes are as they appear on the original list. A likely interpretation is (D) = dealer and (rep.) or (R) = representative. It is unknown what (NL) refers to specifically, but it is likely a distributorship of some kind.

[c]See *Letter series between Arthur Cohen and Folkways Records. Five letters between 9 March 1959 and 4 April 1959.*

Appendix 6 List of Current International Folkways Distributors[a]

Argentina: MCD World Music
Australia: Shock (61) 3 9482 3666
Belgium: Music & Words (31)30 606 76 74
Brazil: RKR
Canada: KOCH International (1) 416 292 8111
Czech Republic: Cure Pink (420) 69 691 6542
Denmark: Olf Music
Finland: Digelius Music (358) 9 622 4804
France: Harmonia Mundi(33) 04 90 49 90 49
Germany: Sunny Moon Music Distribution (49) 761 78622
Greece: A&N (30) 31 283 849
Iceland: Japis (354) 5800 800
Italy: CNI Compagnia Nuove Indye (39) 06 326 511 77
Japan: King Records (81) 3 3945 2134
Luxembourg: Music & Words (31) 30 606 76 74
Netherlands: Music & Words (31) 30 606 76 74
New Zealand: BMC
Norway: Musikdistribution (47) 66965540
Portugal: Mundo de Cancao
Russia: Apostrophe
Slovenia: SRAKA
Spain: ANTAR (34) 91 359 0797
Sweden: MNW (46) 8 630 36 00
Turkey: Acta Musik
United Kingdom: KOCH International (44) 181 832 1800
United States: KOCH International (1) 516 484 1000

[a]*From SI/Folkways page:* <http://www.si.edu/folkways/international_distributers_list.htm>.

Appendix 7 Mail Order Catalog Companies Dealing in Folkways
Records, May 1974

ALESCO: 404 Sette Drive, Paramus, NJ 07652

Children's Music Center: 5373 W. Pico Blvd., Los Angeles, CA 90019

Kaplan School Supply Corp.: 600 Jonestown Rd., Winston-Salem, NC 27103

The Pointer: New Readers Press, Box 131, Syracuse, NY 13210

Lakeshore Curriculum: P.O. Box 2116, San Leandro, CA 94577

Baker & Taylor Co.: box 230, Momence, IL 60954

Book-Lab Inc.: 1449 37th St., Brooklyn, NY 11218

Lyons Co.: 430 Wrightwood Ave., Elmhurst, IL 60126

The Learning Shop: 615 N. Sherman Ave., Madison, WI 53704

Kimbro Educational: Box 246, Deal, NJ 07723

Childcraft Corp.: 964 Third Ave., New York, NY 10022

Charles W. Clark Co.: 564 Smith St., Farmingdale, NY 11735

Cokesbury: United Methodist Publishing House, 201 Eighth Ave., South, Nashville,
    TN 37203

Demco Educational Corp.: Box 7767, Fresno, CA 93727

Demco Educational Corp.: Box 1488, Madison, WI 53701

Educators Purchasing Guide: 34 N. 13th St., Philadelphia, PA 19107

Find Catalog: P.O. box 775, Terre Haute, IN 47808

Hammett's: Union, NJ 07083

Instructional Materials Guide for Lutheran Elementary Schools: Concordia Publishing
    House, 3558 S. Jefferson Ave., St. Louis, MO 63118

Learning Media Corp.: 231 N. 63 St., Philadelphia, PA 19139

Mead School Products: 5005 National Dr., Forks of River Industrial Park, Knoxville,
    TN 37914

Miller-Brody Productions: 342 Madison Ave., New York, NY 10017

Secondary School Materials: Lutheran Church Synod, 3558 S. Jefferson Ave., St. Louis,
    MO 63118

Social Studies School Service: 4455 Lenox Blvd., Inglewood, CA 90304

FAO Schwarz, 745 Fifth Ave., New York, NY 10022.

Appendix 8 Alphabetical List of Foreign Accounts with Price Agreements[a]

ABC Records @ 3.32
Amigo, Sweden @ 3.32
Afrika-Bushhandling, Germany @ 40%
Algert & Co. @ 3.32
Alpha Music, Denmark @ 3.32
Almada, Canada (see folder)
Arnold Busk, Denmark @ 50%
Aubout Books @ 40% (Holland)
Asham, Brazil @ 50%
Artist Sound, Germany @ 3.90
Arne Beendiksen, Norway @ 3.34

Basart, Holland @ 3.32
Book End Folk Bks, England @ 40%
B. O. M. Service, Japan @ 4.20
British Ins. of Recorded Sound, England
(10 & 12" LP's @ 2.51—Ethnic @ 2.83)
Buch. Gerda-Schettler, Germany @ 50%
B. C. Playthings, Canada @ 50%
Louis Barnewitz @ 50% (Denmark)
Bro Records @ 50%
Jean Bernard, France @ 4.20
Best Recording Co., Hong Kong @ 50%
Blue Grass Club of Korea @ 40%

Carina, Australia @ 3.32
(on all records except Ethnic)
Chant Du Monde, France @ 3.32
Circle Records, Argentina @ 3.32
Colletts Records, England @ 50%
Crest Records, Australia @ 3.32
A Casa Do Livro, Brazil @ 3.76
Centro de Medicina, Italy @ List
Cuin Discoteca, 50%
Cultural Assn, France @ 40%
CSA Records, Denmark @ 3.32
Cyress Broadcasting @ 50%

DAC, Japan @ 50%
Danielajazzenwajsfield, Mex. @ 3.32
Dansk, Germany @ 3.32

Discfinders, Ireland @ 3.32
Dial Discos, Spain @ 3.32
Diffusion Artist Musical @ 3.32
Disco Center, Germany @ 3.32
Dischouse, Japan @ 3.32
Downtown OY, Finland @ 3.32
Dragon Records, England @ 3.32
Dobell's Jazz Record, London @ 40%
Dominie Group, Australia @ 4.35

Edelstein Records, Iceland @ 40%
Electrola, Germany @ 3.32
Elstree Mobile Rec., England @ 3.32
Evasion, Switzerland @ 3.32
Encounter Bk Shop, Switzerland [np]

Firma Gerda Schettler, Germany @ 50%
Folkshop Schwenken @ 50%
Folk Variety @ 50%
(bill to: J. Feuss and R. Weize Records
28, Bremen, P.O.B. 11042, West
Germany)
Free Reed Records, England @ 3.32
Frog Music @ 3.34
Fuga Records, Finland @ 3.32
S. W. Foto Musik, Sweden @ 40%

Goteborg Library @ 40%
R. Gudmundson, Iceland @ 3.32
Gleumus & Co. Germany @ 40%

Dr. Ludwig Hantzschel Books @ 40%
Helgeland's Imports, Norway @ 3.32

I. R. D., Italy @ 3.32
Importeurs Van Grammofon @ 3.32
Imsel Imports, Chile @ 3.32
Intl. Band, England @ 50%
Intertaal Boekhandling @ 50%

Jazz Records, Belgium @ 50%

K. K. Creative Toys, Australia @ 50%
King Hing Co., Hong Kong @ 3.32
Kirjavintti Books, Finland @ 50%
Kiwi-Reed, New Zealand @ 3.32
Kultturikanaca, Helsinki @ 3.32

Libresso Buchhandling @ 40%
Louis Barwitz Assn. @ 50%
Lost City Music @ 40%
Al Luciana, Switzerland @ 33 1/3

MAI/AS, Norway @ 3.32
David Mann, Australia @ 3.32
Mexico Intl. Imports @ 3.32
Michael Records, S. Africa @ 3.32
Music Center, Denmark @ 40%
Music-Glier @ 50%
Music Sales, Japan @ 3.32
Melodie-Musik @ 40%

Newman Enterprises, England @ 3.32
   (1000 LP's @ 2.50 ea.
   (3000 LP's @ 2.25 ea.
   (5000 LP's @ 2.00 ea.)
New Welt, Germany @ 50%
New Age Books, Holland @ 40%
Nippon (See Mr. Asch)
Nuis, Holland @ 3.32

Oriel Books, England @ 50%
Osterreichischer, Australia @ 3.32

Pick, Switzerland @ 3.32
Peuples & Continents @ 3.32
Pied Piper House, Japan @ 3.32
Pilar Bravo, Spain @ 3.32
Pinto Leite, Portugal @ 40%
Plane, Germany @ 3.32
Maurice Poulior, Canada
(2.75 for 10" & 12"—3.00 for Ethnic)
Projection Design, England @ 3.32

Rawnpike Records, England @ 3.32
Recommended Rec., England @ 50%
Radio DXCR, Mtn. View College
   (Phillipines @ 3.00—10" & 12"
      @ 3.50—Ethnic)
Record Doctors, Switzerland @ 3.32
Red Clay Rec., Japan @ 4.20
Rock Bottom Dulcimers @ 50%
Rocks on Rec, Australia @ 50%
Rolf Schettler @ 3.32
Rock-A-Billy, Finland @ 40%
C. M. Raynor @ 50% (Australia)

Sacher Music, Switzerland @ 40%
Schoeller @ 3.32
Schott-Freres, Belgium @ 3.32
Shinko, Japan @ 50%
Shinsei, Japan @ 3.32
Sinminchu Pub., Japan @ 3.32
Shiplovers Soc., Australia @ 40%
David Sternberg @ 3.32
St. Olav Bokhandel, Norway @ 3.32
Sussex Univ. @ 40%
Swift Records, England @ 3.32
Swingtown, Finland @ 40%

Talk Tapes, England @ 40%
Toowong Music @ 3.76
Towa Kikau @ 40%
Trikont, Germany @ 3.32

United Bearings & Machine @ 3.32

Vaco Records, Italy @ 3.32
Vedette Records, Italy @ 3.32
Viajes Tejedor, South America @ 50%
Carlos Ortiz Vigon, Spain @ 3.32

Warimex Records @ 3.76

Appendix 9 Transatlantic Records XTRA Sales Figures for 1973, Featuring Material Licensed from Folkways [(?) indicates likely Folkways source, but XTRA title unknown][a]

XTRA Record Number	Sales: January to June 1973		Sales: July to December 1973		Total Sales
	Home	Export	Home	Export	
1004 Big Bill Broonzy, Sonny Terry, and Brownie McGhee: *Bill Broonzy, Sonny Terry, & Brownie McGhee*	162	60	238	8	468
1006 Pete Seeger and Big Bill Broonzy: *Seeger and Broonzy in Concert*	69	30	78	28	205
1007 Art Tatum: *Art Tatum*	1	—			1
1012 Woody Guthrie: *Classic Recordings*	117	90	158	26	391
1016 Pete Seeger: *Broadsides*	22	60	70	33	185
1017 Leadbelly: *The Leadbelly Box (2 LP)*	98	30	122	10	260
1026 Pete Seeger: *The Pete Seeger Box*	1	—			1
1034 Pete Seeger: *Guitar Guide*	20	—	107	70	197
1035 Various Artists: *The Rural Blues*	16	1	112	8	137
1047 Various Artists	3	—			3
1096 Jerry Silverman: *Art of Folk Guitar*(?)	63	—	82	8	153
1098 Blind Willie Johnson (?)	61	—	54	8	123
1099 Sonny Terry (?)	109	17	148	76	350
1110 Sonny Terry (?)	55	40	838	65	998
1111 Jazz Gillum (?)	8	—	173	5	186
1115 Little Brother Montgomery (?)	50	—	54	5	109
1116 Walter "Furry" Lewis (?)	44	—	68	2	114
1126 Leadbelly: *Shout On*	174	6	174	34	388
1127 Lightnin' Hopkins: *The Roots of Lightnin' Hopkins*	66	12	73	20	171
Total	1,139	346	2,549	406	4,440

Total Royalties Paid for 1973 on XTRA sales: $532.65.

---

[a]*Royalty statements to Folkways Records from Transatlantic Records, c.1974. Additional information from <http://www.musictrade.com/label/prog/trans.htm>.*

Appendix 10 List of Board of Education–Approved Recordings Offered by Folkways Records: July 1957[a]

Size	Record Album Number	Title	Board of Education Assigned Number
2-10"	8003	French Children's Songs	—
10"	109	Ride with the Sun	—
2-12"	525	Man's Early Musical Instruments	—
2-12"	504	Music of the World's People	—
2-12"	505	Music of the World's People	—
2-12"	506	Music of the World's People	—
10"	740	Rhythms of the World	—
10"	712	Story of Jazz	—
10"	803	Folk Songs of Hungary	—
10"	48/11	American Heritage	—
10"	48/12	American Heritage	—
10"	731	The World of Man	—
12"	80/2	Songs & Dances of Puerto Rico	—
10"	48/1	Ballads—Revolution (1767–1775)	316
10"	48/2	Ballads—Revolution (1775–1781)	317
12"	420	American Indian Music of Southwest	1044
12"	445	Flathead Indian Music	1048
10"	838	Dutch Folk Songs	1049
12"	454	Greek Folk Music	1050
10"	706	Follow the Sunset	1051
12"	464	Indian Music of Canada	1062
10"	615	Pennsylvania Dutch Songs	1064
12"	401	Sioux & Navaho	1065
12"	51	Dance-A-Long	1071
10"	701	American Folk songs	1076
10"	22	Cowboy Ballads	1083
10"	844	Swedish Ballads	1100
10"	29	French Canadian Folk Songs	1104
10"	708	French Folk Songs For Children	1105
10"	843	German Folk Songs	1113
10"	841	Israeli Folk Songs	1115

[a]*Flyer directed to school principals listing Board of Education-approved recordings. July 1957.*

Appendix 11 Titles selected by Scholastic Magazines from Schedule A of the Option-to-Buy Agreement of 1 September 1966.[a]

Number	Title and Artist
7652	This is Rhythm, Ella Jenkins
7659	Learning As We Play, Volume 1
7307	Music Time, Charity Bailey
7114	An Anthology of Negro Poetry for Young People, compiled and read by Arna Bontemps
7009	More Songs to Grow on, Alan Mills
7308	Call & Response Rhythmic Group Singing, Ella Jenkins
7653	Rhythms of Childhood, Ella Jenkins
7023	Activity Songs for Kinds [Kids?], Marcia Berman
8273	Adventures in Rhythm, Ella Jenkins
7051	Animal Songs for Children, Peggy Seeger
7057	Rhythm & Game Songs for the Little One, Volume 2, Ella Jenkins
7658	More Learning As We Play, Volume 2.
7070	The Downton Story, Helen G. Purdy
7406	Follow the Sunset, Charity Bailey
7029	Skip Rope, 32 songs by schoolchidlren
7006	Nursery Rhymes, Games & Folk Songs, Cisco Houston
7056	Counting Games & Rhythms for the Little Ones, Ella Jenkins
7021	Folk Songs for Young Folk, Volume 1, Animals, Alan Mills
7026	Songs for All Year Long, Gil Slote and children
7036	Children's Songs, Johnny Richardson
7655	Songs & Rhythms from Near and Far, Ella Jenkins
7071	The Laundry & The Bakery Story, Helen Purdy
7025	Gosh, What a Wonderful World, Gil Slote
7651	Dance Along
7208	French Folk Songs for Children
7750	Christmas Songs from Many Lands, Alan Mills
3704	Indeterminacy, John Cage
3434	Eight Electronic Pieces, Ted Dockstader
7053	American Folk Songs for Christmas, Ruth C. Seeger
2191	Heritage U.S.A. Volume 1, David Kurlan
5280	Election Songs of the United States, Oscar Brand
7402	Who Built America? B. Bonyum
5252	Songs of the American Negro Slaves, Michel Larue
7654	American Negro Folk & Work Song Rhythms, Ella Jenkins
9771	Benjamin Franklin Autobiography, Read by L. J. Lemisch
9120	Understanding and Appreciation of Poetry, Morris Schreiber
9119	Understanding and Appreciation of the Novel, Morris Schreiber
9881	Early English Ballads, K. D. Read
9740	Bret Harte, D. Kurlan

9851	Early English Poetry, Charles W. Dunn
9852	The Changing English Language/Changing Literary Style
9792	Anthology of Negro Poets in the U.S.A., Read by Arna Bontemps
7104	The Dream Keeper, Langston Hughes
9840	Tyrone Guthrie: Lecture on Directing a Play
8010	Sounds of Spoken English
6115	The Bird's World of Song, doc.
6120	Sounds of a Tropical Rain Forest in America
6178	Sounds of Insects
6250	Science Fiction Sound Effects
7745	Cantos de las Posades, Mexican & Spanish
7719	Chanton en Francais, Volume 1, Part 1, A. Mills, H. Baillargeon
7720	Chanton en Francais, Volume 1, Part 2
7229	French Christmas Songs, H. Baillargeon

[a]*Letter to Moe Asch from D. E. Layman, Scholastic Magazines, Inc. NYC. 21 May 1968.*

Appendix 12 Schedule "A" List of Recordings and Status, from Folkways/MGM Agreement[a]

Artist and Title	Tape	Cover Art	Linear Notes/ Booklet	Addn'l Comments
Dickens and Foster— no title	Ready— M.A.[b] will check if stereo	None (photo not good)	Available (M.A.) Label—Yes	
Woody Guthrie— no title	M.A. tapes— 2 Wks	None	Take liner from booklet to be made up (M.A.) also label (M.A.)	Never before released
Lightnin' Hopkins— "Texas Blues" (Disc) "Lightnin' Hopkins" (Folkways) Do New Title	We have	Yes (Disc)	Samuel Charters intro from booklet—liner Label—set.	
Cisco Houston— no title	? (M.A.)	None— M.A. has pix	? (M.A.)	New release (England Only)
Leadbelly (Folkways #2004) "Take This Hammer"	We have	No art— M.A. has pictures	Lomax intro for linear notes— booklet available Label—M.A.—yes	
Peter LaFarge Title Not Set (Love Ballads)	Ready (M.A.)	None (M.A. pic?)	M.A. (?) Label—M.A.	
New Lost City Ramblers— no title yet	M.A.— this wk.	Art—M.A. (J. Cohen)	Liner, booklet, label (M.A.)	Never released
Peter Seeger— "On Campus"	Needs work (M.A.)	None—Pic. avail. (M.A.)	Liner, booklet (M.A.) Label Lineup (M.A.)	.
Pete Seeger (Folkways #2003)— "Darling Corey"	M.A.	None	Available (M.A.)	
Broonzey & Seeger (Vol. 1) ("Concert at Northwestern")	OK (M.A.)	None	Booklet & liner ready (M.A.) Label lineup (M.A.)	
Dave Van Ronk— "Dave Van Ronk Sings the Blues"	OK (M.A.)	We have	All ready (M.A.)	
Sonny Terry (with Various Great Artists)—no title	M.A. will edit and make album			

[a]This is the format of the Schedule "A" List as it is appended to the original content.
[b]M.A. = Moses Asch.

Appendix 13 Schedule "B" Recordings for FW/MGM Agreement,
10 March 1965[a]

Number	Title	Number	Title
FA 2003	Darling Corey	FA 2327	Brownie McGhee and Sonny Terry
FA 2004	Take This Hammer		
FA 2006	Sonny Terry's Washboard Band	FA 2328	Big Bill Broonzy Sings Folk Songs
FA 2010	Lonesome Valley	FA 2346	Cisco Houston Sings
FA 2013	Railroad Songs	FA 2348	Andrew Rowan Summers Sings
FA 2014	Rock Island Line		
FA 2022	Cowboy Songs	FA 2351	Dock Boggs
FA 2028	Get On Board	FA 2355	Old Time Music at Clarence Ashley's
FA 2030	Blues by Brownie McGhee		
FA 2034	Easy Rider	FA 2364	The Unquiet Grave
FA 2035	Sonny Terry, Harmonica and Vocal	FA 2365	Mountain Music on Autoharp
		FA 2366	Doc Watson and His Family
FA 2042	Hard Travelin'	FA 2369	On The Road
FA 2043	Pete Seeger Sampler	FA 2370	Progressive Bluegrass and other Instrumentals
FA 2049	Folksongs of Courting and Complaint		
		FA 2371	Roger Sprung, Vol. 2
FA 2306	The Poplin Family of Sumter, South Carolina	FA 2374	Negro Folk Rhythms
		FA 2383	Dave Van Ronk Sings
FA 2314	American Banjoe in "Scruggs" Style	FA 2385	Memphis Slim and Willie Dixon
FA 2315	The Stoneman Family	FA 2386	Memphis Slim and Willie Dixon at Village Gate
FA 2317	Mountain Music of Kentucky		
FA 2318	Mountain Music Bluegrass Style	FA 2395	New Lost City Ramblers, Vol. 5
		FA 2396	New Lost City Ramblers, Vol. 1
FA 2319	American Ballads—P. Seeger	FA 2397	New Lost City Ramblers, Vol. 2
FA 2320	American Favorite Ballads, Vol. 1.	FA 2398	New Lost City Ramblers, Vol. 3
		FA 2399	New Lost City Ramblers, Vol. 4
FA 2321	American Favorite Ballads, Vol. 2	FA 2409	The Country Gentlemen
		FA 2410	The Country Gentlemen, Vol. 2
FA 2322	American Favorite Ballads, Vol. 3		
		FA 2411	The Country Gentlemen
FA 2323	American Favorite Ballads, Vol. 4	FA 2412	Pete Seeger at Carnegie Hall
		FA 2416	California Concert with Rolf Cahn
FA 2324	A Walk in the Sun		
FA 2325	Mike Seeger: Old Time Country Music	FA 2417	Rolf Cahn and Eric Von Schmidt
FA 2326	Big Bill Broonzy—Country Blues	FA 2421	Traditional Blues, Vol. 1
		FA 2422	Traditional Blues, Vol. 2

FA 2426 Jean and Doc at Folk City
FA 2428 Oscar Brand, Jean Ritchie, Dave Sear
FA 2429 Foc'sle Songs & Shanties
FA 2431 Folk Music of the Newport Folk Festival Vol. 1
FA 2432 Folk Music of the Newport Folk Festival Vol. 2
FA 2433 Lilly Brothers and Don Stover
FA 2434 Old Time Fiddlers Convention
FA 2437 Frank Hamilton
FA 2439 Nonesuch and other tunes
FA 2444 The Songs of Mark Spoelstra
FA 2445 American Favorite Ballads, Vol. 5
FA 2450 Pete Seeger at the Village Gate, Vol. 1
FA 2451 Pete Seeger at the Village Gate, Vol. 2
FA 2452 With Voices Together We Sing
FA 2453 Love Songs for Friends and Foes
FA 2455 Sing Out With Pete!
FA 2462 Music of New Orleans, Vol. 2
FA 2467 Son House and J. D. Short
FA 2475 The Old Reliable String Band
FA 2476 Snooks Eaglin
FA 2480 Cisco Houston Sings Songs of the Open Road
FA 2481 Bound for Glory
FA 2483 Woody Guthrie Sings
FA 2484 Woody Guthrie Sings, Vol. 2
FA 2488 Leadbelly Sings Folk Songs
FA 2491 The New Lost City Ramblers—Goin' to the Country.
FN 2511 Hootenanny Tonight
FN 2512 Hootenanny at Carnegie
FN 2513 Sing Out! Hootenanny
FN 2531 Iron Mountain and Other Songs
FA 2534 Peter La Farge
FA 2941 A/B Leadbelly's Last Sessions, pt. 1, Vol. 1
FA 2941 C/D Leadbelly's Last Sessions, pt. 2, Vol. 1
FA 2942 A/B Leadbelly's Last Sessions, pt. 1, Vol. 2
FA 2942 C/D Leadbelly's Last Sessions, pt. 2, Vol. 2
FJ 2841 Jazz at Town Hall
FJ 2842 Yamekraw
FG 3522 An Irishman in North Americay
FG 3524 The Real Boogie Woogie of Memphis Slim
FG 3526 Negro Folksongs and Tunes
FG 3534 American Guitar
FG 3535 Memphis Slim: The Real Honky Tonk
FG 3536 Memphis Slim: Chicago Boogie Woogie
FG 3552 This Little Light of Mine
FG 3554 Barrelhouse Buck
FG 3555 The Barrelhouse Blues of Speckled Red
FS 3812 Arkansas
FS 3817 Big Bill Broonzy, Sonny Terry, Brownie McGhee
FS 3818 Ballads Blues and a Spiritual
FS 3829 Big Joe Williams
FS 3821 Sonny Terry's New Sound
FS 3822 Lightnin' Hopkins
FS 3824 Arbee's Blues
FS 3825 The Women Blues of Champion Jack Dupree
FS 3826 Blues by Jazz Gillum
FH 5251 American Industrial Ballads
FH 5263 American Moonshine and Prohibition
FH 5285 Talking Union
FW 8705 The Kobza
FW 8707 She Was Poor But She Was Honest
FW 8708 British Broadside Ballads
FW 8710 Songs of South Africa
FW 8711 Raasche and Alan Mills
FW 8712 Raasche Sings

FW 8718 Australian Folksongs and Ballads

FW 8719 Folk Songs and Ballads of the British Isles

FW 8723 Cante Jondo

FW 8725 Folksongs of Norway

FW 8727 Folksongs of Mexico

FW 8728 Revival In Britain, Vol. 1

FW 8732 New Briton Gazette

FW 8733 Calypso Travels

FW 8734 New Briton Gazette, Vol. 2

FW 8735 Yemenite & Other Folksongs of Israel

FW 8737 Sephardic Folksongs

FW 8738 Selected Songs of Eliakum Zunser

FW 8740 Ruth Rubin Concert

FW 8744 Songs of the Maritimes

FW 8745 Music of Asia

FW 8748 Traditional Songs of Chile

FW 8749 Music of Peru

FW 8750 Hawaiian Chant, Hula and Music

FW 8752 Exotic Dances

FW 8754 Russian Choral Music

FW 8755 Two Way Trip: Brit. Amer. Song Exchange

FW 8756 Songs of Two Rebellions 1715–45

FW 8757 Scottish Popular Songs

FW 8758 Songs of Robert Burns

FW 8759 Bothy songs of Scotland

FW 8760 Traditional Songs and Ballads of Scotland

FW 8762 Irish Traditional Songs

FW 8764 Songs, Ballads Saskatchewan & Manitoba, Dance

FW 8771 Folksongs of Newfoundland

FW 8773 The Pennywhistlers

FW 8774 Songs of Love, Play, Protest

FW 8775 The Grail Singers

FW 8776 The Borders

FW 8778 Songs of the Auvergne

FW 8781 Traditional Music of Ireland

FW 8782 Traditional Music of Ireland, Vol. 2

FW 8791 Songs of the Phillipines

FW 8801 Songs and Dances of Turkey

FW 8802 Folk Songs and Dances From Puerto Rico

FW 8803 Songs and Dances of Yugoslavia

FW 8809 Songs of the British West Indies

FW 8810 The Canadian Black Watch and U.S.A.

FW 8811 Caribbean Rhythms

FW 8815 Arabic Love Songs and Dances

FW 8816 Songs of Lebanon, Syria, and Jordan

FW 8817 Folk Songs of Chile

FW 8825 Square Dances with Calls

FW 8826 Jigs and Reels

FW 8827 Old Time Couple Dances

FW 8829 Spanish Dances

FW 8837 Austrian Folk Dances, Vol. 1

FW 8838 Austrian Folk Dances, Vol. 2

FW 8839 Austrian Schuhplattler

FW 8841 Argentine Dances, Vol. 1

FW 8842 Argentine Dances, Vol. 2

FW 8844 Dances of Venezuela

FW 8856 Songs and Dances of Iran

FW 8861 Tunisia, Vol. 1

FW 8862 Tunisia, Vol. 2

FW 8863 Tunisia, Vol. 3

FW 8867 Tarascan & Other Music of Mexico

FW 8870 Mariachi Music from Mexico

FW 8871 Field Trip England

FW 8872 Field Trip Ireland (As I Roved About)

FW 8877 Ellie Mao Sings Chinese Folk Songs

FW 8880 Chinese Folk Songs and Opera

FW 8881 Waka & Other Compositions of Japan

FW 8882 The Ruse of the Empty City

FW 8883 Beating the Emperor's Robe

FA 2375	The Phipps Family, Mountain Folk Songs	FA 2404	400 Years of Folk Music
FW 8716	Songs from Kenya	FA 2456	Broadsides—Seeger
FL 9671	Jericho-Jim Crow	FA 2471	Barbara Dane—The Blues
FA 2307	American Folk Ballads	FG 3581	Mike Hurley—First Songs
FA 2408	Red Allen and Frank Wakefield	FW 8761	Music for Classical Oud
FW 8885	Festival of Japanese Music	FA 2492	New Lost City Ramblers Instrumental
FW 8886	Festival of Japanese Music	FJ 2843	Mary Lou Williams
FA 2379	Grand Ole Opry	FS 32834	Mary Lou Williams (FJ 2843 in Stereo)

aCompiled from a catalog with the above items checked off. See *Schedules "A" and "B" of the Folkways/MGM Agreement 1965.*

Appendix 14 Verve/Folkways Releases from FV/FVS-9000

FV/FVS-9000	The Roots of Lightnin' Hopkins	Lightnin' Hopkins
9001	Take This Hammer	Leadbelly
9002	Passing Through	Cisco Houston
9003	Rural Delivery No. 1	New Lost City Ramblers
9004	Peter La Farge Sings Women Blues	Peter La Farge
9005	Who's That Knocking	Hazel Dickens/Alice Foster
9006	Dave van Ronk Sings the Blues	Dave Van Ronk
9007	Bed on the Floor	Woody Guthrie
9008	In Concert	Pete Seeger/Big Bill Broonzy
9009	On Campus	Pete Seeger
9010	Get Together	Sonny Terry
9011	Folk Go-Go	Various Artists
9012	Something New	Herb Metoyer
9013	Pete Seeger Folk Music! Live at the Village Gate	Pete Seeger
9015	Mama Yancy Sings, Art Hodes Plays Blues	Mama Yancy/Art Hodes
9017	Gambler's Blues	Dave Van Ronk
9018	The Times I've Had	Mark Spoelstra
9019	Guitar Highway	Sonny Terry/Brownie McGhee
9020	Little Boxes and Other Broadsides	Pete Seeger
9021	Keep Your Hands Off Her	Leadbelly
9022	Lightnin' Strikes	Lightnin' Hopkins
9023	Granada and Other Favorite Songs	Fritz Wunderlich
9024	The Blues Project Live at Cafe au Go Go	The Blues Project
9025	Dock Boggs	Dock Boggs
9026	Jean & Doc at Folk City	Jean Ritchie/Doc Watson

Notes

Introduction

1. Malinowsky, B. *Argonauts of the Western Pacific.* 1984. Prospect Heights, IL: Waveland Press.
2. The complete Folkways catalog is available online at the Smithsonian/Folkways website: <http://www.folkways.si.edu>.

Chapter 1

1. Read and Welch (1978), p. 31.
2. Ibid., pp. 25, 37.
3. Lee (1995), p. 21.
4. Gronow (1983), p. 55.
5. Noble [1913] in Gronow (1983), p. 58.
6. The development of affordable recording and playback technology in the non-Western world will not be pursued here, but there are clearly a number of important implications. For an excellent example of this phenomenon, see Manuel (1993).
7. Read and Welch (1978), p. 52, 142–3.
8. Sarosi (1993), p. 180.
9. Mazo (1993), pp. 200–201.
10. Gronow (1983), pp. 53–75.
11. Read and Welch (1978), p. 417.
12. I defer to Goldsmith (1998) in the recounting of Moe's family history and early influences.
13. Goldsmith (1998), pp. 43–45.
14. Ibid., pp. 48–49.
15. Young (1977), p. 3.
16. Nettl (1983).
17. Myers (1993), p. 39.
18. Ibid., pp. 42, 43.
19. Nettl (1983), p. 274; also Nettl (1964) and Noll (1991). A particularly interesting work is Meyer's (1993) work on the Nazi influence on music during the Third Reich.
20. Krader (1993), p. 175.
21. Bluestein (1987), p. 298.
22. Kenton G. (n.d.) "Moses Asch and Folkways Records: Global Village Preservation Society." Unpublished manuscript.

23. Young (1977) and Kenton (n.d.).
24. After World War II, antitrust legislation helped break up monopolies held by major companies and allowed greater distribution of independent product.
25. Young (1977), p.4.
26. Goldsmith (1998), pp. 70–76.
27. Young (1977), p. 4
28. Ibid.
29. Moe leased space for Radio Laboratories from the Forward Association at room 304, 117–119 West 46th Street, NYC. The lease ran from 1 July 1938 to 30 June 1939 for $50 per month. The business certificate for Radio Laboratories was filed on 23 May 1938 with the names of Moe Asch and Harry Mearns as the proprietors.
30. The Bagelman Sisters later had minor success as The Barry Sisters.
31. *Certificate of Business Registration issued to Moe Asch as Asch Recording Studios. Issued 15 April 1940. New York County Clerks Office.*
32. Young (1977), p. 6.

Chapter 2

1. Young (1997), p. 4.
2. See Leiter (1953).
3. *Draft statement re: Asch and Stinson. Early 1944.*
4. *Letter contract to Moe Asch from Irving Prosky. 25 January 1943.*
5. U.S. Treasury Department: Bureau of Internal Revenue (1946), Sec. 316.5.
6. *Five IOU notes payable plus payment schedule. 27 May–27 December 1943.*
7. *Accounting information and (partial) tally sheets. Asch Recordings. January 1943.*
8. The title and artist omissions are a result of an incomplete catalog listing of all the recordings.
9. *Letter to Don's Dependable Service, Los Angeles, CA. from Robert Thiele (an example of letter sent to several distributor/dealers). 20 July 1944.*
10. This was a standard distributor cost formula. It was likely presented in this manner for ease of calculation: divide in half and subtract a further 10 percent.
11. A session list from 1944–1945 shows that Asch continued to actively record new acts, primarily jazz musicians, for release on the Asch label; see *Recording Itinerary for Asch Recordings, 1944–1945* (Table 1).
12. *Letter to Moe Asch from Robert Thiele, Signature Record Co. 7 August 1944.*
13. Once a master was made, a series of mothers—negative images of the master, but the same as the positive image of the final recording—are made. The mothers are used to make stampers (negative images of the final recordings) that need to be replaced periodically as a result of wear.
14. Shortly after this date, Scranton became Capitol Records Inc. This change is also noted in the text to avoid confusion.
15. *Letter to Scranton Record Co. from Asch Recordings. 18 March 1943.*
16. *Letter to Asch Recordings from Scranton Record Co. 21 June 1943.*
17. *Letter to Asch Recordings from J. W. Griffin, Scranton Record Co. 22 March 1943.*
18. Older "scrap" 78s could be sold back to pressing plants by labels. The plants would then recycle the shellac and use it to manufacture new items. For this reason, many historic 78s from the 1920s and 1930s were scrapped during the war.
19. *Letter to Asch Recordings from Scranton Record Co. 21 June 1943.*
20. *Letter to Asch Recordings from J. W. Griffin, Scranton Record Co. 29 September 1943., Manufacturing and license contract between Scranton Record Co. and Asch Recording Studio. 10/12 November 1943.*
21. *Contract between Record Syndicate Trust and Asch Recording Studios. 8 December 1943.*
22. *Letter to Asch Recording Studios from Scranton Record Co. 15 December 1943.*
23. *Contract between Scranton Record Co. and Asch Recordings. 28 February 1944.*
24. *Letter to Asch Recordings from Scranton Record Co. 16 August 1944.*
25. *Purchase order to Scranton Record Co. from Moe Asch, Asch Recordings. 24 January 1945.*
26. *Purchase order to Scranton Record Co. from Moe Asch, Asch Recordings. 24 January 1945.*
27. *Purchase request list to Scranton Record Co. (unsigned). 16 August 1945.*
28. *Letter to Moe Asch from J. W. Griffin, Scranton Record Company. 30 January 1946.*

29. *Contract between Moe Asch (Asch Recording Studio) and Irving Prosky and Herbert Harris (Stinson Trading Co.) for sale of masters to Stinson. 22 December 1945.*
30. The 3 December and 22 December agreements restricted the license to fifteen months. This must have been made explicit in the first agreement, because this provision is not in the second agreement: *Letter to Moe Asch from J. J. Corn re: Stinson Trading Co. 13 August 1946.*
31. *Letter to Moe Asch from T. L. Allen, Scranton Record Co. 1 February 1946.*
32. *Letter to Moe Asch from J. J. Corn re: Stinson Trading Co. 13 August 1946.*
33. The list reproduced here is as close to the original in format as possible.
34. *Letter to Moe Asch, Asch Recording Studios from M. Connerton, Capitol Records, Inc. (18 September 1946).*
35. *Letter to M. Connerton, Capitol Records, Inc. Moe Asch, Asch Recording Studios from (20 September 1946).*
36. *Letter to Moe Asch, Asch Recording Studios from M. S. Hardy, Capitol Records, Inc. 9 October 1946.*
37. *Court agreement between Moe Asch (Asch Recording Studios) and Irving Prosky and Herbert Harris (Stinson Trading Co.) signed 7 January 1947.*
38. *Letter to K. E. Knudsen, Dansk Grammofonpladeforlag, Copenhagen from Harold Orenstein, Orenstein and Arrow, Solicitors. 15 June 1962.*
39. In a later letter to Jack Kall at Stinson Records (23 January 1963) the recordings are listed again. The bracketed text indicates differences or omissions in the titles between the first and second letters.
40. *Letter to K. E. Knudsen, Dansk Grammofonpladeforlag, Copenhagen from Moe Asch, 29 September 1962.*
41. *Letter to Jack Kall, Stinson Records from H. R. Etlinger, Orenstein and Arrow, Solicitors. cc to Moe Asch. 23 January 1963.*
42. Others have reported this date as around 1941 (Goldsmith 1998, p. 94). Given that Lead Belly appears on the *Asch Recordings, 1939–1945, Vol. 2* (AA003) singing *On a Monday*, it seems that Lead Belly likely did begin recording for Moe in the early 1940s.
43. Palmer (1983).
44. Pete's father, Charles Seeger, was an esteemed musicologist and is considered by some to be one of the founding fathers of modern ethnomusicology. Stepmother Ruth Crawford Seeger was an important musician in her own right. Sister Peggy had some success as a folksinger, on her own and with husband Ewan MacColl. Half-brother Mike Seeger made significant recordings on Folkways as part of the New Lost City Ramblers and has been an important contributor to American music as a player and documentor.
45. Bluestein (1987), pp. 301–02.
46. Bluestein (1987), p. 302.
47. Bluestein (1987), p. 300.

Chapter 3

1. An interesting parallel to this is a receipt for a subscription to Romeike Press Clippings, presumably to watch for press activity. No search terms are indicated and it is the only evidence that he ever subscribed to such a service. *Receipt for subscription to Romeike Press Clippings. 16 March 1945.*
2. *DISC Press Release (draft). 20 August 1946.*
3. *Contract between DISC Company of America and Charlie Ventura (unsigned). 19 June 1945.*
4. At the same time as Moe was beginning to introduce DISC, he was also checking proofs for a new Asch International label; *Letter to Asch Recordings from Keystone Printed Specialities Co. 5 November 1945.*
5. *DISC Press Release (draft). 20 August 1946.*
6. There exists several different sets of copy written at this time about the role of DISC and the importance of different aspects of promotion, including the importance of booklets (*Copy for a short outline of the importance of booklets in the presentation of recorded material. Appears to be part of "Periscope" copy.*) and the importance of strategy (*Business strategy outline for DISC*).
7. Gottlieb (1947).
8. Asch (or someone in the office) compiled a list of all the DISC recordings that featured booklets, which was the lion's share of the catalog; a hand-typed list exists in the Archive, see *Music on DISC (Anthology of DISC booklets).*

9. *Internal list of political releases by Folkways from 1947.*

10. *Draft copy of editorial for Periscope (tentatively titled "From the Control Room" Continuation of "Humble-Proud" copy for Periscope, Unsorted typed notes regarding artists and sales of DISC records,* and *Copy for a short outline of the importance of booklets in the presentation of recorded material. Appears to be part of "Periscope" copy.*

11. *Continuation of "Humble-Proud" copy for Periscope.*

12. There is a cryptic list of items printed on DISC letterhead that outline "material for Periscope."

13. Nelson Lewis worked as DISC's sales manager for a period of time, although neither the duration or scope of his position is known. *Letter to dealers from Nelson Lewis, Sales Manager for DISC Records of America. 11 March 1947.*

14. *Business strategy outline for DISC.*

15. Goldsmith (1998), p. 200.

16. *Unsorted typed notes regarding artists and sales of DISC records.*

17. Bluestein (1987). In this article, Bluestein lists the dates for DISC at 1946–1951. However, the bankruptcy occurred in 1947–1948 so it is unclear what source he is using to mark the passing of the company.

18. *Creditor letter and (partial?) list of creditor amounts. 1948.*

19. *Operations of the DISC Company of America from its Inception to Date of Proceedings—bankruptcy document.*

20. See especially Mabry (1990) for an analysis of this problem.

21. Unless otherwise noted, the text comes from the draft version of the document. The strikethrough words are as they are in the text. They are included because of the additional information that they provide. Words in square brackets [] indicate hand-written additions to the text. A "?" indicates uncertainty of certain words. Words in braces { } are my own additions in this case only.

22. DISC was still placing considerable numbers of orders with Eastern Record Co; see *Pressing Orders Placed to Eastern Record Co. for DISC in 1947.*

23. This is likely Nelson Lewis. *Letter to dealers from Nelson Lewis, Sales Manager for DISC Records of America. 11 March 1947.*

24. I believe this is the process of "selling" a receivable to the bank for a percentage of amount owed in order to raise capital quickly.

25. A contract exists for March 1947 between DISC and Malverne giving Malverne exclusive distribution in the City of New York, and Nassau, Suffolk, and Westchester Counties. *Contract between Malverne Distributors and Moe Asch / DISC Company of America. March 1947.*

26. *Business certificate for United Record Sales. Filed with the New York County Clerk's Office. 2 December 1946.*

27. *Letter to I. W. Wolfe, Peabody College for Teachers, Nashville TN. from United Record Service. Unsigned. 28 June 1948.*

28. *Letter to F. M. Bennett, Dept. of Education, Div. of Music, Baltimore MD. from United Record Service. 19 July 1948.*

29. Goldsmith (1998), pp. 194–95.

30. *Business certificate for Union Record Co. Filed with the New York County Clerk's Office. 19 January 1946.*

31. Moe, in fact, did this with the release of Solo records. Other than a few recordings in the archive with the Solo label, there is only a contract between Folkways and B&W Record Distributors of Hollywood, California, for the exclusive distribution and production rights to the Solo label. Folkways makes clear that they own all content, but will provide the masters for B&W to press the recordings. The contract is dated 1 December 1948. *Contract between B&W Record Distributors, Hollywood, California, and Marian Distler, Folkways Records. 1 December 1948.*

Chapter 4

1. *Signed, undated affidavit by Marian Distler.*

2. *Business certificate for Folkways Records and Service Corp. 30 July 1948. New York County Clerk's Office.*

3. *Letter To Whom It May Concern, from Frank Borut. 6 October 1948.*

4. See Schicke (1974) for an extensive discussion of the "battle of the speeds."
5. *Invoice from Saul Mildworm to Moe Asch (marked paid) for services rendered in the formation of Corporation—"Records, Books and Films Sales Co." 17 November 1958.*
6. *Moe Asch interview with Ralph Rinzler and Felix Lowe. Assorted times and locations, c. 1983/84.*
7. Goldsmith (1998), pp. 304ff.
8. *Letter from Moe Asch to John Franks, Columbia Special Products. 29 September 1978.*
9. Marcus (1997).
10. Asch (1997).
11. Ibid.
12. Chen (1990).
13. *Interview with Marilyn Averett, Sommerville, MA. With Smithsonian Folkways staff. 30 July 1991.*
14. *Folkways Records catalog and price list. With number changes. 1957.*
15. Goldsmith (1998) provides a more detailed picture of this time, especially in his chapter "Recording the Civil Rights Movement."

Chapter 5

1. *U.S. Treasury Department: Bureau of Internal Revenue. 1946. Regulations 46 (1940 edition) relating to Excise Taxes On Sales by the Manufacturer. (Part 316 of Title 26 Codification of Federal Regulations). Washington: United States Printing Office. Sec. 316.14.*
2. *List of accounts to which Excise Tax refunds were paid. 2 November 1967.*
3. *Larry Sockell. Phone interview with the author: 24 November 1996.*
4. *U.S. Treasury Department: Bureau of Internal Revenue. 1946. Regulations 46 (1940 edition) relating to Excise Taxes On Sales by the Manufacturer. (Part 316 of Title 26 Codification of Federal Regulations). Washington: United States Printing Office. Sec. 316.25.*
5. It is not entirely clear if this is a pressing plant or a company specializing in album covers and sleeves.
6. Predominantly during the Asch–Stinson agreement. The three labels sets ordered from Keystone Printed Specialties Co., were to be used for records pressed by another pressing plant, National Recording Company of Philipsberg, NJ. After 1944 there is no longer mention of National Recording Co.
7. *Order to Globe Printing, NYC. from Disc Co. of America, NYC. 7 April 1947.*
8. *Order to Kaltman Press, Woodside, LI, NY. Author unk. (likely DISC Co.) 4 October 1947.*
9. *Letter to Folkways Records, Attn: Marian Distler from Record Manufacturing Corporation of America, NYC. 16 January 1951.*
10. *Invoice to Folkways Records from RCA Victor Div. of RCA, Camden NJ. for records pressed. 31 March 1955.*
11. *Letter to George Clark, Clark Phono. Co. Harrison, NJ, from Moe Asch, DISC Co. of America. 8 September 1947.*
12. *Letter to Ralph C. Williams, Custom Record Sales, NYC, from Marian Distler, Folkways Records. 21 March 1955.; Letter to Marian Distler, Folkways Records. from Ralph C. Williams, Custom Record Sales, NYC. 8 April 1955.; Letter to Ralph C. Williams, Custom Record Sales, RCA Victor, NYC, from Marian Distler, Folkways Records. 13 April 1955.; Letter to Carl Reinschild, Custom Record Sales, NYC, from Folkways Records. 28 October 1955.*
13. *Price Schedule for Custom Record Sales effective January 1954.*
14. A letter from R. C. Williams of Custom Record Sales to Sam Goody indicates Sam Goody's intention to guarantee a $2,500 line of credit with Custom Record Sales. This says a great deal about the nature of some of the relationships between Moe/Folkways and major record retailers, especially in New York. *Letter to Sam Goody from R. C. Williams, RCA-Custom Record Sales, NYC. 30 March 1955.*
15. *Letter to Moe Asch, Folkways Records from Walter Alshuk, Custom Record Sales, NYC. 14 August 1968.*
16. *Inventory list sent to Folkways by Plastylite Corp. Plainfield, NJ. 4 September 1952.*
17. *Letter to Folkways Records from H. Weinraub, Plastylite Corp. Plainfield, NJ. 16 September 1959.*
18. An invoice from 20 September 1960 shows a single shipment of assorted titles in 12 inch Vinylite (50 cents each) containing 1,343 records. This is one of several invoices still in the archive. Payment is net 30 days. *Shipping order to Folkways Records from Plastylite Corp.*

Plainfield, NJ. 20 September 1960. There are other quotes given for production of various parts of the pressing process. For example, Gem Albums offered price quotes for album covers (*Letter to Marian Distler, Folkways Records. from Meyer Rappaport, Gem Albums, NYC. 5 August 1959.*); Economy Record Co. for pressing 45 rpm records (*Open letter from Paul Noble, Economy Record Co. LI. Reply sent 13 April 1956.*); Allentown Record Co., Inc. for pressing (*Price list from Allentown Record Company Inc. Allentown, PA. Fall 1950; Letter to Moe Asch from Harold L. Friedman, NYC. 18 July 1962*); Arlington Sales Agency, Inc. for Kraft record sleeves (*Letter to Plastylite Corp. Plainfield, NJ. from Arlington Sales Agency, Inc. NYC. 22 March 1956*).

19. *Letter to Moe Asch from H. Weinraub, Plastylite Corp. Plainfield, NJ. 7 October 1963.*

20. What is interesting in this exchange is the fact that Moe is offering a credit guarantee using Pioneer Record Sales as part of the assets supporting the credit for Folkways (*Letter to E. Paull, Credit Manager, Allied Record Mfg. Co., Los Angeles, CA. from Moe Asch, Pioneer Record Sales, Inc. 6 December 1961; Letter to Folkways Records, Attn: Moe Asch from E. Paull, Credit Manager, Allied Record Mfg. Co., Los Angeles, CA. 19 December 1961*). This is very likely part of a larger business strategy that will be discussed later in this work.

21. As suggested by Shore (1983).

22. *Larry Sockell. Phone interview with the author: 24 November 1996.*

23. *Larry Sockell. Personal communication with author. November 1996.*

24. *Personal communication with author, August 1999.*

25. Wholesale Distribution. Import–Export. 7818 S. Stony Island Ave. Chicago, Illinois.

26. *Letter to K. O. Asher, K. O. Asher, Inc. From Marian Distler, Folkways Records. 18 September 1959.*

27. *Letter to Folkways Records re: Lyon and Healy Inc. Chicago, from K. O. Asher. 10 September 1960.*

28. *Signed contract between K. O. Asher, Inc. and Folkways Records/Pioneer Record Sales/Moses Asch. 27 April 1964, with addenda 2 July 1964.*

29. Letter series: *Letter to Moe Asch, Pioneer Records Sales, Inc. from K. O. Asher, K. O. Asher, Inc. 27 April 1964; Letter to Moe Asch, Folkways Records from K. O. Asher, K. O. Asher, Inc. 1 June 1964; Letter to Pioneer Record Sales from K. O. Asher, K. O. Asher, Inc. 23 September 1964; Letter to K. O. Asher, Inc. from Abner Levin, 25 September 1964.*

30. *Letter to Cosnat Distributors, Cincinnati, OH. from Folkways Records. 4 December 1959.*

31. 27 West Court, Cincinnati, OH.

32. "Our terms are: net 30 days, 5% additional discount if payment is make within ten days and 3 percent 20 days. Lists are $5.95 and $4.25 with certain exceptions and your nets are $2.80 and $2.00 and 50 and 10 [%] from the lists on the excepted items."

33. *Letter to Ed Rosenblatt, Cosnat Distributors, Cincinnati, OH, from Moe Asch. 14 February 1961.*

34. *Letter to Larry Sockell from Gene Frawley, Keynote Distribution Co., Cleveland OH. 20 May 1960.*

35. *Memo to Moe Asch from Larry Sockell. 22 February 1961.*

36. 3741 Woodward Ave., Detroit, MI.

37. *Letter to Moe Asch from M. M. Jacobs, Music Merchants, Inc., Detroit, MI. 23 January 1961.*

38. 1718 John Street, Baltimore, MD.

39. *Letter to Kay's Record Distributors, Attn: James B. Klompus from Marian Distler, Folkways Records. 2 January 1958.*

40. Larry confirmed the hiring of a salesman to handle the Northern California Tower Record Stores in San Francisco, San Jose, Berkeley, Sacramento (2 stores), and Stockton at $125/week. *Letter to Moe Asch from Larry Sockell, 30 September 1976.*

41. *Signed contract between Herb Goldfarb Associates, Inc. and Folkways Records. 1 January 1979.*

42. *Letter to Moses Asch from Sid Fox, Children's Music Center. 20 August 1959.*

43. Likely to compensate for the free review copies that are commonly distributed for promotional purposes.

44. Fox also clarifies this to mean south of San Francisco.

45. Fox was also operating out of the Curriculum Center (5128 Venice Blvd., Los Angeles, CA) though it was unclear whether this was a separate entity from the Children's Music Center or a development from it. *Letter to Sid Fox, Curriculum Center, Los Angeles, CA from Marian Distler, Folkways Records. 14 September 1960.*

46. *Letter to Allied Music Co. Attn: Irving Shorten from Moe Asch. 25 April 1960.*
47. There does exist one list that sets out foreign distributors with their corresponding rates in either dollars or percentage (see Appendix 8). This information is added in an appendix due to the lack of other supporting documentation, including a date for the list. An associated set of financial documents lists the commissions paid to various distributors.
48. *Letter to Moe Asch from Ken Lindsay, Agate & Co., London. 18 October 1960; Letter to Moe Asch from Agate & Co. London. 25 October 1960.*
49. *Letter to Nathan Joseph, Transatlantic Records from Moe Asch. 5 September 1961.*
50. Moe makes several references to problems with the increasing cost and inconvenience to doing business between England and the U.S. See *Letter to Marian Distler from Leslie Shepard, London. Notes raids by Board of Trade and seizure of LP's with American labels in London. 5 October 1957; Letter to Moe Asch from Colin Shaw, British Broadcasting Corporation, London. re: fees due to the English Musicians' Union for music clearance and potential BBC licensing costs. 23 March 1960; Letter to Moe Asch from Ken Lindsay, Agate & Co., London. 18 October 1960.*
51. The arrangement with Jupiter was 500 records at 25 cents each up front, 25 cents per record for all records after the original 500, and Folkways pays about £10 (about $US 25) for all tapes. Folkways makes their owns covers and reprints the notes (*Letter to Nathan Joseph, Transatlantic Records from Moe Asch. 5 September 1961*). The year 1962 saw some strain to this relationship with the tough economic climate in the U.S. and poor sales overall (*Letter to Mr. Southam from Moe Asch. Attributed to Jupiter Records. 24 March 1962*). The relationship continued into 1965 with Moe assuring Jupiter that the Scholastic/Folkways deal would not harm them and would, he thought, improve Jupiter's sales via Folkways (*Letter to V. C. Clinton-Baddeley, Jupiter Records from Moe Asch, 28 July 1965*).
52. *Letter to Moe Asch from Nathan Joseph, Transatlantic Records, 5 March 1963.*
53. *Contract between Folkways Records and Transatlantic Records, London. 8 March 1963.*
54. *Letter Agreement between Transatlantic Records, London, and Folkways Records, 16 April 1964. Letter to Paul Cooper, Record Retailers Ltd., London, from Nathan Joseph, Transatlantic Records, 1 June 1964.*
55. *Letter to Moe Asch from Nathan Joseph, Transatlantic Records, 3 July 1963. Reply from Moe Asch, 7 July 1963.*
56. *Letter to Sam Gesser, Folkways Records, from Nathan Joseph, Transatlantic Records, 14 October 1963. Includes list of initial English releases (17 items)* An interesting point about this letter: it is addressed to Sam Gesser at the Folkways New York address. Sam was a long-time Canadian Folkways distributor in Montreal during this time. At about this time, Moe asked him to come help out with Folkways. He was in New York for a short period, but did not stay. *Sam Gesser. Phone interview with the author: 21 November 1996.*
57. There was also the accounting for the ongoing errors on Folkways' part: ". . . one last thing which we have not so far included in our account with you—the cost of at least four telephone calls, at £4. ($US 9.60) per call, to try to clear up errors in documentation by your staff."
58. Moe also seemed to be having problems with other licensing and sales arrangements in England—for example, A. P. Watt and Son, London (*Letter attention Patricia Butler, A. P. Watt & Son, London, from Moe Asch. 18 February 1965*), and Dobell's Jazz Record Shop, London (*Letter to D. A. Dobell, Dobell's Jazz Record Shop, London, from Moe Asch. 11 June 1965*), respectively.
59. *Letter to Moe Asch from Nathan Joseph, Transatlantic Records, 2 August 1963. Reply from Moe Asch, 10 August 1963.*
60. *Letter to Moe Asch from Nathan Joseph, Transatlantic Records 4 June 1964.*
61. *Letter to Moe Asch from Nathan Joseph, Transatlantic Records, 18 August 1969.*
62. Moe released a variety of material on Broadside Records, the audio component of an underground magazine begun in New York City in 1962. Performers ranging from Bob Dylan to Buffy Sainte-Marie to Phil Ochs published songs in Broadside magazine, making it an important outlet for progressive topical music of the day. In September 2000, Smithsonian Folkways released a five-CD box set of 89 Broadside recordings, released from 1962–1988, called *Best of Broadside* (40130).
63. These songs can be found on Folkways 05301: *Broadside Ballads, Volume 1*, Folkways 05315; *Broadside Ballads, Volume 6: Broadside Reunion*, Folkways 05592; *We Shall Over-*

come: Documentary of the March on Washington; and FF-SE107, *The Fast Folk Musical Magazine.*

64. *Letter to Moe Asch from Nathan Joseph, Transatlantic Records 20 May 1964.*

65. The license agreement sounds very similar to the one reported for Jupiter Records *supra*. Transatlantic paid $100 advance on royalties and presumably a flat rate for tapes. The amount is not known.

66. *Letter to Moe Asch from Nathan Joseph, Transatlantic Records 19 October 1964.*

67. *Letter to Moe Asch from Nathan Joseph, Transatlantic Records, 23 December 1964.*

68. *Letter to Nathan Joseph, Transatlantic Records from Moe Asch, 23 May 1965.*

69. Interestingly, it was because of government import restrictions that the licensing deal arose for production of recordings within Spain.

70. Letter series: *Letter to Moe Asch from Nathan Joseph, Transatlantic Records 11 October 1968; Letter to Nathan Joseph, Transatlantic Records, from Moe Asch, 24 October 1968.*

71. With respect to direct deals on Folkways material that was now controlled by Scholastic, there did not seem to be any difficulties with licensing. In a 1969 letter to Nathan Joseph of Transatlantic, Scholastic offers Joseph five titles that "Insofar as rights to these five records are held by Moses Asch and Folkways/Scholastic, they shall be extended to Transatlantic, for the duration of the Asch/Scholastic distribution agreement which expires on August 31, 1971." *Letter to Nathan Joseph, Transatlantic Records from Ernest Schwehr, Publisher, [Scholastic/Folkways?]. 28 February 1969.*

72. *Letter to Moe Asch from Nathan Joseph, Transatlantic Records, 22 October 1969.*

73. *Letter to Moe Asch from Nathan Joseph, Transatlantic Records, 31 October 1969.*

74. *<http://www.musictrade.com/label/prog/trans.htm>.*

75. There is a brief history of Topic Records from the company website at *<http://www.topi-crecords.co.uk/topic_records_history.html>.*

76. *Letter to Gary Sharp, Topic Records from Moe Asch, 29 May 1959; Letter to Moe Asch from Gary Sharp, Topic Records, 11 June 1959.*

77. *Letter to Moe Asch from Gary Sharp, Topic Records, 9 June 1965; Letter to Moe Asch from Gary Sharp, Topic Records, 20 July 1965.*

78. *Letter to Moe Asch from Gary Sharp, Topic Records, 16 December 1965.*

79. There is ample evidence that this is through Transatlantic. Sharp and Nathan Joseph of Transatlantic had communicated with each other on a number of occasions.

80. *Letter to Folkways Records from R.V. Van Lancker, Rose Records, Belgium. 14 January 1957; Letter to Moe Asch from L. P. Mabel, Henry M. Snyder and Co., 7 August 1957.*

81. It is not clear if this refers to the previous discussion of Rose Records of Belgium, or whether it is a different distributor/importer.

82. The little evidence available for this arrangement is a letter dated 5 December 1957 (*Letter to Folkways Records from Hans Gomperts, Les Editions Internationales Basart, Amsterdam. 5 December 1957*) in which Les Editions Internationales Basart, Inc. of Amsterdam asks for 20 copies of FEP 1 "on our account," then pursues a previous request for 45 rpm records: "If you do not have many of these records yet it would be most important for this territory to start such a production immediately." It is not known if production was started to meet the demand.

83. *Letter to Moe Asch from Mike Glasser, Transglobal Music, 12 October 1965.*

84. *Letter to Moe Asch from Natalia Danesi Murray, Mondadori Publishing, includes text of award parchment, 15 February 1962. Reply from Moe Asch, 17 February 1962.*

85. There were a lot of other deals going on at this time, including the Scholastic/Folkways deal that put limitations on the types of licensing that Moe could pursue.

86. *Letter to Folkways Records from Giovanni Fabbri, Fratelli Fabbri Editori, Milan, 30 November 1967.*

87. *Letter to Hachette Company, Paris from Moe Asch. 28 May 1959.*

88. Payment would be at a 35 cents royalty per record.

89. The request includes Lightnin' Hopkins (FS 3822), Brownie McGhee/Sonny Terry (FA 2327), Memphis Slim (FG 3524), Sonny Terry w/ Sticks McGhee (FA 2369), Hilton Jefferson, V.1 (FJ 2292), and James P. Johnson (FG 3540).

90. *Letter to Folkways Records from Hugus Panassie, Hot Club de France, Paris. 15 March 1960.*

91. *Letter to Hugus Panassie, Hot Club de France, Paris from Moe Asch, 24 March 1960.*

92. It may never have come to fruition. This is the only reference I have seen to this company.

93. *Letter to Moe Asch from Hugus Panassie, Hot Club de France, Paris. 14 April 1960.* This may well have been a fabrication on the part of the President label. There is to date no evidence of any contact between Folkways and a company of that name.

94. *Annual application by Folkways for reduction of French taxes on royalties paid by Chant du Monde. Signed and dated 10 June 1974.*

95. *Letter from Moe Asch to Jean Miailhe, Director General, Le Chant du Monde, Paris. 2 June 1978.*

96. *Interview with Marilyn Averett, Sommerville, MA. With Smithsonian Folkways staff. 30 July 1991.*

97. *Folkways Records catalog and price list. With number changes. 1957.*

98. *Letter to A. G. Seidman, Federal Trade Commission, U.S. Court House, NYC, from Moe Asch. 21 June 1961.*

99. Whether it was generated by Moe or someone else is unclear. It has a number of amendments in Moe's handwriting made throughout the document. *Analysis of potential business from the Ethnic Folkways series. 2 November 1948.*

100. For more information about this series, see Chen (1990).

101. Goldsmith (1998, p. 234) discusses this particular document as well, noting that "Moe asked a stewardess for a piece of stationery and wrote out a marketing strategy for the young label." Other than the heading on the stationery—"IN FLIGHT—EASTERN AIR LINES"—there is no evidence to support the particular scenario concerning the writing of the note during a flight as Goldsmith contends; the note could have been written anywhere. Goldsmith offers no other supporting evidence. *Notes by Moe on Eastern Airline stationery re: Folkways marketing plan. 7 April 1952.*

102. Fifty years on, the educational legacy of Folkways Records was marked by a celebration at the University of Alberta, Edmonton, Alberta, Canada, in January 2002. Home of the only complete collection of Folkways recordings outside the Smithsonian, the University of Alberta and the University's Institute for Ethnomusicology organized an event celebrating the educational and research opportunities to be found in the collection.

103. *List of accounts paid from Lee-Myles Associates.*

104. One of the more telling documents is a letter to Lee-Myles Associates from *The New Yorker* magazine. In part, the letter notes that, "As you may recall, this account was submitted to me in 1959 at which time The New Yorker came to the conclusion that it would prefer not to run Folkways Records. . . . Again, we thank you for considering The New Yorker but must again ask that you pass us by as far as this account is concerned." *Letter to R. Miller, Lee-Myles Associates, NYC. from W. P. Baxter, New Yorker magazine. 16 November 1960.* One is left quite curious as to their reasons for refusing Folkways.

105. *Letter to Moe from "Bob" at Lee-Myles Associates.*

106. *Note from S. Sprince, W. Schwann Cataloging, Boston, Mass. 11 September 1956.*

107. *Letter to Phonolog Publishing Co. Los Angeles, CA. from Moe Asch. 6 December 1963.*

108. In one instance with Scholastic Teacher magazine, the editorial staff were nice enough to remind Folkways in time to get an entry into the 16th "Where To Find It" directory for educators across the country. *Letter to Patricia Coleman, Ed. Asst. Scholastic Teacher, NYC, from John G. Vrotsos, Jr. Education, Folkways Records. 12 August 1964.*

109. *Letter to Moe Asch from Molly Harrison, Record and Sound Retailing, NYC. 9 December 1960.*

110. *Letter to Moe Asch from Richard Hill, Notes Magazine, Washington DC. 10 February 1957.*

111. It appears that this refers to a sampler record put out with the magazine.

112. *Letter to Moe Asch from Richard Hill, Notes Magazine, Washington DC. 5 May 1959; Letter to Richard Hill, Notes Magazine, Washington, DC. from Moe Asch. 8 May 1959.*

113. *Letter to Moe Asch from V. Warren, WSEL-FM Chicago IL. 4 March 1960.*

114. *Letter to H. C. Nicholson, The Music Box, Charleston, WV. from Marian Distler. 30 January 1958.*

115. *Letter to C. Freeland, Rebel Recording Co., Mt. Ranier MD, from Larry Sockell, Syosset, NY. 28 December 1960.*

116. *Letter to Sign of the Sun Books, San Diego, CA, from Moe Asch. 7 October 1961.*

117. A good example is the investment that Moe made in "The Pete Seeger Shows" made by Advertisers' Broadcast Co., NYC. An invoice shows $2,800.00 due (8 shows @ $350.00 each). The amount of $1,750 is shown paid, with a copy of a check for $1,050.00 attached. A second invoice shows $2,600 owed on 13 episodes at WNJU-TV Ch. 47, Newark, NJ. *Television*

contract with WNJU-TV Ch. 47, Newark, NJ. via Advertiser's Broadcasting Co. NYC. 12 August 1965.

118. *Letter to G. A. Korobkin, Jewish Community Centers of Denver, Denver CO. from Ed Badeaux, Folkways Records. 17 September 1959; Letter to R. Butler, Iowa State University, Ames IO. from Ed Badeaux, Folkways Records. 27 October 1959; Letter to Ed Badeaux, Folkways Records. from A. Shaffer, Berkeley Area Jewish Community Center, Berkeley CA. 24 February 1960; Letter to H. Darling, Sign of the Sun Books, San Diego CA. from Folkways Records. 27 September 1961.*

119. *Itinerary listed on inside of Conventions '59 folder. 1959.*

120. *Invoice to Moe Asch from R. M. Coles, Book-of-the-Month Club for conference expenses. 7 May 1957.*

121. *Invoice to Folkways Records from Brede Inc. 25 June 1959; Invoice to Folkways Records from Brede Inc. 1 April 1959; Invoice to Folkways Records from Brede Inc. 22 March 1960.*

122. *Invoice to Folkways Records from United Convention Services, Inc. 25 June 1959; Invoice to Folkways Records from United Convention Services, Inc. 17 April 1959.*

123. For example, *Invoice for exhibit space at the Dept. of Audio-Visual Instruction (DAVI) Convention dated 10 February 1959; Letter of confirmation of space assignment to Moe Asch from Music Educators National Conference, Washington DC. 26 March 1959; Exhibitor letter from National Catholic Educational Association, Washington DC. 14 August 1959.*

124. How much convention activity occurred through the 1960s and 1970s is not clear. However, there are receipts from Greyhound Exposition Services for display materials for the MENC conference, Atlantic City, NJ, Feb, 1979 totaling $414.00, and from Legacy Books for display at the American Folklore Society, Cincinnati OH, Oct. 1985, for $247.50. Moe clearly thought that conferences continued to be a useful marketing opportunity.

125. *Flyer directed to school principals listing Board of Education approved recordings. July 1957.*

126. Sam Goody's discount likely reflects, in part, a discount given to them by Folkways, as part of both educational savings and as a general sales arrangement.

127. *Outline of sale terms of Speak English series by PHONOTAPES to Folkways. 18 December 1957*

128. *Flyer directed to school principals listing Board of Education approved recordings. July 1957.*

129. *Letter to Folkways Records from G. W. Seelig, Hamburg, 10 January 1963.*

130. This is known for sure. Hennig may have also provided the material for 6915: *Folk Music of Italy* and 4437: *Flamenco Music of Andalusia* (*Letter to Walter Himmelmann, Hamburg, likely from Moe Asch (unsigned).17 February 1958*).

131. *Letter to Folkways Records from G. W. Seelig, Hamburg, 10 January 1963.*

132. The original contract states: " . . . in so far as your rights and interests are concerned you have no objection to our manufacturing, advertising, publicizing, selling, licensing or otherwise using, controlling or disposing of, in any fields of use throughout North and South America and Japan . . ." *Contract with Musical Sound Books (Paul Lazare and Walther Hennig) and Folkways Records 13 April 1955.*

133. *Letter to Tondienst Hamburg, attn. Walter Hennig, from Moe Asch. 17 January 1963.*

134. Hennig was contracted to Paul Lazare. *Letter to Marian Distler from Paul Lazare, Hamburg. 3 June 1957.*

135. Needless to say, Electrola was also confused about the situation, inquiring about clarification from Folkways. *Letter to Folkways Records from Legal Department of Electrola Gesellschaft m.b.H., Koln-Braunfeld. 11 February 1963.*

136. *Letter to Electrola Gesellschaft m.b.H., Koln-Braunsfeld, Germany, from Moe Asch. 17 January 1963.*

137. Letter series: *Letter to Moe Asch from R. Thalheim, Electrola Gesellschaft m.b.H., Koln-Braunfeld. 18 July 1966; Letter to R. Thalheim, Electrola Gesellschaft m.b.H., Koln-Braunfeld, from Moe Asch. 1 August 1966; Letter to Ernst Schwer, Scholastic Magazines and Books, from F. Schorn, Legal Dept. Electrola Gesellschaft m.b.H., Koln-Braunfeld. 9 February 1967; Letter to F. Schorn, Legal Dept. Electrola Gesellschaft m.b.H., Koln-Braunfeld from Moe Asch. 28 February 1967; Letter to Ernst Busch, East Germany from Moe Asch. 8 March 1967*).

138. It might be said that early on there may have been considerable friction between Hennig, Lazare and indirectly, Moe. In a letter from Lazare to Moe on 3 June 1957, Lazare writes that "Hennig, who used to do our recording work, held us up for a 100% raise in the middle of a recording session about a year and a half ago . . . got thrown out after the session was over

and then claimed that I had promised him a long series of recordings . . . which I hadn't . . . and threatened to sue me . . ." (ellipses in original) (*Letter to Marian Distler from Paul Lazare, Hamburg. 3 June 1957*, also *Letter to Moe Asch, from Paul Lazare, Hamburg. 7 March 1958*).

139. *Letter to Tondienst Hamburg, attn: Gottfried Bergholt, Hamburg, from Moe Asch. 15 March 1965.*
140. *Service Contract: Hsin C. Lee to Folkways Records. 28 October 1955.*
141. *Pete Seeger. Phone interview with the author. May 1998.*
142. Moe is sometimes accused of this practice by the existence of Folkways Music, a publishing company. However, it is well documented that there is no connection between Moe and Folkways Music. In fact, one anecdote relates how the proprietor of Folkways Music, after copyrighting the name "Folkways" (which Moe never did), then tried to sue Moe for the use of "Folkways." Moe clearly had established himself with the name, and nothing apparently came of the suit.
143. *Moe Asch interview with Ralph Rinzler and Felix Lowe. Assorted times and locations, c.1983/84.*

Chapter 6

1. Please note that these documents have not been referenced. The original books are under the same titles as the sections below with the ledgers quite clearly identified. Copies of these documents are held by the author and can be retrieved based on the information presented here.
2. The question remains, however, whether anyone other than "management" could make any sense of Folkways.
3. *Loft Lease Agreement between Leniben, Inc. and Folkways Records and Audio Components of America, Inc. 4 April 1957.*
4. *Invoice from Pearce, Mayer and Greet Management to Ash (sic) Recordings. 30 April 1965.*
5. *Invoice from Times Square Associates to Folkways Records and Service Corp. September 1970.*
6. *Invoice from J. G. Haft & Co. Real Estate to Folkways Records and Service Corp. 27 August 1974.*
7. *Lease Agreement between F. M. Ring Associates, Inc. and Folkways Records and Service Corp. 23 June 1980.*
8. *Invoice from Princeton Brokerage Corporation to Folkways Records and Service Corp. 10 March 1980.*
9. *Statement of coverage from General Accident Fire and Life Assurance Corp. Ltd. to Folkways Records and Service Corp. and Pioneer Record Sales Inc. 10 June 1981.*
10. See, for example, the employee list on *Invoice from Union Central Life Insurance Company to Folkways Records and Service Corp. 24 July 1978*. Moe was either hiring friends and family, including Pete and Toshi Seeger and John and Michael Asch, or he was covering those he knew. Either way, Moe was making sure that such individuals were covered under a life insurance plan.
11. *Balance Sheet and Income Statement for Pioneer Record Sales, Inc. for year ending December 31, 1964. Prepared by Becker and Becker. 14 May 1965.*
12. *Larry Sockell. Phone interview with the author: 24 November 1996.*
13. *Corporate tax report form for Pioneer Record Sales Inc. 28 May 1976.*

Chapter 7

1. *Contract between Pioneer Record Sales, Inc. and Scholastic Magazines, Inc. May 1965.*
2. *Document titled "Questions and Answers for Scholastic Resident Representatives about Scholastic's New Long-Playing Record Program."*
3. The advantage of this arrangement between Pioneer and Folkways has not always been evident beyond merely providing a means of separating and managing accounting. However, in the next section on the Folkways/MGM agreement, the advantage of this arrangement will come to the fore.
4. *Letter to Moe Asch from D. E. Layman, Scholastic Magazines, Inc. New York. 21 May 1968.*
5. *Letter to Miles Lourie, New York, from Moe Asch. 24 May 1968; Letter to Walter Heussner, Scholastic Magazines, New York, from Moe Asch. 24 May 1968.*

6. *Letter to Miles Lourie, New York, from Moe Asch. 24 May 1968.*
7. *Letter to V. C. Clinton-Baddeley, Jupiter Records from Moe Asch, 28 July 1965.*
8. *Letter to V. C. Clinton-Baddeley, Jupiter Recordings Ltd., London, England, from Moe Asch. 28 January 1967.*
9. *Interview with Larry Sockell. November 1996.*
10. *Letter of Agreement between Scholastic Magazines, Inc. and Nippon Columbia, Tokyo, Japan. 4 June 1970.*
11. *Memo to Moe Asch from Carl Sandberg, Scholastic Magazines. 17 February 1972.*
12. *Letter to Hajime Saito, Nippon Columbia from Carl Sandberg, Scholastic Magazines. 5 May 1972.*
13. *Interview of Moe Asch by Ralph Rinzler and Felix Lowe, 1983.*
14. *Unsigned letter of agreement from Sande E. Lichtenstein to Moses Asch and Dr. Barry Lew. 7 February 1972.*
15. *Federal wage and tax statement from Blue Giraffe Ltd. to Moses Asch.*
16. *Application for Additional Extension of Time to File Corporation Income Tax. Submitted by Blue Giraffe. 13 May 1974.*
17. *Notice of New Employer Identification Number Assigned: 06–0963728. 9 August 1977.*
18. *Bank Statement for Aschco Records, Inc. from Amalgamated Bank of New York. 30 April 1981.*
19. *Corporate Resolution of Aschco Records Board of Directors, 17 February 1981.*
20. *Corporate Resolution of Folkways Records Board of Directors, 17 February 1981.*
21. *MGM/Folkways agreement, 1 April 1965.*
22. The "suggested retail selling price" as outline in the contract is $4.98 minus excise tax *actually* paid by MGM.
23. The provision for the termination of the contract was to have MGM return to Folkways all materials related to the schedule A, B, and C masters (tapes, mothers, stampers, booklets, etc.) at no cost to Folkways.
24. *Contract between MGM and Pioneer Record Sales, Inc. 3 May 1965.*
25. The text of the contract indicates that the MGM/Folkways agreement—dated 1 April 1965—was also signed that day.
26. Note the absence of C masters here as well as throughout the contract.
27. An additional clause indicated that if MGM were to release recordings of previously unreleased Folkways material, the amounts for 1971–1972 and 1972–1973 would become $20,000.
28. *Draft of release concerning MGM/Folkways and Scholastic/Folkways contracts.*
29. *License agreement between CBS Special Products and Moe Asch. 22 March 1968 and 5 August 1968.*
30. *Letter to A. M. Stuchiner from Amster and Rothstein. 18 May 1964.*
31. *Letter to Moses Asch from A. M. Stuchiner. 25 May 1964.*
32. *Letter to Walter Alshuk, RCA from Moe Asch. 19 June 1964.*
33. *Guarantor agreement between Pioneer Record Sales and RCA. 9 July 1964.*
34. *Press release for DISC Records. 18 January 1965.*

Chapter 8

1. *Moe Asch interview with Ralph Rinzler and Felix Lowe. Assorted times and locations, c. 1983/84.* Virtually all of the information for the sale of Folkways comes from these interviews.
2. Jon Appleton, a music professor at Dartmouth, had released a number of recordings of eletronic music on Folkways, and was very familiar with the company mandate.
3. *Draft terms of sale to Moe Asch from Robert Dierker, Assistant General Counsel, Smithsonian Institution. 23 July 1984.*
4. *Letter of offer from Moe Asch to Ralph Rinzler, Smithsonian Institution. 9 June 1986.*

Conclusion

1. There are even anecdotal accounts by travelers and ethnomusicologists of Folkways recordings being found in unlikely parts of the world, themselves introducing new sonic ideas to different locations. This also further elevated Folkways' standing within their niche consumer communities.

2. Marx (1960), pp. 399–400.
3. Schicke (1974).
4. Goldsmith (1998), p. 387.
5. *Sam Gesser. Personal communication with author. November 1996. Larry Sockell. Personal communication with author. November 1996.*
6. It must be said that the study of popular records would not necessarily lead to this conclusion. With such a high sales peak in such a short time, the percentage of income gained outside of a very short window of opportunity is very small in comparison to that of a Folkways recording, for example.
7. *Moses Asch Interview: Edmonton, AB: Aug. 15, 1973. Edmonton Public Library. (Interviewer unknown.)*
8. *Moses Asch Interview: Edmonton, AB: Aug. 15, 1973. Edmonton Public Library. (Interviewer unknown.)*
9. *Moses Asch Interview: Edmonton, AB: Aug. 15, 1973. Edmonton Public Library. (Interviewer unknown.)*

Bibliography

Asch, Moses. 1997. "The Birth and Growth of the Anthology of American Folk Music." Notes to *Anthology of American Folk Music*, Smithsonian Folkways, 40090. Pp. 32–33.

Bluestein, G. 1987. "Moses Asch, Documentor." *American Music* 5(3): 291–304.

Chen, Kenneth R. D. 1990. The Ethnic 4000 Series of the Smithsonian Folkways Collection of Sound Recordings: A Contextualized and Systematic Study of Its First 20 Written Documents. Unpublished M.Mus. Thesis University of Alberta, Canada.

Goldsmith, Peter D. 1998. *Making People's Music: Moe Asch and Folkways Records*. Washington and London: Smithsonian Press. Pp. 194–195.

Gottlieb, Bill. 1947. "Cover Art Sells Albums" *Down Beat* 9 April. P. 12+.

Gronow, Pekka. 1983. "The Record Industry: The Growth of a Mass Medium." *Popular Music, Vol. 3: Producers and Markets*. R. Middleton and D. Horn (eds.). Cambridge: Cambridge University Press. Pp. 53–75.

Krader, B. 1993. "Poland." In *Ethnomusicology: Historical and Regional Studies*. Helen Myers (ed.). New York: W. W. Norton and Co. Pp. 171–177.

Lee, Stephen. 1995. "Re-examining the Concept of the 'Independent' Record Company: The case of Wax Trax! Records." *Popular Music* 14(1):13–31.

Leiter, Robert D. 1953. *The Musicians and Petrillo*. New York: Bookman.

Mabry, Donald J. 1990. "The Rise and Fall of Ace Records: A Case Study in the Independent Record Business." *Business History Review* 64:411–450.

Manuel, Peter. 1993. Cassette Culture: Popular Music and Technology in North India. Chicago: University of Chicago Press.

Marcus, Griel. 1997. "The Old, Weird America." Notes to *Anthology of American Folk Music*, Smithsonian Folkways, 40090. Pp. 5–39.

Marx, K. 1960. *Theories of Surplus-Value: Volume IV of Capital*. Part 1. Moscow: Foreign Languages Publication House.

Mazo, Margarita. 1993. "Russia, the USSR and the Baltic States." *Ethnomusicology: Historical and Regional Studies*. Helen Myers (ed.). New York: W. W. Norton and Co. Pp. 197–211.

Meyer, M. 1993. *The Politics of Music in the Third Reich*. New York: Peter Lang.

Myers, Helen. (Ed.) 1993. *Ethnomusicology: Historical and Regional Studies*. New York: W. W. Norton and Co.

Nettl, B. 1964. *Theory and Method in Ethnomusicology*. New York: Free Press of Glencoe.

———. 1983. *The Study of Ethnomusicology: Twenty-Nine Issues and Concepts*. Urbana: University of Illinois Press.

Noll, W. 1991. "Music Institutions and National Consciousness among Polish and Ukrainian Peasants." *Ethnomusicology and Modern Music History.* S. Blum, P. V. Bohlman, and D. M. Neuman (eds.). Urbana/Chicago: University of Illinois Press. Pp. 139–158.

Olmsted, Anthony A. (1999). "We Shall Overcome": Economic Stress, Articulation and the Life of Folkways Record and Service Corp., 1948–1969. University of Alberta, Canada. Unpublished Ph.D. Dissertation.

Palmer, Robert. "How a Recording Pioneer Created a Treasury of Folk Music." *New York Times.* May 29, 1983. Section 2, 1+.

Read, O. and W. L. Welch. 1978. *From Tin Foil to Stereo: The Evolution of the Phonograph.* Indianapolis: Howard W. Sams and Co., Inc.

Sarosi, Balint. 1993. "Hungary and Romania." *Ethnomusicology: Historical and Regional Studies.* Helen Myers (ed.). New York: W. W. Norton and Co. Pp. 187–196.

Schicke, C. A. 1974. *Revolution in Sound: A Biography of the Recording Industry.* Boston: Little, Brown and Co.

Shore, Lawrence K. 1983. The Crossroads of Business and Music: A Study of the Music Industry in the United States and Internationally. Ph.D. Dissertation. Stanford University.

Young, Israel. 1977. "Moses Asch: Twentieth Century Man." Interview by I. Young. Edited by Josh Dunson. *Sing Out!* 26(1):2–6.

Index

Note: Song and record titles are italicized